Morning Jam Sessions

Other Books by Betty Malz

My Glimpse of Eternity
Prayers That Are Answered
Super Natural Living
Angels Watching Over Me
Women in Tune
Heaven: A Bright and Glorious Place
Touching the Unseen World

Morning Jam Sessions

Betty Malz

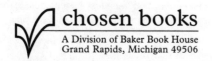

chosen books

A Division of Baker Book House
Grand Rapids, Michigan 49506

A Chosen book

Copyright © 1992 by Betty Malz

Chosen Books Publishing
Published by Fleming H. Revell,
a division of Baker Book House Company
P. O. Box 6287, Grand Rapids, MI 49516-6287
Printed in the United States of America

Unless otherwise noted Scripture quotations are from The New King James Version. Copyright © 1979, 1980, 1982 Thomas Nelson, Inc., Publishers.

Scripture quotations identified NASB are from the New American Standard Bible, copyright © The Lockman Foundation 1960, 1962, 1963, 1968, 1971, 1972, 1973, 1975, 1977.

Verses marked TLB are taken from *The Living Bible* copyright © 1971 by Tyndale House Publishers, Wheaton, Ill. Used by permission.

Scripture quotations identified KJV are from the King James Version of the Bible.

Library of Congress Cataloging-in-Publication Data

Malz, Betty.
  Morning jam sessions / Betty Malz.
    p.   cm.
  ISBN 0-8007-9204-1
  1. Devotional calendars.   I. Title.
  BV4832.2.M3   1992
  242'.2--dc20   92-27969

To my youngest daughter, April Dawn, who never leaves her room each dawn, until first she has read her daily devotional and made her bed.

and

To my daughter Brenda, whose writing and thinking abilities never cease to stimulate my own creativity.

Acknowledgments

To Jane Campbell and Ann McMath. Your prayerful support and enthusiasm sparked my imagination like spurs in the sides of a running quarterhorse.

Costume: Tissy's Boutique, Palm Harbor

Photographer: Dawn at Olan Mills, Clearwater, Florida

Hair Stylist: Jack Cocilova

Introduction

We live in Crystal Beach, a sleepy fishing village on Florida's Gulf Coast. There is no mail delivery; the residents walk to the post office to get their mail. This quaint white post office is situated on Crystal Beach Avenue between the hiking path and Live Oak Park at the waterfront where mullet jump and porpoises play.

About 8:20 A.M. one morning, I was walking briskly, mail in hand heading back home, humming joyously. The sun was remarkably warm for March, and the mockingbirds were not just singing, they were warbling in competitive concert.

Ducking, so that the overhang of Spanish moss above the sidewalk would not hit me in the face (I'm "five-foot-twelve"), I came face to face with Mr. Pitham. In fact, we almost collided. This ancient Englishman was headed for the fishing pier, pole over his shoulder and a couple of chicken wings between his fingers, to cast for crabs.

He stopped short, looked me in the eye, and said: "Tell me what you're about."

"I don't understand," I answered him.

"You're always so happy. Tell me why."

Hoping not to appear self-righteous, I leveled with him. "Mr. Pitham, I had an energy crisis before I started taking daily vitamins—not the kind from a bottle, but from the Word. I read and digest a short devotional from the Bible each morning before leaving my bedroom. This morning I read Colossians 1, verses 10 and 11: 'Increasing in the knowledge of God; *strengthened with all might, according to his glorious power . . . with joyfulness!*'"

"I'll try it" he said, saluted me, then gingerly walked on to the bay nearby.

Why a daily devotional? Psalm 68:19: "[The Lord] *daily* loadeth us with benefits"; 2 Chronicles 31:16: "his *daily* portion for their service"; and Lamentations 3:23, 25–26: "[The Lord's mercies] are *new every morning*: great is thy faithfulness! The Lord is good unto them that wait for him, to the soul that seeketh him. It is good that a man should both hope and *quietly wait* for the salvation of the Lord."

As far back as I can recall, first our grandparents then my parents gathered us children in the living room, first thing in the morning, before the school bus arrived for daily devotions. My dad would read a brief Scripture, then pray for us. Later on I recall their using the devotional *Our Daily Bread*.

It was my youngest brother (at that time), Marvin's job to round us up for this occasion. He would run up the stairs calling, "Betty, Don, Jim, git down here. Time for Daily Emotions." We would laugh. At an early age I realized how important my parents thought the daily devotional book was. I was probably only twelve when I told them, "I'll write one some day!"

My pastor husband, Carl, and I adopted this habit for our family. Then, a few years ago, I was hospitalized in the Houston Medical Center to have five nodes (two large and three small) removed from my voice box. The surgeons explained that I might never talk again. I determined that if I could not *speak* again, I would *write* a daily devotional book to exalt Jesus and thank God for His faithfulness to me. I was talking again in two days.

When I started this project, our friend Ed Schlossmacher handed me his worn, browned copy of President Abe Lincoln's daily devotional. In the front was his famous signature . . . A. Lincoln. It is well known that his daily devotional book was utilized. He quoted from it frequently in public addresses.

I got excited while writing *Morning Jam Sessions* to think that Abe Lincoln thought back then, around a hundred and fifty years ago, that daily devotions were important. He considered Scriptures valuable and vital for daily living. In *Lincoln's Devotional*, Carl Sandburg quotes him as saying: "I believe the Will of God prevails; without Him all human reliance is vain; without the assistance of that Divine Being I cannot succeed; with that assistance I cannot fail. I give thanks to the Almighty and seek His aid. I believe in praise to Almighty God, the beneficent Creator and Ruler of the universe."

10

The school bus had not yet come to a complete stop, when my step-daughter Connie, the youngest of Carl's and my three children, leaped from the orange vehicle, tore down the driveway in a dead run and lunged through the front door. "Mother, hurry! I gotta have your bike and two-sixty-five quick so I can get to Anderson Drug Store before they close!"

Like Connie, all the fifteen-year-old girls at Ellendale High School in North Dakota were using tubes of Fresh Start, that magic product that promised to enhance your looks, stimulate the natural color of your skin tones and reduce acne on contact. She embodied anticipation.

On August 1, 1959, I emerged from death into a second chance at life, following a ruptured appendix, gangrenous organs and weeks in the hospital. The experience is still a "living testimony" of Jesus' resurrection and I feel that every morning starts a new day, a new year, a new challenge. When you have an attitude of anticipation, little things mean a lot.

My Aunt Pearl suffered a heart attack recently, a dangerous acceleration of high blood pressure, followed briefly by no blood pressure at all.

In a few days, however, following prayer on the part of concerned Christian friends and the care of good doctors in the hospital, her heart monitor and tests showed an "all clear" bill of health. The heart murmur she had experienced from the time she was a child was gone, and her cholesterol levels were normal. What good news!

Now she awakes every dawn as if it is January 1—anticipating, listening for the birds' first song, and lingering to hear their last note at eventide.

Whether you are a young lady in your teens, a young woman with a second chance or a young grandmother with a new lease on life, anticipate! Get a fresh start and new beginning—not just New Year's Day, but every day of the 365 you celebrate. Jesus has "put a new song in my mouth—praise to our God" (Psalm 40:3). "Behold," He says, "I will do a new thing" (Isaiah 43:19).

Happy New Year!

Are you suffering from "stressure and press"? That happens when anxious days are filled with pressure and stress. Does it seem that when you awaken in the a.m., you put one foot on a banana peel and the other on a skate board?

I never met Carl's first wife, but right after we were married he took me through Ohio to introduce me to relatives and old friends. Everywhere we went people would ask, "Did you know Wanda? She was a saint!" Now, no one ever called me one of those, so I began to feel inferior by comparison!

One evening, engaging in "pillow talk" just before falling asleep, I got the nerve to ask my husband, "Was Wanda really a saint?"

"Yes," he replied. "She started practicing patience very young, growing up in a most unhappy environment. Later, she was patiently cooperative, willing to move whenever the missions board needed our services and ministry. She died the same way. She suffered untold agony with cancer, but rarely took anything for pain and never complained once."

Wanda showed in a godly way that what you are usually comes through. Let me draw a contrast.

I know a large man who attends a large church. This incident occurred on Communion Sunday. They had recently installed pale blue carpet in the entire sanctuary. This respected elder and board member walked down the aisle with a tray of one hundred individual Communion cups filled with dark purple grape juice, the emblem of Christ's blood.

About the fourth row back, he leaned forward to serve, and stumbled. He flung those cups of purple juice all over the new pale blue carpet and he exclaimed, "O s—!" At first the people who heard the slip of his tongue, gasped an "Ooooh!" Then ripples of muffled laughter broke out like an epidemic. The red-faced man walked out in total humiliation.

People are like tea bags. You really do not know what they are like inside until they get into hot water!

Out of the abundance of the heart the mouth speaks (see Matthew 12:35).

My married daughter has hands that look like mine, but they are much smaller. Her little hands amaze me. She is a good wife and mother. She cooks, teaches piano, plays pipe organ, uses the computer, writes—and throws pots. Do not misunderstand: That does not mean that she has temper fits and flings things! She makes pottery.

After a few lessons, her instructor recognized that she was unusually creative at the potter's wheel. She can take raw, natural North Carolina clay and, with the proper pressure applied by her tiny fingers, is equally good at designing jewelry, even small earrings, clay pots, serving vessels, large salad bowls and compotes.

Her husband moved a quaint little shed onto the back of their property where she has her wheel, her equipment and supplies. She calls it her potting shed, and her clay creations are labeled "Potting Shed Pottery." For Christmas we got a large box from her, accompanied by a note:

Dear Mother and Dad,
This dessert set didn't "fire" exactly as I'd planned, but most clay pieces are uniquely different in appearance. Fired at a high temperature, they are extremely useful. This pottery is food safe and can be used in the microwave, dishwasher, oven or freezer.

Marjorie Rawlings, the author of *Cross Creek*, reminds us that through Adam we were a part of the clay of the earth before we were a part of the womb of a woman. I am amazed at God's creation—so uniquely different in appearance and versatility, but still all from the dust of the earth. "For we know that if our earthly house [clay vessel] . . . is destroyed, we have a building from God, a house not made with hands, eternal in the heavens" (2 Corinthians 5:1).

If we are ever tempted to feel inferior to other human beings, we must realize that they are all just made of mud! And like us, "have this treasure in earthen vessels, that the excellence of the power may be of God and not of us" (2 Corinthians 4:7).

Twenty-six years ago as a young widow, lonely, financially stressed, confused, I made some wrong turns in the road. The Holy Spirit in His mercy has covered my bad tracks left when I detoured into mis-understandings with loved ones, business associates, church friends.

For two years I ran on a low battery by sheer nerve and raw, naked faith in God. I played the organ, taught Sunday school, worked in the nursery, directed and sang in the choir with absolutely no emo-tions. I did not cry, and could not laugh. Those were the longest two years of my life. I prayed and read the Word knowing—not by feeling but by faith—that He, Jesus, the "Fleshed-Out-Word" is our only true foundation.

I have always slept soundly, and rarely dream, but one night I dreamed that I was walking slowly with tired feet down a dusty path. At the foot of the trail was a small potter's shed. Hearing the hum of a man's gentle voice, I opened the door to look in. As I did so, I jarred the wall causing a clay pitcher that the potter was using to fall from his bench onto the floor. It broke into two pieces. Without speaking he picked up the broken pieces. Then with skillful hands, he reached into a basin of warm wax, and mended the pitcher. Looking up at me, he lovingly put the vessel back in its place on his bench.

I shall never forget the "wounded dove" look in those gray-blue eyes when he spoke to me! Pointing first to the plain vessel he had just mended, then to a row of ornate ones atop a shelf, he said, "'Tis better to be a broken vessel and plain . . . forgiven, mended by the Holy Spirit, willing to be poured out and used . . . than to be perfect but not yielded."

When I awakened, my pillow was wet with my own tears. I could cry again. Then "tears of laughter" flowed! The crack in my heart had been mended. I have been laughing, singing, playing, writing, helping, running over with joy ever since that night.

Return to the Potter's Shed. He will turn your mourning into dancing!

"O Lord, You are our Father; we are the clay, and You our potter; and all we are the work of Your hand" (Isaiah 64:8). "Heal me, O Lord, and I shall be healed . . . for You are my praise" (Jeremiah 17:14).

* Dedicated to Peggi

I love giraffes. I have legs like a giraffe, and a neck like a giraffe.

I have been "five-foot-twelve" since I was twelve years old. (I weighed 96 pounds at the time!) All my growing up years I prayed, "Lord, I want to be small." He thought I said "tall"! My brothers called me giraffe, stork and "sisty ugler," which, translated, means ugly sister.

I played women's basketball, not because the coach thought I was good, but because I was tall. People in the bleachers would laugh when one of my teammates would yell out during the game, "Pass the ball to the giraffe! Give the ball to Betty!"

Now that I am mature, I realize that I cannot be any "ammer" than I am. You can change the size of your body, but you can neither add nor subtract from your height (see Matthew 6:27, Luke 12:25).

Recently I studied the giraffe. Did God make a creative error? The giraffe has a long, black tongue—twenty inches long—yet the poor animal is mute. He cannot make a sound, but he can shed tears. The thing I love about the giraffe is that he is in tune with himself. Though his tongue cannot talk or sing, he is content and just "keeps on giraffing."

This would be a great lesson for church volunteers to learn. Have you noticed that those who are willing are not able, and those who are able are usually not willing?

Being out of tune with God bankrupts your joy, for the undeniable sign of the presence of God is joy. Being out of tune with others robs you of eternal rewards from investing in people, loving your neighbor. But being out of tune with yourself is like having dental floss caught between your teeth or wearing underwear that does not fit.

He is rich who is satisfied!

"Godliness with contentment is great gain" (1 Timothy 6:6). Does this mean to be good and force yourself to accept your situation? I think not. I believe this verse is the formula for financial, spiritual and personal success. It may well be the prescription for a private energy crisis.

I know a wife who is so busy working for her husband that she has no time for him. Her husband called me. "My wife will spend two hours getting her hair and nails done, but won't take any time to love me. She knows where every retreat center in the state is located, but has forgotten where the kitchen and the bedroom are. Pray that God will take this super-duper-spiritual-intellectual home to Glory and give me a flesh-and-blood woman who loves, cooks and takes care of our kids."

A pastor's wife called me. "My shepherd-husband is so involved in the mechanics of the ministry that he has no time to minister to the sheep, to me or our children."

Beware that you do not traffic in unfelt truth. The worst rut is that seemingly good one, the religious ritual—going in circles, singing the same songs, quoting the same Scriptures without feeling or meaning.

I heard Dr. Louis Evans, when he was pastoring in the Washington, D.C., area confess to this. He explained that he was forever accellerating, rushing, hurrying. One day looking in the mirror, shaving too fast, he cut his face and the Lord spoke to him.

"Louie," He said, "you are either doing more than I told you to or you are not taking My strength to do it with." That day he vowed to begin eliminating the unnecessary and simplifying his life so that he had time to enjoy God, his family and his church.

Life was meant to be sipped, not gulped. Savor life. Let it, like sweets, melt in your mouth. Don't eat just to fill your stomach. Taste and enjoy!

Solomon, the wisest man who ever lived, yearned after pools, fountains, palaces, wives, concubines, wisdom, riches, gold and silver. His conclusion after much vexation of spirit: that "nothing is better for a man than that he should eat and drink, and that his soul should enjoy good in his labor" (Ecclesiastes 2:24); "live joyfully with the wife whom you love" (9:9); and "fear God and keep his commandments: for this is the whole duty of man" (12:13, KJV.)

I was running late for church. The boating, fishing, golfing traffic on Alternate 19 was constipated. I darted left across the highway and rushed east on Palm Boulevard toward the place where we worship on Sunday.

I almost wrecked my car. I slammed on the brakes in disbelief! In the middle of the second block sitting in a driveway was a purple car with hot pink wheels and a bouquet of hot pink carnations attached to the radio antenna. Pink and purple tassels hung around the perimeter of the interior. On the back of the trunk in bright pink and purple letters, printed seven or eight inches high, was the telephone number of the car's owner. Another bouquet, a bright floral arrangement, was perched atop the mail box on the street, just in case you missed the car in the driveway. At a right angle, by the porch, loomed a large surrey, the wheels bedecked in bold pink and purple. There was no question in my mind, this was obviously a house of ill repute right here in the respectable neighborhood of Dunedin, Florida.

On the way home Carl was with me. I drove by and asked him, "What is this?"

He guffawed, "Oh, my! It's a whore house!"

Writers always have a "nose for a story." I was soon to know for sure.

On Tuesday, leaving the little Key West Plaza in Crystal Beach where I work part-time at Tissy's Boutique, I spotted that pink and purple car stopped at the light. I pulled alongside. I figured she must not make enough money to have air conditioning. Her window was down.

"What is your game?" I called over quickly before the light changed.

With a wide grin, she proclaimed hurriedly, "My work is actually play. I'm a professional clown. I love cheering up kids in orphanages, handicapped children, little people in hospitals. And I perform for the elderly and infirm in nursing homes."

Jesus' own words are written in red letters in John 7:24: "Do not judge according to appearance, but judge with righteous judgment."

In order to "mount up with wings like eagles" (Isaiah 40:31), you must be an eagle, not merely say you are one. To be an eagle, you must be born an eagle. Eagles are born on a rock, live on a rock and die on a rock.

To be a Christian you must be born again of the Spirit, on the Rock Christ Jesus. Eagle Christians that are born on the Rock, living on God's Word by the power of the Holy Spirit, are not afraid of birth, life or death where we will live eternally . . . *on the Rock.*

The mother eagle builds her nest on the rock, on the face of a cliff, in the fastness of the craggy rock (see Job 39:27–28). A baby eagle could look around and to quote Pastor Roger Casey, say, "I've got it made. What a view! Mother has padded my little nest with soft things like feathers, and she brings me all that good stuff to eat like mice and rats!"

But when the right time comes, she nudges him out of that down-filled security blanket and teaches him to fly. "Like an eagle that stirs up its nest, that hovers over its young, He spread His wings and caught them, He carried them on His pinions. The Lord alone guided him" (Deuteronomy 32:11–12, NASB). While God is teaching us, we know that underneath are His wings of love, His everlasting arms.

The Rev. Everett L. Fullam, in his book *Facets of the Faith*, points out that an eagle will not flap its wings furiously to fly like other birds. An eagle "has the ability to lock its wings and wait for the right breeze. When [it] comes along, the eagle simply lets go and rides the wind."

So it is with Christians. The wise Christian will wait for the Wind, the Spirit, and then be "borne aloft" by His power.

Dr. Fullam tells how, when an eagle has a premonition of death, it will fly to a rock and fasten its talons to the edge. With eyes open, it looks straight into the setting sun. When the sun goes down, it dies.

Like Dr. Fullam, at the death of his father, I, too, have seen an eagle die. We drove up a hill, west of town, to the bedside of my grandfather. Gripping our hands, joy on his face, his eyes open looking straight at the *Son*, he breathed the name *Jesus*. He had lived his life in Jesus the Rock and now he was riding the heights home.

When I was a young girl people used the expression, "She certainly is a becoming young lady." Becoming what? I wondered. Now, I suppose it meant developing into an attractive person. Other expressions my mother used were "Give them credit" and "Everyone needs a chance to change." "Therefore if any man be in Christ, he is a new creature: old things are passed away; behold, all things are become new" (2 Corinthians 5:17, KJV).

I sat with my daughter April in a college Sunday school class at First Baptist in Atlanta where Dr. Charles Stanley is pastor. Bobbie, the teacher of that class, put it this way, "Everybody I know used to be someone else." That's a great statement . . . and we need to let them remain someone else, without looking back to penalize them for their pasts.

People change. Circumstance, suffering and God's unchanging mercy change people. When Ruth and Naomi arrived in Bethlehem, "All the city was excited because of them; and the women said, 'Is this Naomi?'" (Ruth 1:19).

The persecutor Saul became the Gospel proclaimer St. Paul. Peter used to be a foul-mouthed curser, but the Holy Spirit indwelt him and with that same mouth he preached the Good News of Jesus as Lord. All of the above used to be someone else.

Every time I see Nicky Cruz witnessing on television for Jesus, I remember that he used to be a gang member who tried to kill David Wilkerson for doing that very same thing, witnessing for Jesus Christ. You cannot meet the unchangeable Christ and not be changed. Everyone you know who has ever embraced Him used to be someone else.

Quiet your spirit and remember where God brought you from, and be thankful.

Mom Perky, my paternal grandmother, called me one day some years ago. "Bets, I hate to eat by myself. If you'll come, I'll go out back, pick six ripe apples off my tree and bake you a warm apple pie for lunch."

"If it's a come-as-you-are party," I said, "I'll be there. Twelve sharp!"

Driving south along the Wabash River through Terre Haute, Indiana, I crossed the bridge, drove through West Terre Haute, crossed Sugar Creek driving through the village of Toad Hop, up Larimer Hill and turned west on the winding road through the hollow. I spotted her little five-room house in the edge of the woods of maples and oak trees. It was a humble sight, but beautiful in the early spring. The red bud and dogwoods were starting to bloom, and I smelled the fragrance of smoke curling from her chimney even before I saw it. God love her, she knows how I love the sight of real wood burning in a fireplace.

I entered without knocking and hugged her in spite of the flour on her hands and all over her old-fashioned, green paisley cobbler apron.

"I can't find my nutmeg," she said by way of greeting. Looking up toward the ceiling, she prayed, "Lord, find my nutmeg."

"Mom Perky, I'll answer that prayer for you," I said. "I'm taller than you. Don't bother the God who is busy running the universe with such trivia!" I looked on the top shelf. I could not find it either.

She rolled out, then imprinted two fern leaves on the top crust, Mother's "trademark." Her name was Fern. We heard a knock.

There stood Bill Green's wife with a box of nutmeg in her hand. "I borrowed your grandma's nutmeg 'bout six weeks ago, and forgot to return it. Just two minutes ago, something reminded me."

After she left Mom Perky smiled at me. "See, I'm not crazy. I pray about everything. You know what's wrong with you, Betty? You're too smart to understand! You sing, 'What a friend we have in Jesus. . . . Oh, what peace we often forfeit . . . all because we do not carry *everything*—not just big things—to God in prayer.'"

Whether you have been *derailed* by inferiority or *sidetracked* by superiority . . . this one's for you!

For ten weeks recently, I dragged through a valley of dry bones. It was especially hard because, due to his work, I was not able to see Carl during that time. But I knew he would be home soon to comfort me and I was grateful for long walks and talks with the pastor's wife, Carol.

The cause of the extra burden during those weeks was a story that appeared in print about me designed to discredit my ministry. It was full of outright falsehoods. And if that were not enough, the reporter dug up a story about me from more than 25 years ago, a failure on my part that has been under the blood all this time. Jesus has already forgiven and forgotten it. It had nothing to do with my current ministry, and I felt it was mean-spirited of her to drag it up now.

Relatives offered money to fund a slander suit and Christian publishers defended my integrity. I decided to let Jesus be my defense. Still, the effect of that story on me was like robbery. It drained me of the fruit of the Spirit, especially my joy. The two gifts of the Spirit that the Lord has given me—messages and interpretations—slumped in me.

During one church service, after the singing, there was a lull and a sweet spirit of assurance rested on the congregation. The Holy Spirit, my coach, prompted me to speak out: "Come unto Me all you who labor and are heavy laden and I will give you rest. Take My yoke upon you and learn of Me. . . . In quietness and confidence shall be your strength. Rest in the Lord and wait patiently for Him." I did not, could not speak out.

Immediately Pastor Casey stood and took as his Bible text Matthew 11:28–30 (KJV): "Come unto me, all ye that labor and are heavy laden. . . ."

Even though I failed the Holy Spirit's prompting, I received the private confirmation that I am not an ugly stepchild, but one of God's loved, forgiven and cherished children. Driving home my Mustang became a private place of worship and rededication.

If you, the reader, are a wounded, lacerated sheep, Jesus is looking for you. He has a hidden, resting place waiting for you. King David found it. He proclaimed for generations to come, "He restoreth my soul!"

It is fun to watch a wee one at a wedding—the ring bearer. And in old movies about medieval times I thrill at the majestic grandeur of the cup bearer or the bearer of the crown. We do not wrangle, however, over the role of "burden bearer." Who wants it?

As part of his Jewish trade, the *atal* or professional burden bearer practiced this vocation up until the end of World War I. Many of these poor people, both men and women, walked around the streets of Jerusalem all day every day, available to ferry goods or deliver large loads of merchandise—furniture, baskets, boxes and burdens of all descriptions—for small pay.

The atal carried a rope in his hand, a harness around his waist and a yoke across his back to steady the loads that were often larger than he was. He made only a meager existence, a poor living. Sometimes compassionate people would help, but many times he would fall beneath the weight. Overturning the goods, upsetting themselves, they would lose the job. Many a man spent an entire lifetime bent over. Bending beneath loads all day, some became deformed and hunch backs.

Many of Jesus' messages were mini-sermons spoken in practical parables like one we can apply here. He became our burden bearer, carried our grief, bore our heavy load of sin up Golgatha's hill, all the way to the cross. And not for hire, but freely. Now He wants to help you lift your load.

Is your back against the wall? Are you bent over with your heaviness? David was there. In Psalm 38 he says, "There is no rest for my bones. My wounds are great. I mourn all day long. I am feeble, broken. Iniquities over my head are so heavy they topped me over. *My burden is too heavy for me.*"

Reader: Let down your load. Roll it over on the Lord. Let Jesus carry it for you. He is *the* authentic, official, initial burden bearer.

"Cast your burden on the Lord, and He shall sustain you" (Psalm 55:22). The "burden will be removed from your shoulders and . . . the yoke will be broken" (Isaiah 10:27, NASB).

My Uncle Earl Rodgers told me this: "If there is such a thing as good choice between the two, I'll take the hurricane over the tornado. It is rather predictable, can be spotted weeks before and the course charted. People can prepare beforehand. But a tornado is totally unpredictable." The one that hit Terre Haute where I used to live dipped down unexpectedly taking 36 homes; then it lifted leaving the next house right next door untouched. The newspaper remarked jovially, "One shall be taken, the other left."

We are reinforced for the predictables in life—birth, puberty, school, marriage, the normal perils of the aging process and natural death. But what about the unpredictables, the "and suddenlies" of life? And suddenly there is a wreck or cancer discovered. And suddenly a divorce or cardiac arrest occurs. And suddenly the unexpected loss of a job or tragic death of a loved one.

We have had many "and suddenlies" at our house in the last couple of years. They came hard and fast. We suddenly moved from a large Victorian house into a tiny four-room house. Our youngest daughter suddenly came back home to live in this tiny house. Carl went suddenly from a salary of $41,000 a year to $5,200 a year working on a foreign missions assignment in Siberia. Suddenly I broke my foot twice in three weeks. And while limping around, suddenly I learned that a misguided reporter had decided to destroy my integrity as a writer and a Christian, even though the late Catherine Marshall first researched and edited my "life after death" story for *Guideposts* magazine.

Can we be fortified for the "and suddenlies" of life? I think so. God does invade our crises. "In the time of trouble he shall hide me" (Psalm 27:5).

Yesterday we thought about the "and suddenlies" that are hardships. But for the believer who trusts God, an "and suddenly" can be a life-saving or life-giving event. Look at some "and suddenlies" in the Bible. In Genesis we read that the earth was in darkness, without form—and suddenly the Holy Spirit moved over the deep and brought order out of chaos.

The earth had become perverted and evil unnatural desires had stained God's perfect world. And suddenly God sent a flood. And suddenly the door of the ark was shut, and eight persons were kept safe.

Elijah debated with the worshipers of false gods—and suddenly the Creator-Living God sent fire from heaven to endorse Elijah and establish Truth.

Elisha was being ridiculed, harassed, persecuted—and suddenly bears came out of the woods and devoured his tormenters.

Daniel was flung into a den of hungry lions—and suddenly an angel came and shut the lions' mouths.

Another time in history, the earth was filled with violence and confusion. During the rule of the wicked King Herod, people trembled under the hand of cruelty—and suddenly there appeared to the shepherds on the hills of Judea a multitude of the heavenly host, singing glory to God in the highest and peace on earth toward men. Jesus, the deliverer Messiah, was born, the One named Wonderful, Counselor, Mighty God, Everlasting Father, Prince of Peace.

Again in history Christians needed supernatural strength—and suddenly there came from heaven a rushing, mighty wind, the wind of Pentecost. They received power after the Holy Ghost came upon them.

Saul had papers in his briefcase authorizing him to kill Christians—and suddenly a light shone from heaven, brighter than the noonday sun, and blinded him. He recognized the power of God and turned aboutface—and suddenly Saul the persecutor became Paul the saint.

We are approaching days when the spirit of anti-Christ shall pervade the peace of this world, when war and turmoil shall seek to destroy mankind—and suddenly Jesus shall come again and receive us to Himself!

Spoken or written words enter the ear or eye gate and are processed through the brain, but music skips the thought process and goes directly to the heart. It transcends the intellect and touches the soul. God reaches us this way . . . through music!

Music is essential. You can use it to express, refine, define and clarify the emotions locked inside. Music will allow you to express to God that which cannot be put into words. Without it, your relationship with Him will be reduced to an intellectual exchange.

How natural and basic music is. Have you noticed how easily and readily young children tap, hum, clap and dance? Language, no matter how hard one tries, cannot express the complete feelings of life. That is the role of music.

And more, music is a powerful connecting rod from this life to the next! Music is heaven's tuning fork, earth's dress rehearsal for heaven. There will be lots of singing there. The fifth chapter of Revelation describes the elders playing harps, ten thousands of angels singing, joined by every creature in heaven that has come from earth; the whole universe will sing to Him, worshiping Him who sits on the throne.

A children's psychiatrist did a survey of reform schools and prisons. He concluded that few children who had had the opportunity to study music or who enjoyed singing or playing a musical instrument were to be found in those institutions.

A resident doctor at a nearby mental institution said, "A patient is not yet hopeless who can be induced to sing and laugh aloud."

No wonder David played for King Saul to lift his depression and evil spirit. And no wonder that Nehemiah commanded that there be singing and music every day while the wall was being built. And no wonder that the psalms exhort *us* to sing, worship and praise with music!

*I am grateful to Paul Hamelink for the content of this devotional.

I had just finished speaking at a large church on a Sunday morning several years ago. The pastor told me, "This was our largest attendance ever. We will mail you an honorarium." This was good news for I had driven quite a distance and had paid for meals on the road.

Three weeks later, on Thursday, a "skinny" check for $50 arrived. I went in the hole nine bucks on that deal!

"I quit," I complained to Carl. "If God can't do any better than that, I quit working for Jesus."

Sunday afternoon the phone rang. It was Larry. He pastored a small-frame, country church a couple of hundred miles away from us.

"Betty, can you help us? Our missionary speaker is in bed with a high fever. Will you come and speak in our church tonight?"

"Larry, I quit working for Jesus last Thursday," I reported.

"I'm sorry to hear that," he said, as I slowly replaced the phone receiver.

Carl had overheard and suggested, "You'd better pray about this assignment, maybe." We prayed together and I called Larry back: "I'll be there."

During the five-hour drive, I reasoned that this was not a smart decision. Our house payment was due in three days and our checking account was low. It was not a good time to be adding to our expenses.

The audience was small but enthusiastic. Two people embraced Jesus as Savior. When it was time for me to leave, an usher handed me a brown paper bag with a rubber band twisted around the top. Grinning he said, "Here's your love offering. I didn't count it, but I hope it meets your need."

When I arrived back home it was almost midnight and I slipped into bed. Next morning I opened the sack, poured its contents onto the bed and started counting. . . .

It came to $438.22. Our house payment was $438. Those recording angels are excellent bookkeepers, even including 22 cents for the stamp to mail the payment!

"For God is not unjust to forget your work and labor of love which you have shown toward His name, in that you have ministered to the saints, and do minister" (Hebrews 6:10).

Rushing fast, almost running, I tried to get ahead of him in line to be first at the teller window of our little branch bank. I lost the race. That wispy, bent, little old man was swift.

Poorly dressed in a faded green sport shirt, atop a wrinkled pair of khaki walking shorts, he whispered confidently, "Myra, I want a bank draft for $30,000. I need to make a real estate investment."

Without looking up, the teller pushed a familiar button on her trusty computer, then went to work writing out the written "big request."

It was my turn, and I stepped to the window and whispered confidently, "Myra, I want a bankdraft for $30,000. I need a Mercedes."

Shocked, she looked up at me, pressed a few keys on her computer and replied, "Betty Malz, you crazy woman! You only have $112.33 in your account. The difference between you and Mr. Miller is the fact that he has been making small deposits over a long period of time. So, when he comes in and makes a big demand, we are familiar with his account and we give him what he asks for."

I cry about every two years whether I need it or not, but I cried all the way home from the bank. This is the way heaven's bank operates. The voice that the Father hears most frequently is the voice he recognizes most quickly. Like a parent. If a child phones often he is easily recognized, whether day or night. We will readily answer his or her request. Those little deposits (calls) of love are rewarded with a big supply of our love.

Carry on a running conversation with your Lord, as you do with a neighbor, or friend traveling in a car with you, or your doubles partner during the course of a game.

"Pray without ceasing" (1 Thessalonians 5:17).

My late husband, John, owned a Sunoco Service Station at 2030 Gulf To Bay in Clearwater, Florida. After his death following heart surgery, I tried to operate the business, but had to sell out. I had a twelve-year-old daughter, insecure without Daddy, and I was ill from grief and morning sickness: I was four months pregnant with our second child when he died.

I nearly miscarried but the tiny premie was born, and the two girls and I survived on Social Security and bouillon cubes. I wrote letters to individuals and businesses who owed my husband money, explaining that he did not have insurance, and shared my financial plight. Some replied, "We owed your husband. He is dead. We do not owe you anything." I went to small claims court and collected only one $50 account.

We were living on a two acre, mini-horse farm on north Summerdale Drive near Countryside Mall. Early one morning, bitter and wounded in spirit, I read in the Bible about forgiveness. I took printed records of $6,000 worth of accounts receivable out to the trash burner and struck a match. As the smoke ascended so did my prayer, "Lord, I forgive these hard-hearted debtors. Help me to forget their names." It felt so good to forgive people who did not deserve to be forgiven!

Sunday morning as I got into my car with the girls after church, I wondered, *Are there any just, honest, unselfish men left in this world?* Suddenly a man knocked with his knuckles on the car window. It was Shorty Osborn with two, one-dollar bills in his hand. "Wait!" he yelled, holding up the bills.

"What's this?" I asked, rolling down the window.

"For tires," he reported. "I told your man I would give him two dollars every week until my set of tires was paid for."

"Shorty, I don't have any records. Do you want a receipt?"

"Don't need one. Me and him, we had an understanding. He trusted me and I trusted him. I know how much I owe, and when I git it all paid off *you'll* know, 'cause I'll quit bringin' you two dollars on Sunday morning."

And he did—pay off his debt and restore my faith in *man*kind.

When you pray, forgive.

Proverbs 22:6 says, "Train up a child in the way he should go, and when he is old he will not depart from it." He will remember the memories. I have just returned from a women's retreat in Winnipeg, Canada. Some of the material used for one session, "Survival by Our Faith and Prayer," was taken from *Prayers That Are Answered*. Kathy Penner, from Ames, Manitoba, told me a story involving that book and her son.

She was propped up in bed reading it one evening before retiring. Her little four-year-old son, Braydon, who was suffering from a bad cold, crawled up on her lap and asked her to read to him.

She told me, "It's an adult book, but I accommodated him, just to soothe him, doubting that it would have any lasting effect on his mind. Before tucking him into his bed, I prayed for his cold and promised him that God would always answer his prayers if he would ask, then trust the Lord."

Next morning Braydon was indeed better and went next door to play with his friend Andy. Near lunchtime the two little guys came running in, chattering excitedly, to report a most curious experience. They had found a baby eagle lying lifeless in the grass. Braydon informed his friend that if they would pray, God would make it fly away.

"Mom, you'll never believe it! The bird flew away!" Andy nodded in agreement, speechless, his eyes wide with wonder.

I am quite sure that if two adults had seen a young eagle lying lifeless, they would have stared at it, and then buried it or left it lying there. But the faith of a child . . . an elementary, trusting type of faith. I do not even know if God would have performed such a miracle for adults. Perhaps He did it for two children to launch them on life's journey of faith.

Oh, for that simple, trusting faith, that "except-ye-become-as-little-children" faith!

"From the mouth of babes. . . ."

When my two older brothers and I were in high school, our baby brother, Marvin, was born. Under the influence of older siblings, he developed mentally beyond his years. Every morning my mother and dad always had family devotions, dubbed "family emotions," as I mentioned earlier, by Marvin who was three years old at the time. They read from *Our Daily Bread*, then they prayed with us before we boarded what Mother termed "the big orange monster that swallows up my children": the school bus.

One morning only a few days after renaming our family altar times, the doorbell rang. Mother was frying chicken and had flour on her hands. Looking through the window she saw "Bea," a large, lazy, "busy-body" neighbor.

"Marvie," Mother said, "will you be Mommie's helper and get the door please?" Little Marv loved to be helpful. He went to the door and invited the lady in. When Mother arrived, he pointed to our grandfather clock in the hall, and turning to her said, "Mommie, her face did *not* stop an eight-day clock."

Mother had no idea that little ears had been listening when she had remarked about Bea months before, "That woman was hit with an ugly stick. Her husband is not bad looking, but she has a face that would stop an eight-day clock."

We lived in an old two-story house in New Castle, Indiana. There was no heat in the upstairs bedroom, and one below-zero night, Mother heated a comforter and hurried to tuck little Marvin in for the night. We heard him singing, as gustily as a three-year-old can, the old hymn, "The Comforter Has Come." Not a bad sermon application.

"Take heed to yourself, and diligently keep yourself, lest you forget the things your eyes have seen. . . . And teach them to your children" (Deuteronomy 4:9).

Sometimes our children become the teachers.

When I was seventeen, I fell in love with John Upchurch, a "Kentucky Wonder" whose family had moved to the small Hoosier town of New Castle, Indiana, where my father, Glenn Perkins, pastored a small church on South Eighteenth Street.

We were married two years to the day, at Thanksgiving time, in a private service at my parents' home. I had just started working for Edwards Jewelry Store and he had been hired at the Chrysler factory.

We were so happy as we drove 124 miles to the annual Thanksgiving dinner held every year at my grandparents' home in Terre Haute. Thirty-one relatives were present to congratulate us and admire our shiny, new wedding bands, which I had obtained wholesale from my new boss.

Then a neighbor put a hole in our air balloon. She was a large, redheaded, freckled, gossipy woman living near my parents. She had worked overtime, I learned, going about our little town convincing neighbors, a few church members, and a couple of employees with whom I worked that it was a plain fact that I had to get married! She was certain that I was pregnant before wedlock. Otherwise, why did I have a private wedding instead of a church wedding, since my father was a pastor?

I was devastated. My dad told me that maturity was to suffer without complaining, and be misundersood without explaining. He went on to discuss with me the Virgin Mary.

The young mother of Jesus did not have to advertise the fact that she was indeed unmarried and with child. She kept the secret and waited silently, knowing that time would tell the truth—that she was pregnant, but also, eventually, that she was God's servant.

I decided to use the Mary technique in reverse and wait out the storm, knowing that time was on my side. Everyone would know the truth in nine short months. (I admit they did seem long, though.)

In the meantime, while reading the Bible my eyes fell upon a Scripture concerning Jesus found in Isaiah 53:7. Jesus was oppressed, but He did not open His mouth.

When our first child was born four years later, the same people who had laughed *with* the talebearer were now laughing loudly *at* her.

January 22   *The Best Things in Life Are Free*

In the morning, as the sun comes up, open your east window and view without cost the glorious sunrise. Next take a deep breath of fresh air, no charge, an unseen gift: Try living without it! You also get today, without asking, sixty minutes in each hour and 24 hours. Now, beside that open window, prop up in bed and sip a fresh cup of rich, dark, coffee, Stockholm blend, while listening to a twenty-minute concert directed by God, the divine Maestro. No ticket necessary to hear the mockingbird sing.

If you are as fortunate as I am, just by driving to the Gulf of Mexico you can "rent" for nothing waterfront property that sells by the frontage foot, million-dollar property with more than a million-dollar view. You can pick up antique shells and take them home to look at and enjoy permanently. While there you can even scoop up some white sand with cake flour texture. No one will arrest you for taking these sea treasures.

Wherever she traveled, my mother collected beautiful rocks for her rock garden, for free. In the Dakotas, after the great runoff when the snows melt, stones wash from the streams and surface from the soil. Some people even make a pretty good living in the spring "picking rocks."

Here in Florida no one will bill you for the marvelous fragrance that wafts freely from the orange blossom groves. You may pick a wild periwinkle in pink (blue??) or white. These tiny volunteers come up uninvited annually, sometimes blooming between the cracks in the sidewalk or on dusty roadways in out of the way places. You may dip your toes in a cool creek, fish in the Gulf or go crabbing—all without paying.

And there is no admission charge to go to God's house on Sunday to worship.

But, by far, the greatest free gift of all is eternal life, received by believing on the Lord Jesus Christ.

"Whoever desires, let him take the water of life freely" (Revelation 22:17). The best thing in life is free!

"What have I gotten into? . . . This is the worst trial of my life. . . . I see no way out of this mess. . . . I'm on a dead end road, I've reached the end of my rope. . . . My back's against the wall, Satan has me cornered. . . . I'm misunderstood by my friends. . . . Trouble seems to come, not singularly, but in litters. . . . Where is God? The heavens seem like brass when I pray. . . . My tears won't stop flowing. My troubles are many and my friends are few."

Have you heard these exclamations? Have you even quoted them to, or about, yourself?

If you are suffering opposition from the marketplace, or hurt in your own home, if you need healing, help and hope, He is your *now* God.

If you have gotten yourself into a dilemma because of your own ignorance or transgression, if Satan and his foul, opposing spirits are harassing you, rejoice that you have that kind of reputation in hell, that those opposing forces deem you a threat to their evil kingdom.

Psalm 46:1 says, "God is a very *present* help in trouble." God is in our midst. We can be still and know that He is God.

Hebrews 13:8 says, "Jesus Christ is the same yesterday, today, and forever." This qualifies Jesus as your counselor, your healer and deliverer from every circumstance.

Let's look at His *yesterdays*. He raised Lazarus from the dead. He cured leprosy and every kind of disease. Let's consider His *forever*. He is coming again to air-lift us out of this wicked world to heaven, His forever home and Kingdom.

You can trust the Creator of the vast universe with your *nows*. His map never leads to a dead end.

"No temptation has overtaken you except such as is common to man; but God is faithful, who will not allow you to be tempted beyond what you are able, but with the temptation will also make the way of escape, that you may be able to bear it" (1 Corinthians 10:13).

*I am grateful to Pastor Roger Casey for the content of this message.

Life is not always fair. Look around you at the injustices, the inequalities of life. All men are not created equal. Perhaps you have been fired from a job, falsely accused, or someone has stretched, shrunken or inflated something you said to twist its meaning and bring you sorrow. You may be suffering a wounded spirit and you picked up this book looking for a formula for how to get even. You've got it!

Everyone will not like you. Even though Jesus was perfect, not everyone liked Him. They pulled out His beard, spat in his face and killed Him. When He was accused, railed upon, "He did not open his mouth." He refused to act as they acted.

He said, in effect, you do not have to hang around people who do not like you. On at least one occasion He could do no miracles because of the people's unbelief in Him. He took his disciples aside and gave them a little pep talk:

"Boys, they don't like us here. They have disdain and disrespect for us and for God. If you go to places like this and even have some sand in your shoes, shake it out and get on to believers where you can do some good."

Personally, I believe we waste a lot of time being sidetracked with people who have closed their eyes. None is so blind as he who closes his eyes. You can expend and exhaust your time and energy on a few parasites who are not going anywhere. You could spend less time feeding a hungry heart, speaking to a listening ear, with a thousand times the results. I have wasted two hours on a phone trying to convince one paranoid, negative, nitpicking, legalistic, mentally overfed person, when I could have spent that time using my gift, writing words that would be read by a number of anxious, positive, receptive hearts.

Ask the Lord through the Holy Spirit to help you discern sincerity. Check for genuine motives. Do your best, then God will make up the rest. And when you run into difficult people, remember that Jesus also said, "Love your enemies, bless those who curse you" (Matthew 5:44).

Would you like to have twice as much as you have ever had in your life before? You can double your pleasure, get double for your investment. The formula for this is chronicled in the book of Job.

Job's "luck" ran out. His misery was multiplied. He was sick, had boils, lost property, and when he went to his wife for comfort, she told him, to paraphrase loosely, "Job, why don't you curse God and die, and get me out of *my* misery."

He found that many of his neighbors were miserable comforters. His friends and acquaintances accused him of sin and rebellion.

Job did not need a formula; he had the Father. He did three things.

One, Job never did blame God. He was respectful of the difference between the things he did and did not understand. (We would do well to reverence this as well instead of trying to figure everything out in our own mentality. We must refuse to let the things we do not understand rob us of the things that we know.)

Two, Job acquainted himself with God. He spoke of God "what is right" (Job 42:7). Even so, when God revealed Himself to Job, Job was stunned by His greatness.

Three, Job prayed for the friends who had let him down, instead of getting even, and, as he did, God reversed his misfortune into a fortune. God gave him *twice* as much as he had before! He doubled his pleasure. Jesus offers you this marvelous investment opportunity, you, the modern, contemporary reader and investor! Realize that God understands, even when we do not. Realize, too, that God is bigger than we can imagine. And pray for those who hurt you. God will work it for your good.

I rummaged through the Bible quickly, window-shopping for a "sharp, two-edged sword" verse to cut down my mother-in-law. She had gone too far this time. I was out to get even, get revenge. I was only nineteen, as I have mentioned, when I married John, her first son, her pride and joy. And she and I had a competitive encounter right off.

There were religious and age differences, too, and now I realize that I was secretly jealous of her cooking ability and the 22 years of motherly influence over my husband.

I found it! She was an old-fashioned Methodist and I knew she would be impressed if I fought back with Scriptures. I would meet her words of criticism with Psalm 141:3. I picked up the phone and prepared my little speech. I would tell her, "Before you 'pop off' to me again, quote this: 'Set a watch, O Lord, before my mouth; keep the door of my lips'" (KJV).

My verbal gun was loaded for her, both barrels. I dialed her number but the phone only rang once, when the plot backfired on me. I put the phone receiver down quickly, and never did deliver my message. The word had condemned me. I was about to criticize her, and God had put a sentry at the door of my lips to keep me from hurting her, placing my husband in an embarrassing situation and jeopardizing my communication with her for the rest of the sixteen years I was married to her son before his death.

One day, many years after that episode, I was running through the Minneapolis airport, briefcase and small carry-on luggage in hand, when an obese woman yelled out to me, "I just recognized you. You're Betty Malz! Give me a word from the Lord to help me lose weight." I learned then that Scripture can have two meanings.

Now, I am not patient with people who think they are God's fortune-tellers; people who want to hear from the Lord should just dial direct. But it was too good an opportunity to miss. I answered her with the mother-in-law verse: "Psalm 141:3," I shouted. "Set a watch, O Lord, before my mouth; keep the door of my lips . . . to guard me from overeating!"

While on vacation in the summer of 1959, I was hospitalized in Morton Plant Hospital in Clearwater. A spicy old lady in the next bed to mine introduced herself. "My last name is Ill. With a name like that, I've been sick all my life."

In junior high, I rode the school bus with a boy named Small who was quite large, and a girl whose last name was Butts—and she wished it weren't.

In my age group, parents named their boys Gordon, Paul, John and David. The next generation had an epidemic of Brian, Keith, Chris, Rick and Mike. Names are popular in cycles.

Scanning through the Bible, I read where Abraham had a brother named Nahor, who had baby twin boys. The nephews of the famous Abraham were named Huz and Buz (Genesis 22:20–21). Now those are unique names. I have never heard of any people naming their kids Huz and Buz.

Before our first baby was born, I told my husband, "If this baby is a son I think I'll name him 'Benaiah' and call him 'Ben.'"

His reply was, "You're joking, right? What's wrong with John or David—some 'out front' Bible names? Who is Benaiah, anyway?"

I feel sorry for Benaiah. No one names a boy after him, and he was a great man. Just because his name is mentioned in the Bible only once, people overlook his fame and bravery. He was one of the three most honorable of King David's warriors. He slew two lionlike men of Moab; he went down and slew a lion in the midst of a deep pit, on a slippery, snowy day; and he had enough bravery to attack an enemy Egyptian, wrench the spear from his hand and kill him with it (2 Samuel 23:20).

If your name is not a popular one, take courage. I believe that in heaven some generic-named people will be celebrated for their courage and faith. And they will be given new names to hold proudly for the rest of eternity.

I began a prayer journey several years ago when I realized that others had tremendous testimonies of answered prayer and it seemed that I prayed a lot, but got few results. My journey came to a screeching halt one day when, through jest, a remark got my attention.

Carl and I were playing tennis with a neighbor couple. The husband (I'll call him Chuck) had a profane mouth and his five-year-old daughter was picking up his habit of cursing. I mentioned this to Chuck and told him teasingly, "I'm going to pray about your big mouth."

He leaned on the net, grinned and replied, "Aw, Betty, I cuss a lot and you pray a lot, but neither one of us really means what we're saying."

That remark gripped me. He had hit close to home.

The following morning I was wrestling with my weekly newspaper column, trying to come up with a new topic, when the phone rang. It was one of my brothers. "I've got a great idea for your column. Title it: 'Americans Waste Words,'" he said and then gave a couple of examples.

I liked the idea and and after dropping the column off at the newspaper office, I dropped to my knees and prayed, "Dear Lord, Americans waste words in conversation and Christians waste words in prayer. Forgive me for falling into the same routine with words. If You will begin to answer prayer for me, I will remember that You are too busy running the universe to shift into neutral while I let my mind wander. From this day on, I will say what I mean, and mean what I say. Amen."

Prayer is not conquering God's reluctance. It is not worrying out loud. Prayer is praise for what He has already done, then laying hold of His willingness to do more. As James tells us, the effectual, fervent prayer of a righteous man or woman avails much (5:16).

Shortly after my new prayer pact with the Lord, I started getting answers to my simple, concentrated praying. I prayed for a young woman who could not have children. Weeks later an ultrasound showed she was pregnant. Two of Carl's and my daughters found their mates and married within the year. I prayed for firewood and we received an abundance.

"Now, Lord, about Chuck. . . ."

The apostle John saw four angels standing on the four corners of the earth holding back the four winds (Revelation 7:1). One of our astronauts clarified this. No, the earth is not square. It is round from up there in space, but there are four ridges several hundred miles long, spaced like corners, positioned on the surface of the earth.

I got a letter from a young bride and a picture she had taken from the window of an airplane. She and her husband had never been on a plane before and, on their honeymoon, when they flew for the first time, she was so fascinated that she took a whole roll of film from the porthole. The topside of the clouds looked to her like Kool Whip. Then the pilot's voice came through the intercom and warned, "Please be seated and fasten your seatbelts. Our monitors show about twenty minutes of severe turbulence ahead."

The honeymoon couple, so frightened, became instant "white knuckle" flyers. As the plane dipped and dove her husband cried aloud, "O God, don't let this plane crash! Send angels to hold this plane upright and keep us safe!" Everyone turned to look at the greenhorn fliers but they did not care, they were so afraid.

Suddenly the choppy wind subsided. The second officer got on the intercom and said, "Folks, we have up here in the cockpit what we call an unexplainable. The monitor showed twenty minutes of turbulence, and it was over in two minutes. We don't understand, but it sure feels good."

The couple knew that their prayers had been answered but not how, until they picked up their photo prints at the Anderson Pharmacy the following week. In one of the pictures in the center of the cloud formation was an enormous angel.

That couple believes that they were helped by one of the angels that John saw, spoken of in that passage: "I saw four angels standing at the four corners of the earth, holding the four winds of the earth, that the wind should not blow."

Bill, his wife, Bev, and their two children were vacationing near Big Bear Lake in California near Apple Valley. First night there, they built a fire and were cooking dinner, having a cozy, family time. Before eating in the great outdoors, Bill read from the Scriptures, thanked the Lord for the food and prayed that the Lord would protect them and keep them safe in that remote location and return them safely home.

As Bev and the children began eating Bill took several pictures by the light of the campfire. Suddenly five men roared up on motorcycles and one pulled a gun. "Put your wallet and purse on the ground." They did as they were ordered.

The men suddenly seemed frightened. Rather than pick up the money, they jumped on their motorcycles and left as quickly as they had arrived.

All the way home the kids could talk of nothing else. Little Billy kept saying, "It didn't make sense. They had every advantage. They had a gun. We did what they said, but they didn't take our money." The young father tried to explain to the children that unseen angels indeed do protect those who love the Lord.

It was not until they returned home from the vacation that they fully realized this truth. The invisible became highly visible. They had their pictures developed and in one photo a large, protecting angel was standing directly behind Bev and children. That is what frightened the men away.

Isaiah 63:9 says, "The Angel of His Presence saved them." Psalm 35:5 says, "Let the angel of the Lord chase them."

I grabbed my pelican beach towel and raced toward Clearwater Beach. It was my last opportunity to walk along the shore in the soft white sand and warm sunshine before flying to Canada where they still had snow.

I made one quick "pit stop" at Eckerd Drug Store and bought suntan oil. The label read, "Invisible Protection SPF 2."

Humming down Highway 19 in my old MGA, I read a bumper sticker: "Pray for Me. I Drive on Highway 19." Not a half mile farther I read another one: "Pray for Yourself. . . . I LIVE on Highway 19." The traffic is getting worse here—not just from the snow birds in winter, but year-round.

Those two hours in the sun energized me to return home, pack and head for the Tampa airport. My young friend Sonja came by to drive me. It started to rain as we loaded the last box of books. The sky looked angry.

Crossing the Courtney Campbell Causeway over Tampa Bay, the winds were gusting walls of water over the highway. We thanked the Lord that Sonja's little two-year-old, Stephanie, had fallen asleep in her carseat. Cars were drowned out. Lighter weights had washed off-course and were stalled alongside. The van seemed top heavy. I watched the intent look on Sonja's face as she strained to hold the van on the road.

It was strange, but I remembered crossing that causeway years before to hear Ethel Waters sing the old classic song, "When the storms of life are raging, stand by me. God who rulest wind and weather stand by me."

By the time we reached the Tampa airport, it was paralyzed. We sat for hours, restless but unaware that tornado winds at a hundred miles an hour ripped and dipped around us, bringing destruction.

Sonja, baby Stephanie and I had experienced God's invisible protection that April day. King David, long before, had asked the Lord to "hasten my escape from the windy storm and tempest" (Psalm 55:8). Generations past had learned that God was Abraham's invisible shield (Genesis 15:1).

Now, I have never really cared for worms.

Mind you, I am not the typical woman who squeals at a mouse and shrieks at a roach. In fact, I riddled to pieces two snakes in my yard with the lawn mower, and enjoyed it.

I have always wondered where the old saying "The early bird gets the worm" came from. I asked an old salty fisherman from the quaint fishing village of Ozona, Florida, near here. He explained, "If you want to get good fishing worms for bait, you have to get up early in the morning and dig into the soil when the earth is cool from the night air and moist from the early morning dew."

While talking to him, I recalled a Scripture that I believe is a clue to getting some of our best answers through prayer: "Those that seek me *early* shall find me" (Proverbs 8:17).

I believe this verse has three meanings. One, pray early in the day before cares and doubts crowd in, before our logic and faith can be diluted by the devil's negative input of bluff and deception. Two, pray early at the onset of a crisis before the situation gets out of hand. Three, learn to pray at an early age, flexing your faith muscles while you are young so that you may mature into a full-fledged prayer warrior, at whose voice in prayer the enemy fears, trembles and flees.

You do not wait until after an accident to go buy auto insurance.

There is a classic illustration that says it best: Two old Christian pioneers, forging westward to seek a better life for their families, came to a river with a great many crocodiles along the bank. One man rushed in and swam quickly across the river to safety. The second man stopped to pray, and when he tried to swim across was nearly eaten by four hungry crocodiles.

"Don't seem right," the second survivor complained to his companion. "I'm the one who took time to pray, yet you had safer passage. How do you explain that?"

"Easy," the first man replied. "I prayed early this morning, before the onset of the journey. I didn't have to stop when the crisis came."

February 2   Prayer, the Long-Range Investment

We were sitting in the little deli at the corner of Old Tampa Road and County Road One, licking a frozen yogurt, when Sonja, my new neighbor from Nebraska, told me a most amazing story about prayer on a long-range basis. Here is the story she told me.

Sonja's little four-year-old brother was full of mischief. She said that her mother was usually very mild, but this time he had really misbehaved. For punishment, he was to sit on the couch for one hour and be denied the privilege of going outside to play. While she sat explaining the discipline to him, Sonja's mother noticed a story on the front page of the newspaper lying on the couch nearby.

The wirephoto in the Nebraska paper showed two tiny little girls in Indiana, badly beaten by a drunken father. In his rage, he had taken a large pine branch from a tree and nearly killed them both. The alcoholic father was to be imprisoned for one year.

After the hour was up and Sonja's little brother went out to play, their mother's heart was touched and she felt divinely compelled to pray for the mother of the children in the newspaper story, and for the two little girls. She prayed, "Lord, heal their little bruised bodies and remove the emotional fallout so that they may grow up loving and free from fear. Save this young family." She kept that clipping and prayed for the girls for sixteen years.

Over those years her little boy grew up and one day announced to his family that he was going to be married. He had fallen in love with the daughter of a new family from Indiana.

Later, when the couple began making wedding plans, his fiancee took his mother aside and told a most curious story. Marrying into such a fine, loving family, she feared they would be offended if they learned later that her father had been in jail for a year for his alcoholic abuse. Sonja's mother learned that she was one of the little girls in the picture!

The couple is still happily married. What joy! Sonja's mother had no idea that she was praying for her own sweet daughter-in-law—a loving and suitable bride for her son! Prayer pays!

There is no hurt so painful as a family hurt. I can handle criticism and rejection from strangers pretty well, but I need the vote of my husband and kids.

Evidently the famous comedienne Carol Burnett experienced some "close at hand guff." I heard her advise parents, "Love your kids enough to let them hate you for two years until they get their heads screwed on straight."

I heard a speaker last Father's Day misquote the verse, "What shall it profit a man if he gain the whole world and lose his own *son?*"

As a family counselor, Carl spends many hours praying for those with broken hearts and wounded spirits inflicted by relatives, friends and lovers. Zechariah 13:6 asks the question, "Where did you receive these wounds?" The answer, "I was wounded in the house of my friends."

We expect wounds from enemies, but are totaly unprepared for the kind of hurt we receive from those closest to us. Jesus knew this kind of wound. How His tender heart of compassion was wrung out by the betrayal of Judas, one of the Twelve. Peter's denials hurt, too.

In John 11 we read that Jesus raised Lazarus after he had been bound in his grave clothes for four days. What an impossible miracle of miracles!

Yet instead of his close associates being joyous about this, the scribes and Pharisees, the church folks, tried to kill Lazarus to destroy the evidence of Jesus' miracle. If strangers and foreigners had done this, it would not have hurt so deeply. Scripture tells us that Jesus came to His own, but His own received Him not.

I am sure this is why Jesus told us to "Love your neighbor as yourself."

"Impart grace. . . . And be kind to one another, tenderhearted, forgiving one another, even as God in Christ forgave you" (Ephesians 4:29, 32).

One Sunday I spoke in Pastor Davidson's church in Frankfort, Illinois. Just before he introduced me, the congregation sang the song "Channels Only," followed by the chorus "Lord, Make Me an Instrument." My mind raced ninety miles per hour. We are only channels, not power surge cables. Jesus is the director, we are merely His extension cords.

While looking for a scrap of paper to write on, I spotted in my briefcase two things that I carry with me from my past: a rusty brass bank, my first Christmas present in 1929 as a baby during the depression, costing fifty cents, and a hand-signed letter from Madame Chiang Kai-shek. She had read my book *My Glimpse of Eternity* in the Chinese language and wrote to thank me for removing her fear of death. The bank is my humble "downer" if I feel a wee bit proud; the letter from Madame C. is my "upper" if some snooty looks down on me.

Humility is recognizing that God and others are responsible for the achievements in my life. "And what do you have that you did not receive? Now if you did indeed receive it, why do you boast as if you had not received it?" (1 Corinthians 4:7).

Many ministers could well take a lesson from the traveling salesman who was so busy boasting about his position with the company that he forgot to take orders, forgot to fill orders, forgot the boss for whom he was working—and lost his job. It is not our Church, but God's.

Many years ago my Uncle Cecil left Indiana for a new life in California. He bought a restaurant and a deep sea fishing boat to supply fresh seafood. The sixteen-year-old girl who babysat for them a few hours each evening during dinner was also the babysitter for Lucille Ball and Desi Arnaz' children. When she was supposed to be tending to my uncle's children, she actually spent so much time on the phone, calling and bragging to her friends about the celebrities that she worked for, that she had no time left to do her work. She neglected the children she was being paid to care for, and was fired.

You cannot fool a praying mother. Carl and I were sipping cups of hot chocolate with a big, fat marshmallow floating and melting atop, and discussing this matter.

When I was a junior in high school, I thought I had "arrived." I was dating a graduating senior, the high point man on the basketball team. I wore his class ring and continued seeing him when he came home on furlough from the Navy. He wrote regularly, a letter once each week.

Jumping off the school bus one day, I ran into the house and inquired, "Mother, did I get a letter?"

"Yes," she replied solemnly, "but this one is not a good letter. The Lord seemed to whisper to my mother's heart that you should read this one very carefully, and respond the way God would have you to."

"Mother, I can't believe you read my letter! You have never read my mail before. Why did you violate my privacy?" She was quick to assure me that she had not opened the envelope, but while in prayer felt cautioned.

Later in my bedroom, I slowly read his words: "When I come home this weekend we will make physical love like mature adults, or you can give my class ring back. We are no longer children playing kissing games." I mailed his ring to him, and did not wait for his next date to tempt me to sin against virtue.

At our house it became a family joke among my brothers and me: "Be careful. God tells Mother *everything!*"

My husband laughed while I recounted the above. He said he was always big for his age, and felt like a big shot. One night he and some of his friends believed they could go to a tavern, pass for 21-year-olds and buy drinks.

Before retiring, his mother and dad knelt to pray. Rose Malz felt a prompting that her son Carl was about to get into trouble. How did she know which tavern of the many in Cleveland, Ohio, to march into? She just knew, and when she entered it she spoke only one word, "Carl." He followed her home.

When mothers talk to God, God talks back to mothers!

My friend Karen Siddle loves to walk along the north shore from Palm Pavillion to the tip of Clearwater Beach. Strolling along, she silently prays and receives messages, or "telegrams," in the form of practical parables. She keeps them in her mental computer for future reference and delivers them at women's retreats or when she speaks at churches.

Karen walked by my pew one Sunday morning and dropped a rock into my lap. On one side was printed "Betty's." Turning it over, I saw two words printed: "Giant Killer."

After church I asked for an explanation. She said it was related to 1 Samuel 17. A *known champion*, a warrior of the Philistine army, had defied the army of Israel, the children of the living God. An *unknown boy* accepted the challenge. Goliath was nine feet nine inches tall and wore a brass helmet. His protective coat of mail weighed 166 pounds. He carried a spear and had a body guard to go before him with a shield. Little David insulted the champion when he flung *one* stone. Only a rock, but it was directed in the name of the Lord, hit the mark, killed the enemy. The Lord was the rock that David threw at the giant.

When giants loom large in your life, His name will be enough. He is the source who will send help, or the resource who can create what you need. Use the Lord, *your rock*, against your financial enemy, the giant of sickness or marital strife. Find yourself a little rock to keep in your pocket, on your desk, in your car, as a monument, a reminder, a token. Put your name on one side and Giant Killer on the other.

All you will ever need is God and the rock of His name. The name of the Lord will always be enough. In Psalm 18, beginning with verse 1 and following through to the last verse of the chapter, verse 50, David transfers to all generations the key to win any battle to come: The Lord is my rock for great deliverance forevermore!

When Carl left a pastorate with a generous, guaranteed salary and took a missions assignment in Russia with a *faith school* my financial wheels began to whirrrrrrr. I began to do what I always do in a crunch or pinch—search the Scriptures.

Wow! I found two wealthy verses! Deuteronomy 8:18 says, "Remember the Lord your God, for it is He who gives you power to get wealth." (I was a little disappointed that it did not say *keep* it.) Then I found another. I have found that the more I pray, the more "coincidences" happen; the less I pray, the fewer "coincidences" happen. It was no mere coincidence that Deuteronomy 8:18 and Proverbs 8:18 are almost alike. Proverbs 8:18 says, "Riches and honor are with me, enduring riches and righteousness." That is good. Not just temporary help and blessing, but durable, lasting riches. Sounded all right to me.

I read on to the end of the chapter: Those who love the Lord will inherit substance; He will fill their treasures. Blessed are those who love Him and keep His ways." I qualify. I love the Lord.

That same week I received a letter from two friends of mine in Texas. Their boutique was suffering because of the oil recession and they asked for prayer. Unless God came to their rescue to the tune of $10,000, they would have to liquidate and give up. May 10 was their cut-off day. I called several trusted friends to pray. The morning of the 10th the Lord came through for them. Funds came in and their business turned around and is prospering.

Recently I needed new clothing to travel, speak and do telecasts. The women I prayed for guessed at my size and taste, and sent me lovely things to wear that have brought joy to me personally.

Now come the durable riches. As I have traveled, not only has God blessed me, but people have given generously and I have been able help Carl invest in souls for eternity in the Russian revival.

Get wealth; don't keep it. This is the way to durable, long-lasting eternal investments.

Philippians 4:19 says that God shall supply all my *needs*, not my *greeds!*

Was it a misprint? Is it possible to be whiter than snow? I read and reread Psalm 51:7: "Wash me, and I shall be whiter than snow."

David ought to know. He sinned grossly and publicly after he became famous, yet the Lord forgave him and later said, "David is a man after My own heart." It is possible to be forgiven and cleansed.

David was appreciative and thankful for this mercy from his God. He went on to say:

> Make me to hear joy and gladness, that the bones you have broken may rejoice. Hide your face from my sins, and blot out all my iniquities. Create in me a clean heart, O God, and renew a steadfast spirit within me. . . . Restore to me the joy of Your salvation, and uphold me by your generous Spirit. [If You will do this for me, God,] then I will teach transgressors Your ways, and sinners shall be converted to You. . . . And my tongue shall sing aloud of Your righteousness.
>
> Psalm 51:8–14

David's soul was soiled, but it became whiter than snow.

I talked to a chemist and he assured me that indeed the image is no misprint. He told me how each flake of snow is first a speck of dust. As it falls toward the ground, it picks up moisture and humidity and becomes coated with frost as it passes throught the cold atmosphere. It arrives soft, awesomely white and magnificently unique from all other snowflakes.

But not as white as a redeemed soul in Jesus' care.

Our God "is able to do exceedingly abundantly above all that we ask or think" (Ephesians 3:20).

Jesus had been preaching to large groups of people and sought some privacy to regroup and refresh Himself, but the multitudes followed. They were hungry and there was no place to buy food. A boy had brought a lunch with him of five loaves of bread (probably slices) and two fishes. Out of the generosity of his heart, upon the request of the disciples, the little fellow offered to share it with that immense, hungry crowd.

Jesus had the people sit on the ground, picnic style, in groups of fifty. As I read this account, I thought, *There is no way five loaves and two fishes will feed more than a few people.* I buy smoked mullet to serve my small family of three. But after 5,000 men were fed, their wives and children, too, they had twelve baskets of bread and fish left over! That's an embarrassing abundance!

When Carl taught at Trinity Bible College in North Dakota, Bob Brenneman went there to study. He wanted to be a missionary.

Upon his graduation he received his first appointment—not overseas, but in Chicago with Teen Challenge, working to help young people overcome addictions to drugs and alcohol.

Bob and his fiancee, Sherry, wanted to get married before he went to Chicago, but they had no money. Carl got up in chapel service one morning and took a love offering for them. They were thankful and appreciative for the $700 received.

Later on that same day a young woman came to Carl's office. She told him, "My husband died suddenly and I decided to come to Bible School. I sold our farm and put the tithe, amounting to $3,400, in a savings account and have prayed for two years asking God what I should do with it. I've heard a lot of speakers in that time and listened to many appeals, but never felt they were right. This morning I knew God's will. I want to give it to the Brennemans, but anonymously." And she did.

This was an embarrassing abundance for Bob and Sherry. They did go to Chicago, then on to the foreign mission field where they along with their three darling children are now serving God.

Looking in the mirror one day I remarked to my husband, "I look like a Yankee. I am so white, people on the street would never know I was a resident Floridian."

We had had a lot of company, making it necessary for me to be indoors cooking and entertaining; we had had a lot of rain for a long period of time with little sunshine; and the previous two weeks had been spent helping Carl get ready for his trip to Siberia where he would spend two months helping establish a Bible school.

I enjoyed celebrating his 69th birthday and our twentieth anniversary the Friday before he left. The following morning at 6:20 A.M. I drove him to the Tampa airport and kissed him goodbye, then headed for Caladesi Island near Dunedin Beach.

I sat on the soft, warm sand in the early morning sun watching a young pelican plunge his strong, gray beak into the shallow water, fishing for his breakfast. Perched on his head was a determined sea gull. Once, after pulling up a small fish, the pelican tried to shake the pest off his head and, in the attempt, the sea gull grabbed the fish before the pelican could swallow it.

I recalled an illustration that Jesus used once while he sat in a small boat just offshore, teaching the people who were sitting and listening: "If you have ears, listen! Some see but do not perceive; some hear but do not understand. Satan does not want them to comprehend lest they be converted and their sins be forgiven them. He tries to steal the words of life before they receive them. The sower sows the word by the wayside; but when some have heard, Satan comes along immediately and takes away the word that was sown in their hearts" (Mark 4:9–15, paraphrase).

Preaching is important for hearing, music is integral to inspiration, but "[God's] word have I hidden in my heart, that I might not sin against [Him]." Satan cannot snatch the word away if it is written on our hearts, preserved where it cannot be forgotten.

I broke my foot. For the next six weeks during the recovery process I must have heard every possible broken-foot joke. "Did the preacher step on your toes this morning during his sermon?" (ha, ha!). "Did you kick your husband out of the house?" (ho, ho!). "It's hard to kick against the goads, isn't it?" (ho, hum). Even though I wearied of the corny jokes, they did trigger my imagination. I read the Lord's words to Saul in Acts 9 about kicking against the goads and started musing.

I thought back to a time when my youngest, April, was four years old. (Now, if you like kids when they are four, you really like children.) Whenever I insisted that she do something she did not like she would threaten to run away from home. When I put out her patent leather shoes one Sunday she hid them in the refrigerator and insisted on wearing her sneakers. I found them but she threatened, "I'm going to run away."

One evening we had to retire early so that we could get up and start the long trip from Missouri back to Florida. After I explained this and started helping her get ready for bed, April challenged again, "I don't want to go to bed. I want to stay up. I'm going to run away from home."

This time I called her bluff. "Good," I replied. "I'll be glad to see you go, you've acted so badly lately. Here, I'll help you pack." I put her Mrs. Beasley doll, an apple and her pink pajamas in her little pink plastic suitcase, and shoved her very gently out the back door onto the porch.

"Bye, Mommie," she called out cheerily as I closed the door.

It was a hard lesson for me to teach her. I knew she was safe but it was a cold evening and there was snow on the ground. In about five minutes—it seemed like an hour—I heard a faint, "Mommie, I'm cold." I turned off the lights in the kitchen and held my breath. A minute later the front doorbell rang and a sweet little voice quoted Mother Goose: "Little pig, little pig, let me come in. Got snow on my chinny chin chin."

I flung the door open wide and she ran in and hugged my legs tightly. "I was just kidding, Mommie. I'm not gonna ever run away."

How much like four-year-olds we are sometimes with our heavenly Father. We whine, get stubborn, kick against the goads. . . . We would do well to obey Him. The shelter of His house is best.

A rough-spoken old Irish preacher, rambling in his heavy brogue, stumbled onto a startling truth, "Know why the palsied man was healed? He was *sick of* that palsy." The story is told in Matthew 9:2. Jesus approached, forgave the man's sins, healed him, and the man got up and walked all the way back home.

Shortly after that when Peter was preaching in Lydda, he met Aeneas who also had palsy and had been in bed with it for eight years. He remembered how Jesus treated palsy, and had the courage to do the same. Peter said, "Jesus Christ makes you whole! Arise, make your bed!" He arose immediately, a physically complete specimen of health.

Our friend Eleanor Olson has recently moved to Mesa, Arizona. While living in Leonard, North Dakota, she suffered for thirteen years the side effects of palsy, now known as multiple sclerosis, or M.S. She first used the walker, then a wheelchair. She suffered with slurred speech and could not control her bladder.

She decided to learn to live with this handicap. At a time when her faith was running low and she could no longer cope or hope, an evangelist came to town. Not knowing her circumstance, he had a heart-to-heart talk with Eleanor. He accused her of resigning to her fate, staying in the comfort zone of her handicap. He accused her of using it to her advantage, as an escape from obligations. She did not even have to attend church regularly.

It made Eleanor angry when he asked her a very blunt question, "Do you *really* want to be healed, to be *well* and return to the world of serving, of duties and obligation?" She went home that night, half-challenged and half-mad, but she started searching her own heart. The following night she told her family, "I'm going back to church tonight, *to be healed*." And she was!

Are you sick of being sick? Try again, one more time *right now* as you read. As I write I have prayed for every reader, for *you*. Bristle against the odds. Let your faith reach out to Jesus. Let Him show you the depths of your heart. And be healed in His name.

I have mentioned the old Victorian house in Springfield, Missouri, that I had the opportunity to buy. A landmark, its basement had harbored slaves running for freedom. I had no working capital of my own, so I borrowed $10,000 from a Christian friend, with no interest, until I got some funds of my own to repay him.

Have you ever been so "down," so low, so depressed or oppressed that you could not have faith for your own need? Have you ever had to borrow faith from a friend? It is biblical. Bear one another's burdens, the Bible says. The strong shall bear the infirmities of the weak. Pray one for another that *you* might be healed.

One Wednesday night Sara Douglas put her hand on the back of a young woman who had come for prayer, too depressed even to pray for herself. While Sara, without words, touched the woman in faith, something happened to Sara, the prayer. The following morning when Sara went for surgery to have a cyst removed from her colon, it had dried up and surgery was not necessary.

Paul Davidson had faith in two young couples at Bible School in whom most of us did not see much potential. He loaned them his faith; he believed in them. They made it and are successfully winning souls overseas in missions right now.

Jesus held a cottage prayer meeting: He taught the Word in the house of a friend in Capernaum (see Mark 2:1–12). People were even standing in the doorway listening. There was no space left, not even standing room. A man who had been sick for many years, and had no faith, borrowed faith from four of his friends. They had zealous, energetic, reckless faith. They could not get near Jesus to ask Him to heal the friend, so they lifted the tile off the roof and let the man down through the ceiling in front of Jesus, who healed him. Theirs was active, loaned faith that brought results. The man carried his own bed back home. The crowd was amazed.

Valentine's Day should occur more than once a year. Surprise your date or your mate with a homemade valentine about once a month. It may be corny, but it will be sincere. It doesn't take much time or money. (I saw some valentines this year for $3.50!) Carl was traveling and doing some fundraising for the college. Perhaps a week before Valentine's Day I received an original looking envelope in the mail. Inside was the following:

Dear Betty,
              Dis is a pome. Can't wait till I git home!
                                All my heart, Carl

I will treasure this. He didn't sign it *half*heartedly, but *All my heart*. A heart donor doesn't will half his heart, but the entire organ. A half-hearted romance is probably more hurtful than loneliness. A half-hearted marriage will weaken, then die. "I will praise you, O Lord my God, with all my heart" (Psalm 86:12). God wants one hundred percent of your spiritual allegiance. Your mate deserves one hundred percent of your loving loyalty. A heart divided against itself cannot stand. Do your ordinary chores with extraordinary heart.

Put your heart into your marriage and your body will follow. Be intimate, affectionate, speak lovingly, touch. Avoid selfishness. If both people are in love with the same person, someone is left out. That is a lop-sided marriage. 1+1=1. The two shall be one. Set one shining goal in marriage—permanence.

The right angle from which to approach any problem is the *try* angle. Keep at it. Avoid the rut. Be creative. Treat your mate the way you respect your employer at work, or your best-paying customer.

A sense of humor is a *must*. Sitting at the table during a Valentine's banquet I overheard married couples jesting. One lady asked, "What are you getting for Bill for Valentine's Day?"

Sue quickly replied, "Make me an offer!"

The pastor asked Dennis, "How will you and Pat spend Valentine's Day?" The comeback: "The same way we spend every day . . . eating each other's heart out."

"My times are in Your hand" (Psalm 31:15).

Stepping to the microphone, Pastor David Davidson said, "Before Betty comes to share with us, we have a singer who was previously scheduled two weeks ago. We are glad she finally made it." Her song was a powerful one—"God Has Been Faithful to Me."60

I had just come through three of the hardest weeks of my life and wondered if God had forgotten my address. The singer was two weeks late, but *on time* for me.

Flying home I reflected on my life. This occurred several years ago when Carl and I were pastoring a church in a large, busy city. The children and I did not complain, but longed for the country. Our horses were boarded miles away where we could not really enjoy them. I never discussed it with Carl, but prayed secretly that some day we could live and breathe in the good, clean out of doors.

A few days after that prayer, I was taking part in a television interview. The host introduced Lowell and Connie Lundstrom. I was busy with my notes, and thought the music was a tape. At the close of their song, the curtain parted just behind my chair and there was Lowell. He whispered that he would like for Carl to help him at Message for America with the ministry, counseling, marriage seminars and magazine. Carl accepted the assignment and we moved very shortly to South Dakota, onto a lovely 21-acre farm with a creek and a pond, overlooking the picturesque Red River Valley.

My appearance date had been changed twice. God had coordinated it to coincide with Lowell and Connie's schedule. I was late, but on time.

In John 11 we read that Mary and Martha called Jesus when their brother, Lazarus, became sick. When Jesus came, Lazarus had been dead four days. They mourned, "If you had arrived earlier he would not have died."

Jesus was not late, but right on time. A resurrection is more dramatic than a healing. He said, "Lazarus, arise," and Lazarus came out of the grave very much alive. Dear reader, if God ever denies your request, He will give you an answer of greater value. He might pry a ten-dollar bill from your hand to replace it with a twenty!

It was 7:00 A.M. I went into the little pink bedroom to awaken Brenda for breakfast. The school bus would be coming soon to take her to Otter Creek Elementary School in North Terre Haute, Indiana, where she was in the second grade. I had her breakfast prepared, and had packed a nutritious and attractive lunch in her "Snow White and the Seven Dwarfs" lunch box, before I went into her bedroom to get her up.

After I kissed her cheek good morning, she replied without even opening her eyes, "I'm not going to school anymore. I quit school yesterday. I told my teacher when I got on the bus to come home."

She began to cry as she told me that the lessons were getting harder. She wanted to give up and drop out. *In the second grade?* I thought. *She has a long way to go yet.* I told her to roll over, sleep in, take the day off and we would talk about it at dinner with her daddy.

That evening a couple of her little school friends came over to play. Another child called to see if she had been sick. By the following morning she had resolved her conflict and was ready to go back to school.

She graduated from Jamestown College with a music degree, married, and now both her children enjoy school and are making good grades.

Life is like this: As you mature, the lessons get more difficult. The assignments get progressively harder.

Even the great King David longed to back out, drop out. There are stories chronicled in both First and Second Samuel. Saul's jealousy frightened David and he hid in a cave. Later David again found himself stationed in a cave with a different enemy. He was tired of the battle with the Philistines and told his warriors, "Oh, that someone would give me a drink of the water from the well of Bethlehem, which is by the gate!" (2 Samuel 23:15). This was not to quench his thirst. It was an expression of a deeper longing: "I don't want to be famous, I don't want to be a warrior or a king. I want to quit, go back to the simple life of a shepherd and drink from the water in the meadows of Bethlehem."

We can never go back. The key to survival and victory is the word *rely.* "The children of Judah prevailed, because they relied on the Lord God" (2 Chronicles 13:18).

"Put two grains of corn in each hill, make the hills twelve inches apart and use the hoe to cover the seed with three inches of soil." It was the voice of our dad instructing my two brothers and me. We wanted to make some money so we could go to the circus that was coming to town. He had hired us to help him plant the corn in our garden.

At first it was fun being hired, doing a job, and I remember being glad that we did not have to live in a parsonage next door to the church like most preachers' kids. We had an orchard, a pony, a dog, a cat, chickens, guineas, turkeys and space to play ball.

Have you ever noticed that people who do not have enough to do, always want to spend time with people who have too much to do? Well, this happened to us Perkins children. Wanetta Murdock came across the road and asked us to come over and play in her yard. We wanted to go. She had a real baton to twirl, unlike my makeshift one made from a cut off, sanded, painted broomstick. They had a fish pond, and she had lots of toys.

My dad told us we could go as soon as we finished planting all the seed corn that he had given us. A short while later, when we were through, he said he was amazed at how quickly we had finished the job and he paid us the sum he had promised. We hid our money safely in bureau drawers in our rooms, jumped on our bikes and were off for fun.

Three weeks later, the truth was out. After warm sunny days and a lot of spring rains, Dad found, at the end of one row, a huge clump of corn growing. This particular hill did not have two shoots as we were instructed to plant, but actually contained hundreds of shoots. To save time, we had dumped the last three pounds of seed into a single hole.

One evening after dinner, Daddy rook the three of us out to the garden for an object lesson. He quoted from the Bible, "He that *covereth* his sins shall not prosper: but whoso confesseth and forsaketh them shall have mercy" (Proverbs 28:13, KJV).

His first impulse was to ask for a refund, then mercy prevailed and, after we said we were sorry, he let us keep our undeserved wages.

I grew up in the "big band" era of Tommie Dorsey, Count Basey, Glenn Miller and Johnny Mercer. I think that Johnny Mercer's song, "Accentuate the Positive" should be on page one of every church hymnal, alongside "All Hail the Power."

It was written by a secular songwriter, and people bounced to the big apple and danced to its rhythm, but the circumstances under which it was written intrigue me.

When Johnny Mercer's father died, he was facing bankruptcy. After looking over the books, this son right then decided to make good and recompense for his father's debts. He wrote letters to all the people his father owed money to and promised them that if they would be patient, he hoped to pay all of the debts. It totaled $300,000. That was a lot of money back then.

Johnny was a daydreamer, and wanted to write a hit song. He began working on the lyrics of the song mentioned above, "You gotta accentuate the positive." The catchy, rhythmic beat that accompanied the message made an impact on the American public and he earned a gold record by selling more than a million "platters" (33 1/3 r.p.m. records). His attitude equaled his energy which equaled his faith which produced the money that made the dream come true. And with the money, he did indeed pay off his father's debts!

I have friends who have so much to be thankful for, but complain a lot. We live in a beautiful spot in Florida, attend a wonderful Bible Church, reside among caring family people. I hear many people talk about the negative, look at the unpleasant when they are amid so many beautiful things. We tend to follow our gaze. Exhort means use the language of encouragement. No wonder emphasis is placed on Philippians 4:8: Whatever things are pure, lovely, true, good, just, virtuous . . . think on *these* things.

I got a poster in the mail. The caption was, "I think I'm having stress!" The artist's illustration was a zebra with his little head hanging down, and the stripes were falling off his backside.

Each age imposes stress. Even children are under pressure to learn at accelerated levels. I believe there are three stages of man: school tablet, aspirin tablet, then stone tablet!

When I was a pitiful young widow, people ran to my aid, felt sorry for me. Now that I have a good husband, am a writer and speaker, dress a little better, weigh a little more, stand tall and erect, no one seems to think I have any needs.

Probably the most needy people we know are leaders in their fields, such as teachers, ministers and counselors. Pray for your leaders. Even feeders need to be fed!

One denomination has several rehabilitation centers around the world to help young people escape drug abuse. To avoid the danger of "compassion fatigue," a director usually serves only two years at a time.

This syndrome strikes ministers, doctors, social workers and therapists, draining their ranks. It weakens people who take on too many of other people's burdens, leaving little energy for their own functions. They sleep too little, work too long and sacrifice their families. It is often the best, the brightest, the most committed and energetic who burn out. Even Jesus took an occasional break, pushed off in a boat or went to the mountains.

I read of a Catholic priest who left a Boston hospice program after helping the terminally ill for ten years. "That's heavy emotional material," he said. Many people are afraid of being looked down upon if they acknowledge they are stressed out. He now owns an Italian restaurant, by contrast.

Take a vacation; take lunch away from your desk; don't work at night; go to church Sunday, God's breakaway, and to Wednesday night prayer meeting.

Refreshing from the Lord is rest for the weary (see Isaiah 28:12).

My kids used to love Oreo cookies—well, sort of. They would pry them apart, eat the sweet cream center and then leave the two chocolate wafers lying on the table by their napkins. Did they realize that it was those two wafers that made the sweet center possible, that held together that good stuff that they so much enjoyed?

I believe prayer is like this. I pray first thing each morning before getting out of bed. The last thing at night, after I kiss my husband goodnight, I pray silently until I fall asleep. Prayer at the beginning and prayer at the end are the two wafers. My days are sweet. God fills the middle of my day, all day, with that good, sweet stuff in between.

David used this Oreo concept too. "Evening and morning . . . I will pray, and cry aloud, and He shall hear my voice" (Psalm 55:17). The beginning of David's life was devoted to prayer, praise and singing unto God. At the end of his life he blessed the God of his fathers. All in between David's life was filled with sweet prosperity, fame and honor. The only time it did not work for him was when he transgressed God's Law.

Recall the sweet center of his life. He married the king's daughter and won the praise of the people as a warrior. He became a national hero as a lad when, in the name of the Lord, he slew the giant Goliath. David became a renowned writer. Read the Psalms, passed down for generations, famous for their inspiration. David had wealth, a palace, servants, armies and chariots. He had a son born to him who was the wisest man who ever lived.

You cannot experiment any sooner than today. There is only one way to begin, and that is to start. Tomorrow begin your day with prayer and end it with prayer. Let God invade every day of your life with His bountiful blessings all in between.

Try it! You'll like it!

It was at a Wednesday night prayer meeting in Clay City, Indiana, when a large-framed, red-headed, freckled Irishman stood to testify. I would almost bet even his toes were freckled. He held up his Bible and read verse 5 from the Twenty-third Psalm. *Oh no, I thought. This can't help but be boring. Entire books have been written on the Twenty-third Psalm. What new insight could this brother hope to squeeze out of that over-used, over-worked, over-quoted Scripture?*

His red face beamed, and his voice transmitted genuine joy as he declared with surety, "My cup runneth over and so does my saucer. Since Jesus came into this wicked, sinful heart, I have had joy unspeakable and full of glory that I can't contain. It just keeps spilling over and over and over."

I thought immediately of the great inspirational writer Catherine Marshall. She was a solemn lady, but in her jovial moments, she used an expression to convey a certain meaning. "He's just full of beans," she would say. We Hoosiers used a couple of similar expressions: "He's full o' bologna" (pronounced "boloneee"), or "He's full of hot air."

The more the Irishman talked the more I realized that you can only run over with what you are *full of.* If you are full of depression, negative thinking, criticism, restlessness or self-centeredness, that is what will spill over and affect your children, your mate, your boss, your employees, your neighbors and everyone around you.

Perhaps you cannot help your feelings. Your world may be upside down right now. Well, perhaps God has turned you upside down to empty you of your self so that He can cleanse you. No one wants to drink from a dirty cup.

I walked into a cafe in Ellendale, North Dakota, one day and ordered a cup of coffee. The mug had egg on the side. I knew I had not eaten an egg, and returned the cup. The waitress apologized, "We are having trouble with the hot water in our dishwasher."

Wait in God's presence and let Him empty you of self, wash and fill you to overflowing with the Holy Spirit, with joy, mercy, sympathy and peace.

Never underestimate the faith of a child when she prays. In Matthew 18 Jesus commends a child's faith as the greatest in the Kingdom. The following was written about Carl's resolve and our daughter April's prayer, when she was only eight years old. We lived in Texas at the time.

"I now announce, I now proclaim,
So to my voice give heed!
I'm sick of country living,
I've sowed my final seed.
In summer . . . sweat, in winter . . . freeze,"
I heard my husband say,
"It's just too much—A buck and half
For just one bale of hay!
We'll sell that horse and eat that cow,
The chickens we can freeze,
I'll sell this farm, move into town
And live a life of ease."
That night I heard a muffled sob,
Beside a ruffled bed,
A tiny voice addressing God,
And this is what she said:
"I'll live in a tree or brooder house,
If worse should come to worse.
I'll do anything for Daddy—
But help me keep my horse!"
              * * *
"We're rural bound forever
I'll never be the boss.
Pull the earth from underneath us,
But *April keeps that 'hoss!*'"

We stayed on the farm, and when we moved the next time, at great work and expense, we rented a horse trailer and moved that mare and her colt to North Dakota. She kept that horse.

What Do You Leave, When You Leave?

David Mainse and his wife, Norma Jean, took a much-needed break at noon time. Having just finished the daily telecast at 100 Huntley Street in Toronto, they walked through the little city park close by, to empty their mental computers.

They both smelled it at once and with the same breath asked each other, "What is that wonderful fragrance?" Walking on a short distance, it became more prevalent. Sitting on a park bench were four young ladies chatting while they ate their sack lunches during noon break.

"What is that lovely fragrance?" David asked them. They responded with a puzzled look and, after a pause, laughed. A small brunette replied, "We work in the perfume factory. We are in this aroma eight hours each day and didn't realize we exude it."

When you leave a room, a reunion, a church service, your job, your own house or a home after you have visited, have you ever wondered what you left of yourself with the people you have just been with? When you die, what will they remember most? Will your family be glad to be rid of you?

Do you leave fond memories after your phone calls? Is your hospitality unforgettable, or will people only remember your "display" of furniture and house decorations? These things will remain on this temporary earth, but the impression you leave that helps and elevates the spirits of people, you take with you to the eternal Kingdom, and your investment will follow you with great rewards. Those recording angels are excellent bookkeepers.

Pray: "Jesus, fill me with Your self, Your presence, Your attitudes, so people will know that I have been with You."

Jesus said, "Peace I leave with you, My peace I give to you" (John 14:27). What are you giving, what are you leaving with people? Confusion and unrest? Or do you exude hope, rest, peace and joy?

February 24   *What I See by Me . . . I'm Three*

Not only did Jesus have a love for children, but He gravitated toward them and gave His love to them, held them and blessed them when He was on earth. He left a word of caution, of warning: "Whoever receives one little child like this in My name receives Me. But whoever causes one of these little ones who believe in Me to sin, it would be better for him if a millstone were hung around his neck, and he were drowned in the depth of the sea" (Matthew 18:5–6).

Children do not need to be indulged or pampered, but they do need to be understood. From the vantage point of an organ bench I developed a sympathy for kids. Try stooping down to their level. You look at the songbook rack or the back of heads in church. Pews and seats are too high, and their little legs dangle until their feet become numb. Walking in a crowd, they see fat stomachs and the rear view of adult hips.

What I See by Me . . . I'm Three

Parades pass me by. Can't see too high.

What do I see?

I see navels and knees, hip pockets and keys, trunk lids and trees.

"Now sit still. Keep quiet." (I've started a riot.)

I can't touch the floor; my feet are asleep; I can't take any more.

I see window sills . . . and dress hems, slip frills,

Tumbles and spills. I see car dashboards,
The underneath side of tables, Joe's toes, and Mable's,
Belt buckles, and knuckles.
Squat down to my level, I'm not such a devil.
Won't somebody have pity on me?

Come down to my level, And see what I see,

I'm missing a lot. Have patience with me.
You see, I'm just three.

It is remarkable that I remember almost everything I heard, saw and experienced at youth camp. Every summer from the time I was very young I went to the youth camp sponsored by our church. It was an annual oasis in my life. My brothers and I grew up in a small town where we were the only young people in our church, and the minority of Christian young people in the community. Those ten days in July every year sustained us from summer to summer and insulated us against temptation.

One year our speaker was a young cartoonist with a jolly ability to communicate. He held us spellbound as he sketched a nearly naked bird, six feet tall. The bird had one feather left on his top knot, one fuzzy feather at the tip of his behind, and one feather on his left leg, dangling like a ragged pantaloon. We laughed at the startled expression on the bird's face, a worm hanging lopsided from his beak. Looking in a mirror, he saw his own body, plucked naked with pock marks in his sagging skin.

This was the story. A lazy bird was given the opportunity to trade one of his feathers for a worm. This seemed to be a smart trade-off. He would not miss one feather at all. The idea appealed to him so much that the next day he gladly traded another feather for another worm. Then he suddenly realized the trade-off had become a rip-off. He stood naked and ashamed. When he tried to fly away to hide, he discovered he could not fly! He had traded his ability to fly for temporary pleasure, food for satisfaction. Worms were not wings.

His basic assumption was "I want to live in the 'now' with a full beak. You can't eat feathers." He forgot something, though: You cannot fly with worms. It is good to confront and challenge our basic assumptions of life and find where they will ultimately lead us.

Many a young person has enjoyed a sexual fling, then hoped to marry a virtuous mate. How many politicians "carry on," hoping that the voting public will never know? Parents live loosely, then wonder why they cannot keep a tight rein on their children. One pure example is worth ten lectures.

Where are your assumptions taking you? Don't trade your feathers for worms! "For what will profit a man if he gain the whole world, and loses his own soul?" (Mark 8:36).

Remember Veronica Lake and Marilyn Monroe? Because they were movie stars, their figures—voluptuous and round—were "in." Then when Twiggy came on the scene, to be "in" required you to have a shape like a stick, bony, lean and wispy with no bust. A great percentage of Americans do not know how to be themselves, have no creative imagination, can only imitate. They have forgotten how to read and television has set the standards. They are "dupes" and "carbs"—that is, duplicates and carbon copies.

A missionary friend recently returned to the U.S. after being overseas for fourteen years. He exclaimed, "When I arrived in New York, I thought the plane had gotten off course and had dropped onto a strange planet. Everyone was following after Ninja Turtles instead of human beings, or patterning after some other animated character. Some had hair that sprang upward like a bed of nails on top. I learned they were imitating Bart Simpson."

He went on, "Now, this may be okay for kids, but some of these big hulks look ridiculous. I found one black T-shirt that I did like. It said, 'In a world full of copies [picture of a photocopying machine], here's an original.' One man dared to be himself."

I spoke recently at a bankers' convention. I was not aware that a reception was being held in my honor, upon my arrival, and was whisked off to a cocktail party.

I was the only person there who did not drink! They laughed when I ordered a 7-Up, but then applauded loudly and cheerfully.

God has been faithful to me and I want to be faithful in my testimony to Him. Every day each one of us must beware of compromise.

The Bible tells us, "Do not be conformed to this world, but be transformed by the renewing of your mind" (Romans 12:2).

As a little girl growing up, I remember my dad always waking up happy. He would whistle when he woke up early each morning. He took us with him to work in the garden, to pick apples in the orchard, to haul trash in the old pick-up truck to the city dump, and some- times took us to Lake Placid to help clean up before the camp meet- ing would begin.

I grew accustomed to his voice. He also was my pastor. When I was small, Mother made sure that I sat still in church and listened. I am not sure how much I heard, because my father's voice was so famil- iar to my brothers and me. As I grew a little, I would sit with friends and eat Kraft caramels while he delivered his sermon. In high school I may have heard his messages, but was mostly looking for boys and I am not sure how much soaked in.

Of all the hundreds of Sundays I heard the Reverend Perkins, I *do* remember *one* message, the sermon on boats. His text was "Let not your heart be troubled" (John 14:1). This text is repeated in John 14:27, "Let not your heart be troubled, neither let it be afraid." He illustrated it this way: "When the boat is in the water, that is good news; but when water gets in the boat, that is bad news. Trouble in the heart, like water in a boat, will cause it to sink."

There is trouble in your neighborhood, in your city, gross trouble in the world. You must guard against trouble getting inside your heart. Then you will not sink but will soar above it.

He went on. "Jesus is the shore patrol, the lifeguard, the keeper of the lighthouse on the stormy sea of life. 'We have this treasure in earthen vessels, that the excellence of the power may be of God and not of us. We are hard pressed on every side, yet not crushed; we are perplexed, but not in despair; persecuted, but not forsaken; struck down, but not destroyed'" (2 Corinthians 4:7–9).

"Insulate the walls of this house with peace, Lord, that we may all have a good night's sleep."

My parents prayed this prayer each night before tucking us Perkins children into bed. Before we went to school they prayed, "Lord, we ask the angels of the Lord accompany them all day, keep them safe, help them study, and return them to the sanctuary of this little harbor house. 'Let the words of our mouths and the meditations of our hearts, be acceptable in Thy sight, O Lord, our strength and our redeemer.'"

"Not in the house!" Mother would say when we would quarrel. We could get rowdy and loud in laughter, fun or frolic, but they would not allow dissention within the four insulated walls of the house of peace.

We were never allowed to hit each other. We could "tattle" and our parents would do the punishing, but we never struck each other. Many times I saw my brothers argue, and it would become heated, nearing the fight level, and one of them would say, "Not in the house. Let's go outside and settle this." Usually they would laugh at Mother's rule and not be mad at each other anymore by the time they went out.

My dad had a home-grown Scripture, "Blessed is the *peacemaker*, not the *pacemaker*." Even when I was grown and would babysit my little brothers, I could report, but I was never allowed to spank them. Discipline was Mother or Dad's department, exclusively.

I look back with fond memories of long hours of uninterrupted restful sleep in the home of our parents. That is not a bad rule. Our homes can be insulated with Jesus' peace. We can have that kind of insulation, insurance if we contend for it, invoke it, pray for it.

"'In this place I will give peace,' says the Lord" (Haggai 2:9).

"Peace be within your walls" (Psalm 122:7).

"And great shall be the peace of your children" (Isaiah 54:13).

When Carl taught at Trinity College he started a jogging club. He called it "wings and feet," a 100-mile club. Students interested in physical fitness and/or losing weight would meet each morning at 6:30 for prayer first (wings) and then for a three mile-run (feet).

Now, Carl has a motto, "Anything worth doing is worth doing fast." My motto is, "Anything worth doing is worth doing outdoors." For the twenty years we have been married, I have told him, "Do, but don't overdo." He was not interested in just reaching the one hundred miles, but reaching it first and fastest. He ended up with a hernia.

After surgery, when he was ready to return home, the doctor gave him a prescription for pain medication. There was a caution on the side of the pill box: "Do not drive a vehicle. The side effects are dizziness and drowsiness."

Before my dad became a Christian he noticed that every time Mother's old-fashioned Pentecostal Uncle Arch Brown would come to visit when he had a headache, when that godly visitor came in the door, Dad's headache would disappear. My great uncle was so full of the Holy Spirit, that he radiated Jesus, His joy, His peace, and produced the side effects of Jesus' healing virtue. It was more than remarkable. It was miraculous.

We read in Acts 5:15 that the apostles produced such side effects after having been with Jesus. The people actually laid sick people on beds and coats and brought them into the street so that the shadow of Peter might fall on them and heal them.

I read a discussion in a medical journal between a chemist and psychiatrist. They rationalized that two people cannot walk into the same room and merely exchange glances without both persons being changed just a little.

Does your presence cause any positive side effects?

March 1
Fashions Fade, Yet History Repeats Itself

One of our daughters rushed into the house in a dead run. "Can we get downtown before the stores close? I need shoes. All the kids at school are wearing a new kind of shoes. They're penny loafers. They come in black, brown and oxblood, and in the front is a slot where you put a bright new copper penny! Can we? Can we?"

She did have a cardboard layer inserted in her shoe and did indeed need new ones, and, yes, we made it to Montgomery Ward before closing time at 5:00 P.M.

New trend? Hardly. In 1947 and '48 I wore penny loafers, and also the black and white or brown and white saddle oxfords that were popular again twenty years later. As one designer said, "If you have closet space, store your things for twenty years, for as sure as day follows night, fashions will return. There are only so many things you can do with a dress or a shoe."

About this same time long skirts almost to the ankle were the style, followed by the mini skirt. During the mini era, you were "really up a crick" if you were as tall as I am. I will always remember how shocked the congregation was when I approached the organ bench in a "sack" dress, with the long waistline just below the knees. Necks stretched, heads turned, frowns appeared and old hens clucked at how dreadful new styles were. It was not long before everyone was wearing them.

Men used to wear wide ties and double-breasted suits, which returned years later. Back then, around 1950, men were in only if they wore long side burns and a bow tie. They wore Bryll Creme on their hair to make it look shiny and slick. Now "dudes" are back to the wet look.

I remember in school when the short clipped hairdo was a sure indication that the kid had "cooties" or lice. Then the G.I. haircut and the flat top were in vogue. Now, forty years later, we once again have that straight up, spiked look.

The world will pass away and the fashions thereof, but he who does the will of the Father shall abide forever. Jesus said, "I am the Lord. I change not." He is our authority, our eternal guideline.

I sat recently in the front porch swing talking with my dad on his eighty-fourth birthday. I asked him what he thought about the disappointment we have witnessed in some of our Christian leaders recently.

He placed an arm around my shoulder and said with a confident smile, "Aw, Bets, don't look at people. Keep your eyes on Jesus. Even if Billy Graham should run away with Liz Taylor, and Oral Roberts have an affair with Tammy Faye Bakker, even though people fail and let you down, Jesus will never disappoint you. God will always remain the same unchanging constant, faithful and sure." Pretty sharp answer for an old man!

Our unchanging God is the answer for our changing world. Jesus is still transforming sinners into saints, rehabilitating fallen mankind. He is the changeless one who changes lives.

We in this life can be "changed from glory unto glory." Then one day, "We shall all be changed—in a moment, in the twinkling of an eye, at the last trumpet. For the trumpet will sound, and the dead will be raised incorruptible, and we shall be changed" (1 Corinthians 15:51–52).

It is fun to give to small children. They are so simple in their tastes and basically easy to please. My friend Karen Siddle calls it "peanut butter and jelly faith." They do not try to manipulate God, but are simple in their appeal. They are generally content with the supply for their needs, not their greeds.

Carl rarely picks up hitchhikers, but one evening as it was getting dark the temperature dropped to 42 degrees below zero, and he saw a man walking along Highway 1 north of Sisseton, South Dakota, about two miles from town. He stopped and gave him a ride. After driving a great distance out of his way to deliver the man to his home, the man asked, "Could you give me two dollars for a gallon of milk?"

Carl reached into his billfold and handed him, not two dollars, but seven. Taking it quickly the man grumbled, "Only seven dollars, and you call yourself a Christian?" and went into his house without even a thank-you.

By contrast, I talked last week to an elementary school principal. The first day of school here in Florida, we had a severe, tropical storm that wiped out all electrical appliances in the school kitchen. The cooks had the chicken prepared to go into the oven, and large vats of vegetables waiting to be cooked. When Florida Power failed to get the power on by twenty minutes before lunchtime the principal purchased a large amount of peanut butter and several jars of jelly at the nearest supermarket.

In the nick of time, each child passing through the line received a peanut butter and jelly sandwich, a small bag of potato chips and a can of Coca Cola. The principal felt bad to serve such a meager lunch, but did the best he could in the emergency.

Right after lunch a first-grader came into his office. With an intent look on his little face he said, "Mr. Bates, I just want to let you know I'm glad to go to a school that serves such wonderful home-cooked meals." Evidently this is all the lad got at home from Mama, and was pleased.

No wonder Jesus loved the children, and commends adults who have childlike appreciation. Humble yourself like a child to be great (see Matthew 18:4).

Sunday morning Pastor Casey used a phrase that riveted my attention. He said, "God never meant our churches to be Holy Huddles or Exclusive Religious Clubs where people of like beliefs come weekly to stroke each other."

I have attended a few services that were lopsided health clubs. They are heavy on healing, but light on holiness. Some contend for miracles, but do not know the Word. One country songwriter has done a number titled, "You Can't Stand on the Promises If You Don't Know What They Are." It is so good if you can repeat this Scripture: "Thy word have I hid in my heart that I might not sin against God."

Our churches should say with the Statue of Liberty, "Send us your poor, your needy, your wounded." Instead, many religious clubs are saying, "Send us your rich and those increased with goods who have need of nothing."

Our houses of God should not be hospitals for long stay, but clinics in which people can receive on-the-spot help and be dismissed to go out and serve in turn. We should rescue the perishing, lift up the fallen, so that chords that were broken can vibrate once more.

Jesus said that we should be the salt of the earth, and the lights of the world. "Don't hide that light under a bushel basket," He said, "but put it on a hill for good visibility, to safeguard those walking in darkness" (see Matthew 5:13–15). Light is needed in dark and fearful places.

We need fellowship to keep in tune, but avoid the Holy Huddle. The church building is God's house, the filling station to receive the fuel we need to go out and serve. It is the pit stop to get our spiritual batteries charged.

We lived near a rancher who herded sheep. Early in March I heard that familiar, annual sound, fluttery, weak and high pitched—the sound of the bleating of baby lambs. Our family jumped in our Renegade Jeep, and was off like a herd of turtles. Down the hillside, over the little dam and near the pond we found them, newborn babies, shivering and shaky in their new environment, the outside world.

We have two friends who both love lambs. They consider themselves mother sheep; both of their houses are filled with stuffed, woolly lambs, all sizes, colors and textures.

Be good to the lambs. Jesus, our Shepherd, said, "If you offend one of the little ones it would be better that a millstone be tied around your neck and you be cast into the sea. Beware of the wolves that try to criticize, wound and lacerate young Christians and children in general. God loves His children. He said He would bless those who bless you and curse those who curse you."

We had a bachelor friend who called children rug rats. Carl and I were offended, for we have had kids at our house stretched over a period of years. Our last one is in college. "Behold, children are a heritage from the Lord, the fruit of the womb is a reward" (Psalm 127:3).

We attended one church in Missouri with the name "Sheep Shed" above the foyer door. Their concept is that lambs are born to sheep who love. Love the lambs, train up a child (Proverbs 22:6) and appoint yourself as a missionary to the church of tomorrow by giving yourself as a mentor to the youth.

When we were small my parents never hired a babysitter. They simply did not go places where it would be bad for children to be, or where children were not welcome. It is true that they were poor, but I heard them say on several occasions, "We just don't go places where we can't take the kids."

It was only when we were a little older that they would go away together without us. Once a year Mother and Dad would attend the district council, a ministers' business meeting and convention.

A variety of women stayed with us, but our favorite was Irene. She was a large, lazy young woman with no physical drive. She could not have cared less what we did or did not do. We were free to jump on the beds like trampolines, eat whatever and whenever we wanted, or not at all. We went to bed at the hour we chose and we never had to take a bath. I recall eating nothing but cantaloupes one day (we called them muskmellons in Indiana) and ate so many of them that I got "foundered" on them and vomited for two days.

We expected our parents home late Friday night. The phone rang around noon, and it was Mother. "Bets! It's so good to hear your voice. Did you keep plenty of fresh water for the horse? Did you make your beds?" She was full of questions without giving me time to give her the negative answers. Was I relieved!

Then she said, "If you and your little brothers have been good, I have souvenirs for you. I have to go now. We're coming home early. Daddy is pumping gas while I make this call. We're about twenty minutes from home right now. I love you. We'll see you soon."

Like three white tornadoes, we picked up, cleaned up, got ready. Jesus said, "Behold, I am coming quickly, and My reward is with Me, to give to every one according to his work" (Revelation 22:12) and "You also be ready, for the Son of Man is coming at an hour you do not expect" (Matthew 24:44).

As it was in the days of Noah, so shall it be at the coming again of Jesus.

An Amish farmer named Noah Troyer, a preacher in the state of Iowa, lay for over a month seriously ill, seemingly unconscious, before he died. Over and over again his wife heard him talking, preaching, and his message was always the same. After he repeated it several times, she called together family members and the deacons from their local church. Nineteen different times he gave the same warning. Together they witnessed, made notes and recorded this message:

"God gave Noah 120 years to caution the people to repent before He would destroy the earth with a flood. The people scoffed at Noah, but it happened as God had said. God has come to me, another Noah, with a message. America is sinning the same sins as in Noah's day. God will destroy the world this time, not with water, but with fire. He is giving us 120 years to repent before He will come again and pour down wrath upon the sinful and unbelieving."

The year of this prediction was 1878. Add 120 years to that and it would put the year of Jesus' Second Coming at the year 1998. Could old Noah Troyer be close to right? Many believe that every 2,000 years has brought in a new dispensation in church history. I personally am not interested in making prophecies concerning His Coming. The last word Jesus left with us is that He will come again. Be ready! Play it safe.

True, the Bible says in Matthew 24:36 that no one but the Father knows the day or the hour of Jesus' Return. But it does not say they might not know the year.

"For as the lightning comes from the east and flashes to the west, so also will the coming of the Son of Man be. . . . Heaven and earth will pass away, but My words will by no means pass away. . . . Therefore you also be ready" (Matthew 24:27, 35, 44).

It happens in the best of families. Your seamstress may have an illegitimate son. The mailman could be having an affair. Presidents, even royalty, have skeletons rattling around in the closet. Every family seems to have a "Humpty Dumpty" that threatens to break its gentility open and display a well-kept secret.

Even the great St. Paul had a "thorn in the flesh," something that rubbed his fur the wrong way, irritated his vitality.

I have known parents to do everything right and their kids still go wrong. You may have a picture sitting on the mantle over the hearth that brings a tinge of sorrow, sadness or guilt to your merry heart.

What to do when you have a skeleton in *your* closet?

First, clean out the closet so that you do not give just cause for others to criticize. Ask God to "air out" the closet, to open the door that no man can shut, and to shut the door that no man can open, once and for all. Then *you* leave the closet door closed.

Second, do not judge others, nor condemn, for God has a pin just the right size to puncture your proud family balloon.

Humpty Dumpty sat on a wall,
Humpty Dumpty had a great fall.
All the king's horses and all the king's men,
Could not put Humpty together again.

Maybe they should have asked the king to glue Humpty Dumpty back together again.

We can. God, our great King, can fix or repair anything, any situation, but we must offer Him all the pieces. "If anyone is in Christ, he is a new creation" (2 Corinthians 5:17). We are made new, made righteous in Him.

Sometimes God Himself does the repairing. He may send along another person to help with the mending, through professional counsel or prayer ministry. But many times the skeletons and Humpty Dumpties, those outside pressures, actually become the vice that holds the family while God cements it back together again.

Popularity is always temporary. If you are experiencing applause and approval right now, enjoy it. Wear it like a loose garment with no buttons. Keep in mind that admirers are often fickle and their praise, for the most part, is fragile and fleeting.

Sometimes the transition from approval to disapproval is only a phone call away. A beautiful movie star is adored until she gains weight. Jesus was perfect. On the occasion that we have named Palm Sunday, they proclaimed him Messiah, hailed him with Hosannahs! Some of that same crowd later chanted, "Crucify Him." More than one president voted in by the majority soon learns how fleeting his popularity can be. All it takes for that to change is for some reporter hungry for gossip to climb his family tree, pick one small rotten apple and blab his flaws to the world.

There are so many quips that slam these fair-weather friends: He'll loan you his umbrella—on a sunny day. You can always depend on him to depend on you. He remembers what he gives and forgets what he gets. You will always find him on the dock when any of his friends' ships come in.

Jesus warned us to beware when all men speak well of us. Colossians 2:8 cautions, "Beware lest any man spoil you through philosophy and vain deceit, after the tradition of men, after the rudiments of the world and not after Christ" (KJV). Evil men will disdain you and disapprove of your doing good. With this in mind, remember that "The spirit of a man is the candle of the Lord" (Proverbs 20:27, KJV). Build on things of the Spirit and improve on those things that are eternal. "Wrath is cruel and anger a torrent, but who is able to stand before jealousy? . . . The kisses of an enemy are deceitful" (Proverbs 27:4, 6).

While walking in the glow of your accomplishments, think on the words of the old song, "Build your hope on things eternal, hold to God's unchanging hand."

March 10 Cast Thy Bread (Or, Your Chickens Always Come Home to Roost)

My family will readily tell you that I have a vivid imagination, but no teacher had satisfied my curiosity concerning the "cast thy bread" verse. "Cast your bread upon the waters, for you will find it after many days. Give a serving to seven, and also to eight, for you do not know what evil will be on the earth" (Ecclesiastes 11:1–2). Perhaps experience is the best teacher after all. It was while reading an article by Jamie Buckingham that my memory began to teach me.

Jamie played football for a tiny Florida town. Following every game, even when they played poorly, the coach would encourage them and tell them "Good game!" He taught them morality, not to cuss, to attend church.

In spite of the fact that the team had two undefeated seasons, the beloved coach was fired. Some businessmen had met together and decided that he was not qualified to coach and had simply fooled a bunch of folks.

I remembered that during the embarrassing "Watergate" scandal, I sent President Nixon a handwritten letter and told him that I admired him and believed in him. I wondered if he would even receive it. About that same time Catherine Marshall invited me to her home in Virginia where she interviewed me for an article for *Guideposts* Magazine entitled "My Glimpse of Eternity." Later I wrote a book by that same name, which was translated into several languages, including Chinese.

Upon my return home from Virginia I found that I had received a letter from Nixon's secretary: "The president was much encouraged by your kind letter of confidence and asked me to write for him and thank you."

I have mentioned that a reporter set out recently to disprove my testimony. One morning while "licking my wounds," I grabbed my briefcase to do some writing. The lid was not fastened, and all the contents sprawled wildly in every direction.

In the mess I found the letter from Madame Chiang Kai-shek.

Encouragement is a two-way street. Cast thy bread. It shall return.

My friend Sandra Parker told me the following story:

"Our daughter believed that maturity was synonomous with being able to drive the family car. She was sixteen at last! The day had arrived! With a genuine driver's licence in her billfold and the keys in her hand, she was going to drive the car all by herself for the very first time. She talked of taking the car to school, parking in plain view for all to see, dropping those wonderfully, noisy car keys into her purse and listen to them jingle all day. This was that ultimate milestone.

"My husband and I laughed aloud, then breathed a sigh of apprehension as she pulled out of the driveway. It was hard to believe that our 'little girl' was making her maiden voyage, her solo venture into the adult world.

"Exactly one hour later, the telephone rang. A faint, frightened young voice spoke. 'Mom? I've had an accident in the school parking lot.'

"I resisted the impulse to scream into the phone. After learning that she was not hurt and that the car was drivable, I took a deep breath and said calmly, 'Come straight home from school. Don't worry about it. Just try to enjoy the rest of your day at school.'

"At 4:05 a very nervous and embarrassed young lady walked in the front door. 'I'll never try to drive that stupid car again. You probably wouldn't let me if I wanted to, after having a dumb wreck on the first day.'

"I looked over the car and said, 'The accident isn't that bad. Drive again tomorrow. We can take it to the shop over the weekend.'

"She was ecstatic. 'Mom,' she beamed, 'I can't believe you would give me a second chance.'

"She learned caution from that mishap so early in her driving career and has lived up to the trust that I placed in her. And, I learned the importance of a second chance. The finest place for longsuffering and forgiveness is not long distance, but close at home."

Ephesians 4:32 encourages us to "be kind to one another, tenderhearted, forgiving one another, even as God in Christ forgave you."

Better to Be a Freshman Than a Stalemate

I read of a college freshman who had his faith challenged. A chemistry professor, every year for fifteen years, on the last day before Thanksgiving holiday, would stand in the huge auditorium and lecture against prayer. He was sarcastic, funny and made the students laugh. He would end his lecture by asking, "Does anyone here still believe in prayer? Now, before you answer, I'll tell you what I am going to do."

Then he would pick up a glass flask. "If someone believes in God, I am going to ask you to stand and pray that when I drop this flask, it won't break."

A certain freshman enrolled in that chemistry class one fall. He learned early in the year about the professor's challenge. When he asked, "Is there no one on this campus who believes that God answers prayer?" he was told that a certain Mr. Harvey was a praying man.

The freshman knocked at Mr. Harvey's door and told him that he intended to stand up to the professor. "I need you to pray with me, since you and I seem to be the only two here who believe in prayer." They agreed to pray every day until Thanksgiving break that he would have the courage to pray in class and that God would answer his prayer.

The day came. The professor was building toward the climax. As he asked sarcastically, "Is there anybody here who still believes in prayer?" the freshman stood up and declared, "I believe in prayer."

"My, my, isn't this great. Well, I am going to take a flask and drop it. You pray that it won't break when it hits the floor. Are you ready?"

The young man lifted his trusting face heavenward and said, "Dear heavenly Father, in the name of Jesus Christ I thank You that You have heard me. For your honor, don't let the flask break. Amen."

The professor smirked, held the flask at arms' length, opened his hand and dropped it. The flask fell at a curve. Instead of falling straight down it bounced off the professor's shoe then rolled around on the cement floor—without breaking.

As the professor's face registered absolute disbelief, three hundred students rose to their feet and began to cheer.

Those who put their trust in the Lord will never be ashamed.

"Who is that kid who comes by every day after school? He's a nuisance. He's gonna get killed." The drivers of the heavy equipment at the construction site were aggravated by the little kid who was so fascinated by the huge equipment.

Who was he? Clive, the boss's son. His eyes would grow wide with wonder as he wandered around those earth-moving vehicles, weighing from ten to fifteen tons each. The huge tires stood easily eight feet tall.

Young Clive so much wanted to ride on one of them. One day he dared to do it. He stepped in front of one monster, raised both arms and signalled *Stop!* The driver, Leo, was a soft touch. After letting Clive climb up beside him, Leo explained how dangerous it was to do what he had just done. "You know," he said, "if you were not the boss's son, you would be in big trouble right now."

Clive is now grown, married and has a child of his own. He knows that he enjoyed a special privilege back then because of his relationship with his father. It was not earned by experience, but gained by grace and mercy.

Like that little boy, we, too, have access to the promises and privileges of heaven's resources, because of our relationship through Jesus the Savior to our heavenly Father, creator of the universe. Ephesians 1 and Romans 8 bear out the wonderful discovery of truth, the authority of the believer. We, too, are influential, sons of the living God. In the midst of danger, opposition and earth-shaking obstacles that Satan puts in our way, we can stop his progress because of who God is, and who we are . . . the sons of the boss. We are heirs to the throne of the Kingdom to come!

Are you unhappy? depressed? Quick! Give something away. It works.

Whenever you visited her, "Mom Perky," my paternal grandmother, whether you were relative or neighbor, friend or foe, she always gave you something to take home with you. It might be a quart of homemade buttermilk, a pat of fresh-churned butter, products of the milk she lovingly extracted from the cow in their pasture. She might give you a couple of warm, freshly baked cookies from her oven, dried flower seeds, fresh cucumbers from the garden out back, a rose picked from the bush by the drive or homemade marmalade.

Once when she had nothing special for me, she gave me a couple of clipped coupons for grocery savings, and a piece of left-over apple pie for my husband's dinner.

When I was younger I looked forward to her little "giving goodies." As I matured, I once asked her, "Why are you so giving to people?"

"Oh," she answered, "it's not for them, but for me."

Later, on one particular visit, noting the time I had to rush away, I kissed her wrinkled cheek quickly and jumped into my car. Driving down the dirt lane toward the highway I looked into my rearview mirror. She was running, chasing me. When I stopped, she said breathlessly, "I didn't give you anything." Then she untied her apron, tossed it through the window onto my lap, blew me a kiss and with an "about face" she and I parted.

There is nothing new under the sun. God merely renews it and reveals it to each new generation through some simple, loving person who has a listening heart.

Jesus told us the secret cure for any need when He said, "It is more blessed to give than receive" (Acts 20:35).

I had never realized the powerful effect of light until I made my first trip to Alaska during the long winter season when the days are short and the dark nights are long.

A few weeks later I took a trip down memory lane back to the place of my birth in Indiana. I loved the green foliage, the hills and streams, but I had forgotten that after a rain those Hoosier skies can remain gray for days. When I deplaned at Tampa and headed toward home, it rained for twenty minutes, then the clouds lifted and brilliant sunlight broke through. I felt as though God was smiling! My spirits lifted, too.

"Then God said, 'Let there be light'; and there was light. And God saw the light, that *it was good*; and God divided the light from the darkness" (Genesis 1: 3–4).

Calvin came to Carl's office at the church. "Pastor, I'm at the end of my rope. My wife, Lillian, is so negative and depressed." Carl prayed with Calvin, and for Lillian.

Soon after this, their family doctor discovered borderline anemia in Lillian and put her on a good diet. One of their neighbors, a good, practical, Christian psychiatrist, made a friendly house call and suggested this: "Open the drapes," he said. "Let the light stream into this house. Get rid of those dark avacado drapes and furnishings and replace them with light colors. Your house is in a shady location. Install strips of lighting in the ceilings. Lighten up this place where Lillian spends all day every day, and you will see the difference that light makes."

They did. And in three weeks she had become a different person, a cheerful companion.

It is no wonder that John calls Jesus by two words, the *light* and the *life*, interchangeably. "The entrance of Your words gives light" (Psalm 119:130). Jesus is the Word made flesh. It was prophesied of Jesus before His birth that He would be the dayspring from on high, to give light to them that walk in darkness, to guide us in the way of peace.

Let there be light!

God came down in the cool of the evening to talk with, walk with and commune with His newly formed creation, a man whom He named Adam.

Adam loved the beautiful paradise where he resided. But on one walk on one particular evening I fancy that Adam confessed to God something like this: "I love what You have given me, and I worship You, but what I really want, what I need is a woman."

God told Adam, "I will do it. I will give you your desire. I will make you a woman. She will be beautiful, she will be perfect, and she will do anything you want her to do, but it will cost you an arm and a leg."

After thinking a moment Adam asked, "What could I get for a rib?"

We may laugh, but it is no joke that many modern men have lost respect for their mothers, wives, sweethearts, sisters. It has caused many women to feel undervalued. But they are still just as valuable to God as at the start. Have you even wondered why Satan, when he decided to mess up God's perfect world, set about to trick Eve instead of Adam? The devil must have realized that women have clout.

Women should also recognize their worth in the fact that, when God decided to redeem the world after the Fall, He did it through the womb of a woman. He could have sent the Savior in any fashion, but He chose that Redemption be incubated in the body of a gentle, loving and godly woman.

Carl took a survey and found that ninety percent of the men he tested in marriage seminars are there because a wife put her gentle hand on the middle of her husband's back and persuaded him to go. Polls show that more than eighty percent of inspirational books sold are purchased by women. More than sixty percent of church members are women.

Dr. Paul Yonggi Cho, pastor of a 750,000-member church in Seoul, Korea, attributes that population explosion to home prayer cells. These are often headed by women in a country where tradition has considered the female as a second-class citizen.

I believe the verse "One shall chase a thousand and two put ten thousand to flight" can well be applied to the coupling of a man and a woman. A man can be ten times more effective, linked to a life's mate and partner. Her value is far above rubies (see Proverbs 31:10).

To me, the "Luck o' the Irish" is a four-letter word spelled P–R–A–Y.

Growing up, I thought that Saint Patrick was a tiny, dwarfed leprechaun, wearing a green velvet derby and smoking a round, clay pipe.

While writing *Prayers That Are Answered*, I stumbled upon a classic illustration of St. Patrick. While he walked across France with a group of surviving, but starving footsoldiers, the men began to rail on him.

"Where is your God?" they charged. "Your prayin' don't work, else, why are ye' starvin' like the rest o' us heathen?" They had not eaten for days. Out of desperation, Patrick cried to the Lord, "Send us food!"

From nowhere, out of the thick forest, a herd of wild hogs came pawing, then running and snorting crossed their dusty path.

The soldiers raised their firearms and shot more ham than they could ever consume. It took them two days to dress and prepare the meat! Those unbelieving men became acquainted with God's abundance.

"The love of Christ . . . passes knowledge. . . . [God] is able to do *exceedingly abundantly* above all that we ask or think, according to the power that works in us" (Ephesians 3:19–20).

Do you realize what it means when we as Christians are called the "children of God"? That means that God is our Father, and that by inheritance all He has is ours. We have rights to have everything that He has!

In Genesis 12 God promised Israel, "I will make you a great nation." In 1948 Jews established the Statehood of their native land and, encouraged by the recent, astonishing toppling of governments, are returning there from every nation on earth.

In that same chapter God said, "I will bless them that bless you and curse them that curse you." We become heirs of Jesus, Jews by adoption, when we believe on Him as our Savior and receive His blood's atonement for sin. By the blood, we are in relationship with Him, in union with Christ. He is wrapped up in His people, entwined with His children, tender toward us, and directing our destiny. He is sensitive to our private, individual needs. He was "touched with the feeling of our infirmities" (Hebrews 4:15, KJV).

Some day soon, He will come again for us that we may dwell with Him forever. The wrath of God will fall on the unbeliever. Israel will finally see the Messiah and accept Him as her King.

Then the great white throne judgment will begin in which God will separate the sheep from the goats (Matthew 25:32–34). I believe that this refers not to individual judgment, but His judgment of the nations. The countries that bless Israel will be blessed and those that are unkind to the Jews, God's chosen people, will be cursed.

As God's children who have overcome, we shall rule and reign with Him in the great Millennial reign, when He sets up His Kingdom on earth.

Every healthy human is equipped with five senses. A sense of smell, taste, touch, sight and hearing. Everybody also needs a sixth sense—a sense of humor!

One day I was on my feet for seven straight hours, dressed up in high heels, working at Tissy's Boutique. I came home to a house full of company and fell into bed Saturday night, exhausted. I awakened early Sunday morning and went to church to learn that the organist had been called to Pennsylvania. I played the organ for the song service then slumped into the pew, off my feet at last, and picked up the church bulletin.

The Royal Rangers (a boys' organization) had placed a notice in the bulletin, and this is what it said: "Wanted, new or used bowels, utensils, etc. for camping." Now what could these little fellows possibly do with donated *bowels*? Obviously they meant to write *bowls*, but I shook uncontrollably from controlled laughter. I needed a good laugh. It was like a tonic for me. I finally had to put my head down near my lap so people would not see me shaking from the roar of the guffaw I could not let out. Our secretary, Maria Foran, is so efficient I am sure one of the little boys had written this plea himself.

Carl was in Pittsburgh for a church service that weekend, so I sat alone, ate a quiet lunch and read the latest booklet of "Life Change" by Teen Challenge, published in Cape Giradeau, MO. Their theme of the week was humor. To laugh or not to laugh? That is the question. Should we identify only with Jesus' sorrows, focusing on the sinful aspects of this evil world? Should we contemplate only the crime, perversion and war news we read? Or should we have hearts filled with the humor that comes from true joy? They concluded that everybody needs that sixth sense, a sense of humor.

Yes, focus on joy. It is fitting to be sorrowful in the presence of sin, but there is an appropriate time for humor in God's joyful world.

Carl is the proud owner of a Volkswagen van, a small home on wheels complete with stove, refrigerator and shower. We took it in for an emission control inspection, and the young man checking it for exhaust leaks exclaimed as he looked at the little beds in back, "Whee! A partymobile!"

I told him, "My husband is a missionary and uses this vehicle to travel and raise funds." The kid seemed shocked that a minister and his wife knew how to have fun.

"Puritanism is the haunting fear that someone, somewhere may be happy." So wrote agnostic journalist H. L. Mencken. But rather than describing the Puritans, he caricatured them. Many people today think of Bible believers in the same way as Mencken thought of the Puritans—as humorless, Victorian prudes.

But, in fact, God's people have always known how to party. In Old Testament times, each Israelite family was required to save enough money to attend a nationally sponsored holiday: the Feast of Tabernacles. It was a memorial of the time Israel spent in the Sinai wilderness and a celebration of the fall harvest. It was not characterized by solemn reflection, but was a back-slapping party filled with joy and whoop-it-up type fun.

And the celebration did not stop after the cross. After the Holy Spirit was poured out at Pentecost, believers had such jubilation that the outsiders thought they were drunk on new wine. The New Testament harvest party began.

"You shall eat there before the Lord your God, and you shall rejoice, you and your household" (Deuteronomy 14:26).

I grew up in a happy environment, and we really got happy when we celebrated ten days of "heaven on earth" at Lake Placid Family Camp in Hartford City, Indiana. We sang camp meeting songs and joyous revival choruses like, "What a thrill I feel when I get together with God's wonderful people! What a sight to see, the happy faces, praising God in heavenly places!"

It is easy to sing and laugh when your past is erased, your sins forgiven. There is no haunt of guilt and you know where you are headed—that perfect destination, heaven.

I glanced into a gift shop window one day and spotted a needlepoint pillow. Stretched across it was this boldly stitched message: "One day I shall burst my bud of calm and blossom into hysteria." If I were rich I would I would rush into that little shop and order ten thousand of those pillows and pass them out to the first ten thousand people I met. We need to be set free from our bondage of inhibition and become free spirits like children. A man or woman who can clap easily, tap readily and laugh heartily will never be old.

If you are attending an "Organized Religious Funeral Club" each Lord's Day morning, relocate. Find a group of Bible teaching, happy, singing, testifying, rejoicing believers and enjoy the genuine joy that Jesus gives. Prove the nay-sayers wrong. Celebrate life in Christ with the humor that flows from a redeemed and joyful heart.

"The joy of the Lord is your *strength*" (Nehemiah 8:10).

Have you noticed that laughter is often at another's expense? If the experience had happened to the "laugher" the effect would be reversed and it would then cease to be funny.

Mark Twain, who wrote some of the funniest stories ever written, made a surprising comment. He said, "Everything human is pathetic. The secret source of humor is not joy, but sorrow. There is no humor in heaven."

Not all humor is based on pathos; sometimes humor is based on joy.

The Bible tells us that there is "a time to kill, and a time to heal; a time to break down, and a time to build up; a time to weep, and a time to laugh; a time to mourn, and a time to dance; a time to cast away stones, and a time to gather stones; a time to embrace, and a time to refrain from embracing" (Ecclesiastes 3:3–5).

In this passage of opposites, weeping, a sign of sorrow, is the opposite of laughter. Laughter and the humor that produces it, can be an expression of passionate joy.

Are you acquainted with joyless Christians? Carl, at age nineteen, passed by a church with a somber "funeral" reputation. An elderly man with a troubled frown on his face and the expression of "Digger O'Dell, the friendly undertaker," stood at the entrance and invited Carl and his friend to come in. They answered him, "No thanks. We have enough trouble of our own."

There is a time for humor. There is a time to unleash the joy within you and break out in laughter that is loud, long and clear. A person who loves to laugh is a person who is easy to love.

My Aunt Gwen is the youngest great-grandmother I know. Last Thanksgiving Day following dinner, as she was leaving, she fell down the flight of twelve steps from our sun deck. It knocked her out, hurt her hip, and through her bleeding lips she smiled and told Carl when he picked her up, "I'm sorry I ruined your holiday. Next time I won't go down the steps, I'll slide down the bannister."

When John Hinckley, Jr., tried to assassinate President Reagan in 1981, the world waited tensely, hoping the president would not die.

President Reagan himself broke the tension with his endearing sense of humor. It was revealed at a press conference soon after the shooting that when the barely conscious president was wheeled into the operating room, he looked at the doctors and nurses and said, "I hope you're all Republicans."

What's more, the first thing President Reagan said to his wife when she arrived at the hospital was, "Honey, I forgot to duck!" . . . a line borrowed from Jack Dempsey when he lost the Heavyweight boxing title to Gene Tunney in 1926.

Have you noticed that being around a person with a positive attitude makes you feel better about life? "A merry heart makes a cheerful countenance" (Proverbs 15:13). "And a good report makes the bones healthy" (Proverbs 15:30).

Be a person who has a positive impact on others. In so doing, you will bring health to their bones and glory to your Lord. Laughter and joy are contagious. Are you infectious?

Most Americans are suffering from some degree of stress, anxiety and tension. People who do not care about much in life are stressed for absence of funds to have fun. Those who do care suffer compassion fatigue and empathy bankruptcy.

Stress is saying yes with your mouth when your good sense is whispering *no*. Stress is big news. Everybody experiences it; nobody likes it; and sometimes it seems as though nothing can make it go away.

But researchers have found that people who have a good sense of humor are more likely to bounce back and are less likely than humorless folk to become depressed during periods of stress.

A person with a sense of humor has a therapeutic effect on others. And, according to the writer of the Proverbs, people who have the ability to laugh also help themselves: "A merry heart does good, like medicine, but a broken spirit dries the bones" (Proverbs 17:22).

Laughter actually has important physiological effects on the human body, protecting organs such as the heart from the harmful effects of stress. In other words, those who laugh loudest just might live longest!

A cheerful heart is a healthy heart, a heart that is filled with the good medicine of joy and laughter. Do you have such a heart?

As a Christian, you have more cause to be cheerful than the general public. After all, the God who is your Creator has become your Father through His Son.

The next time something in your life strikes you as funny, don't hold back. Laugh out loud, knowing that God has given to you, prescribed, and administered the miracle medicine of laughter.

A sense of humor has a double reward: more fun for more years.

My neighbor Sara teaches a Sunday school class of second graders. One morning she opened with a question, "What would make you happy this morning?"

One scrawny little eight-year-old boy with a cherubic face quickly answered, "If I had some money to put in the offering during morning worship today!" She gave him a dollar bill and, later during the service, glancing out of the corner of her eye, saw what joy it brought to the little fellow as he dropped the money in the red velvet offering bag as it passed down the pew to him. It started a trend with her.

Every Sunday she would inquire of the children whether or not they had something to give. It was no large investment for there were only from four to ten pupils. From then on she found herself praying, "Lord, you said to covet earnestly the best gifts. I covet the gift of mirth. Give me something to give away to bring mirth and joy to others."

Other great people have prayed the same prayer, with different words. Joseph Scriven was a young song writer living in Ireland. The evening before his wedding, his bride suddenly died. It broke his heart. He got on a ship and sailed to Canada, trying to run away from his grief. His sorrow followed him. Alone in his room one night he screamed out to God, "Visit me!" Immediately the Holy Spirit gave a song to him, gave him joy deep in his heart to pass on for generations to come. The song was "What a Friend We Have in Jesus."

The apostle Paul prayed for the gift of mirth. "[We] are fellow workers for your joy" (2 Corinthians 1:24). What a valuable gift! He was willing to give because he had received. In 1 Corinthians 16:18 he names three men who came to him and "refreshed my spirit and yours."

Jesus is the joy of living and giving. Covet earnestly this great gift. Don't keep it, spread it around!

I was sitting on our sun deck, in the early morning sun, sipping my first cup of coffee listening to the birds sing their early songs. Suddenly a young man, about sixteen years old, appeared out of nowhere. I did not hear a car, so he evidently was walking.

With a confident grin, he asked me, "Pretty lady, are you the queen of this castle?" Immediately I thought of several expressions I recalled from growing up, such as preaching politician, smooth talker, smooth as silk, soft as butter.

The boy's next line: "Are you in love with this ugly mold on your sun umbrella and the mildew on your deck floor?" Before I could reply, he whipped a spray bottle of liquid magic potion from a bag, and whisked off the mold with one sweep of the rag in his slight hand! His trick was as quick as his tongue.

Of course I wanted to buy some! He informed me that it was $40 for a gallon, but that it was highly concentrated. And "No, ma'am." I did not have to pay him in advance. He would deliver it the following day. I reasoned, "This swift-talking kid is really honest."

After delivering the goods, he left and I sprayed the stuff on my porch furniture full strength, I let it set for a half hour, then scrubbed, rubbed and sprayed again. Nothing happened! I sloshed some in my eye. It did not hurt, though the caution printed in red said, "Avoid contact with eyes."

That was two years ago. Just this morning I started to unlock the garage, when I was heard a smooth voice say, "Pretty lady, are you the queen of this castle?"

"No," I blurted out, "I don't want to buy your forty dollar a gallon anemic nothing!" He looked as though he would throw up, then darted down the street. He did not realize he had covered this territory before.

Satan beguiled Eve with his evil smooth talk. We must be prepared with an answer from the Word that will put him to flight. The Holy Spirit will bring an answer to mind if we know the Word.

What kind of faith are we to have? Following faith. Sometimes it takes more faith to follow than it takes to lead. I have always had an abundance of energy and vitality. For me, stopping is harder than starting, and God has more trouble with getting me to wait than getting me to go.

I believe it takes a finer quality of faith to accept the closed door, than it does to walk through an open one. Many of our old American traditional sayings and quotes are Bible-based. Henry Ford put faith in perspective with belief when he said, "Whether you believe you can or believe you can't, either way you're right."

God is always leading, but we are not always following. God knows the way; God shows the way. I rest in this realization. I have no fear, no anxiety. With God there is always a way. The great hymn writer Fannie Crosby expressed it this way:

> All the way my Saviour leads me;
>   What have I to ask beside?
> Can I doubt His tender mercy,
>   Who through life has been my Guide?
> Heavenly peace, divinest comfort,
>   Here by faith in Him to dwell!
> For I know, whate'er befall me,
>   Jesus doeth all things well. . . .

At church we sing, "Where He leads me I will follow." It is easy to follow during the fresh start, but what about the long journey? Please stop, reflect, meditate upon the following Scripture, pray it aloud and mean it with all of your heart: "You are my rock and my fortress; therefore, for Your name's sake, lead me and guide me" (Psalm 31:3).

He leads; you follow.

I remarked with a laugh one day as we lifted off from the little runway in Sisseton, South Dakota, headed for Wisconsin, "Well, I've always wanted to be rich enough to own my own private plane. My dream has come true. I can pretend." Little did I know that this dream was to become a nightmare. In just minutes, we flew through fog, then freezing rain and blinding snow.

"We're losing altitude and the wings and flaps are getting heavier with ice." It was the cool voice of Ed Arness. I use the term *cool*, which is an understatement. The Dakota temperatures were below zero and we were flying in a single engine Moonie without de-icing equipment. Ed shouted over the roar of the engine, "Our directional gyro just went out. In a blizzard like this you can be totally disoriented. We can't go on into Wisconsin. We are making a forced landing. I only hope we can keep altitude long enough to find a landing strip, or a good, wide highway." Then his lips moved in prayer.

I will never forget how forcefully the old song my grandparents used to sing, kept hammering my mind and spirit. It became my point of contact and concentration, my faith focus, to keep from panic: "The Lord knows the way through the wilderness, All I have to do is follow; Strength for today is mine always, And all I need for tomorrow. The Lord knows the way through the wilderness. All I have to do is follow."

Psalm 37:23 says, "The steps of a good man are *ordered* by the Lord." I prayed silently, *Ed is a good man. O God, give him orders, and help his following to be wise!*

Suddenly a voice from a control tower burst from our radio: "Here are your orders. Since your directional gyro is out, we are going to talk you down. Follow the instructions carefully. Do not trust your own judgment." They actually talked us down through the blowing ice and snow onto a runway that was invisible to our human eyes.

We made it!

Following dinner (known as "supper" in Indiana), when the sun went down, and the fireflies (lightning bugs) came out; when Mother and my grandmother Mom Burns washed the dishes; when Dad and my grandad Dad Burns sat in the porch swing as our live audience, my brothers, my Aunt Pearl (Pib), who was close to our age, and I would play "blind man's bluff" in the front yard.

We loved to fool each other. Taking a towel, or someone's shirt, we would tie it tightly around the head of the person who was "it," turn him or her around ten times until he or she got dizzy, lost direction (or if they ate too much supper, lost that), then we would lead them to a spot, stop and make them guess where they were. Once "it" I became the object of a dirty joke. I wondered why the trip was so long and why the two brothers who were leading me laughed so hard. When I smelled something awful and took the blindfold off, they had run away, leaving my two feet planted in a large "cow dab" that old Betsy had deposited in the pasture. I had no idea they would do that. I trusted them to guide me safely.

Faith walk. It takes no faith to believe in the past. It does take faith to walk forward and to keep believing that there is a future. I think that in each of us there is born a spirit of adventure, a hope and anticipation of things to come.

Jesus is our guide. Sometimes He *leads* us, sometimes He *makes* us.

"He *makes* me to lie down [to stop] . . . He *leads* me [to go]" (Psalm 23:2).

No daily devotional would be complete without the old faith walk classic "If We Could See Beyond Today" by Norman J. Clayton.

If we could see beyond today,
    As God can see,
If all the clouds should roll away,
    The shadows flee;
O'er present griefs we would not fret,
    Each sorrow we would soon forget,
For many joys are waiting yet,
    For you and me.

If you do not think little things mean a lot, get dental floss caught between your teeth or break the smallest toe on your right foot, the foot with which you press the brake and gas pedals in your car or the foot pedal of your sewing machine.

Or leave out the period on a check. It is only a little period, but it suddenly changes the amount from $1.00 to $100. Another little thing, a small piece of silver-colored metal, that tiny ignition key, commands a large bus, starts up an eighteen wheeler. Lose that small key and your progress is paralyzed.

One hot summer day, Carl came home suddenly in the middle of the morning, wearing a heavy winter topcoat. "Carl, you gotta be crazy," I said. "You're so sweaty. It must be 92 degrees out there!"

Without reply he turned around and bent over. The entire seat was split out of his trousers. He took them off and in four minutes, with the aid of a little thing, a needle, and another small item, #8 thread, I spared him further embarrassment and saved his day. Little things mean a lot.

Scripture tells us, "Go to the ant, you sluggard! Consider her ways and be wise." (Take coaching from a small thing, like an ant.) Floridians know how much clout the small ant has. Have you ever stepped into a seemingly harmless, sandy ant hill of fire ants? Your eyes can swell shut, your ears close up till you cannot hear, your heart will race and you can become very sick.

Little things mean a lot. Anything you do 35 times becomes a habit. If you do not want to be an alcoholic, never take the first little sip. To prevent a smoking habit, never light the first little match.

The Bible talks about a little thing that can do great good or harm. "The tongue is a little member and boasts great things. . . . And the tongue is a fire, a world of iniquity. . . . No man can tame the tongue. . . . Out of the same mouth proceed blessing and cursing" (James 3:5–6, 8–9).

Small things, even small jobs, are important. Do not be afraid to take the small assignment. God can then trust you with a larger one. In the parable of the talents Jesus said, "Well done, good and faithful servant; you were faithful over a few things, I will make you ruler over many things" (Matthew 25:21).

Jesus said, "Be of good cheer!"

This was an exhortation, a command and a promise, all in one. He could afford to command us to "be of good cheer" for He *is* the ability to bring cheer into any situation. Jesus carried His cheer around with Him, inside of Himself. He offers this same joy to you and me.

Paul found the source of creative cheer from God. While he was a prisoner he wrote over and over again: "Rejoice in the Lord always. Again I will say, rejoice!" (Philippians 4:4). David said, "You will show me the path of life; in Your presence is fullness of joy" (Psalm 16:11).

The Gospels show us three particular instances in which Jesus said to be of good cheer.

Sickness. A woman in a crowd had suffered from an issue of blood for twelve years. She had spent everything she had on doctors but they could not do anything to help her. When she saw Jesus and said to herself that if she could just touch His robe she would be made well. So she reached out and touched the fringe. Jesus, perceiving that power had gone out from Him, looked at her and said, "Daughter, be of good cheer; your faith has made you well. Go in peace" (Luke 8:48).

Darkness. Jesus sent His disciples by boat on to Bethsaida while He sent the crowds away and went up to the mountain to pray. When evening came He was alone on the land and saw His disciples straining at the oars because the wind was against them. So at the fourth watch of the night He came to them, walking on the water. The disciples were terrified, supposing that He was a ghost, but He called out to them and said, "Be of good cheer! It is I; do not be afraid."

World turmoil to come. In one of His last long talks with His disciples, Jesus told them that they would be scattered by the world's accusations and He would be left alone. "These things I have spoken to you, that in Me you may have peace. In the world you will have tribulation; but be of good cheer, I have overcome the world" (John 16:33).

Three cheers for Jesus! He will heal your sickness, calm your fears and be with you in any future trouble.

I love the month of April, its promise of spring, blossoms and the return of the robins. I even enjoy jokes on people the first day of April.

One April Fool's Day our neighbor Rick was reading the morning paper, when his wife, Beth, said quietly, "Today my attorney will be serving you with divorce papers." When he dropped the paper in shock, she laughed and said, "April fool!"

This morning I spotted a poster at the bookstore. It was of two giraffes standing taller than a host of other animals in the same meadow. The caption read: "Leadership: Seeing further down the road than those around me can." At the bottom was Proverbs 24:7, "Wisdom is too high for a fool" (KJV).

I had just finished speaking on a college campus in Minnesota and invited the students to ask questions. Without raising his hand for recognition, one young man with a bad complexion and a husky voice blurted out, "Mrs. Malz you keep talking about God. Now, I've never seen God, but if you will introduce Him and let me shake hands with Him, I will believe there is a God."

Some students laughed. Others gasped. He had my back against the wall. I paused a moment and in my heart whispered, *Jesus?* Then I told him, "If you'll stay after class I'd like to talk. I think I can help you."

"Help me?" he retorted, "If you really want to help me, see if you have a couple of aspirins in your purse. I have a helluva headache."

I saw my chance. The Holy Spirit is the one called alongside to help.

"Hmm," I said. "I have never seen a headache, but if you will introduce me to your headache I will believe and buy you a whole bottle of aspirin."

"The fool has said in his heart, 'There is no God'" (Psalm 14:1).

The Bible says that we will be held responsible for every careless word we utter. How frightening to think of the results in eternity of words spoken purposely to destroy another!

I believe that hiding wounding words in the guise of righteousness is just as criminal as pouring poison into someone's food. Solomon said, "Keep your heart with all diligence, for out of it spring the issues of life" (Proverbs 4:23). Thus, we must always weigh our motives. Are we really seeking righteousness? Or is some deeper contention at work?

The tender heart will look for answers, not flaws.

It seems to me, generally, that the people who spend their energies trying to pry others apart do not have strong commitments of their own. I have seen well-meaning people hurt because someone chose to rake them over the coals, someone who might better have spent the time seeking God for a wonderful experience of his or her own.

Strange as it may seem, cannibalism is still practiced in the twentieth-century! Reports of Congolese soldiers eating the flesh of their victims shocked the civilized world. But what is even more shocking is instance after instance in which people who call themselves Christians are practicing *spiritual* cannibalism. It is true that we cannot abide blatant sin in the Body of Christ, but more often we need to lock arms in love and not fight each other but Satan.

Webster defines *cannibalism* as eating one's own kind. The desperate act of starving men who try to save their own lives by eating the flesh of the dead might be excusable. That is not as sinful as devouring another human's integrity.

Paul warned against this evil practice: "For all the law is fulfilled in one word, even in this: 'You shall love your neighbor as yourself.' But if you bite and devour one anther, beware lest you be consumed" (Galatians 5:15).

Jesus commanded us to love one another. Let's forgive. And forget.

Most Americans tend to turn to food for fun, entertainment or recreation. Food is *fuel*, necessary nutrition to energize and motivate the body and mind to do its work. The excessive consumption of food causes obesity.

I saw these two bumper stickers on the back of a blue Toyota pickup truck: "Love Thy Neighbor, But Don't Get Caught" and "Save Water, Shower With Your Neighbor's Wife." Now, physical love within the confines of marriage with your life's mate is the next best thing to heaven. Love out of bounds, however, with the wrong peson becomes merely lust. God calls it sin. The wages of sin is death. That kind of love will kill your soul.

I have a miniature green house, an atrium, attached to my east kitchen window. I decided I would make those window plants a real show piece, a traffic stopper on my street. I overdid the fertilizer. They did not grow; they burned up, turned brown and ugly, and all died.

The Bible must be read and followed, but we can become Pharisees in our scrutiny, legalistic and unforgiving. "The letter kills, but the Spirit gives life." Any tire that is overinflated makes for a bumpy ride.

My family used to love to waterski down the Wabash River. That river flowing peacefully within its banks is beautiful to behold. But a river out of control becomes a flood, a raging, damaging force.

Fire is fine for cooking a rib eye steak, or crackling in a fireplace on a wintery night. But fire out of control burns up everything in its way. It consumes and destroys. Even religious fire can flame into fanaticism.

Excessiveness is rarely good.

Paul said that everyone who "striveth for the mastery is temperate in all things" (1 Corinthians 9:25).

In the mail we received a most impressive bright green folded advertisement. Opening it fully I read, "The key to happiness can take many shapes. This could turn out to be a *key* decision to take out a loan. We can help you with a *key* to an addition to your home, the *key* to a new car, a *key* to a college dorm, the ignition *key* for a new boat, or a *key* to a beautiful hotel room for an exotic week in the Caribbean.

The ad failed to inform us about one flaw: Paying back the loan with interest will not bring as much happiness as the *key* it buys!

Most people equate peace and contentment with happiness. *Happiness* has as its root the word *happen*, forcing happiness to depend on what happens. True joy is different.

When my first husband opened his new Sunoco service station and automotive parts store in Clearwater, Florida, in 1961, he prayed for a key for success. Early one morning he exclaimed, "I've found it! The key to success!" He read Joshua 1:8: "This Book of the Law shall not depart from your mouth, but you shall meditate in it day and night. . . . For then you will make your way prosperous, and then you will have good success."

Every morning at five minutes before seven, John inserted the key to the front door of that business with his right hand, held the Bible in his left hand and read that Scripture aloud before opening the door for business. That actually became his key to happiness. God directed traffic on that busy corner. The business propspered for the next four years before his death, until we hardly knew what to do with all the money. It was the only time in my whole life when I was wealthy.

We do not need a formula when we have the Father. He not only knows the source, but *is* the source of all comfort, our deliverer and our Great Physician. Jesus Christ is the same yesterday, today and forever. He was the compassionate healer when the walked the earth and is still the functioning Physician yet today. Jesus is the author of peace, and what He gives is not temporary happiness, but eternal joy, joy in the Holy Ghost. Small wonder that Isaiah calls Him the Wonderful Counsellor, the Everlasting Father, and the Prince of Peace.

Take the keys Jesus offers—the keys of the Kingdom.

Beauty is only skin deep, but ugly is to the bone! The kitchen cabinets around our refrigerator are covered with insulting bumper stickers: "You have a striking face. How many times were you struck there?" "She's so ugly, when she comes in the room, mice jump up on chairs." And our personal favorite, since there are just three of us left in our family now: "Ugly strikes one out of three."

I got a book of insults for Christmas. Here are three more gems: "She's so ugly, the Peeping Tom reached in and pulled down the window shade." "He has Early American features. He looks like a Buffalo." "She has not only kept her girlish figure, she has doubled it."

Americans are certainly "looks" conscious. Think about it. Suppose "The Sleeping Beauty" had been "The Sleeping Ugly." There would have been no kiss and she would still be dead.

My parents tried to change this attitude when we children were growing up. I shall never forget when Dad appointed an overweight, homely, depressed woman to teach a boys' Sunday school class to encourage her. One of my kid brothers told him, "Yes, you'll encourage one woman and discourage fifteen boys!"

Still hoping to change our perceptions, Mother appealed to my brothers' Christian charity. "Please ask Dorothy out. She's new in the church." They replied with horrid jokes: "She's straight and narrow. If it weren't for her Adam's apple, she would have no figure at all. She has a good job though, modeling for thermometers."

As a last appeal Mother said, "Beauty is only skin deep." Don to Jim, "O.K., then, Jim, you hold her and I'll skin her."

The British have a saying, "Even God has His dear ones and His queer ones." (The word meant "frumpy" or "dowdy" then.)

The Bible should have the final word here. "Man looks at the outward appearance, but the Lord looks at the heart." Some of those stunning "lookers" might not be so stunning after all.

Several years ago, during our move from Texas to South Dakota, April and I were driving the Ramcharger, pulling the trailer with the mare and colt. Nearing Dallas we were to take 35W, but sudden, heavy sheets of rain hit us. As hailstones pelted down on the truck and metal trailer, terrifying the mare and colt, we missed the exit. Suddenly we found ourselves headed for downtown Dallas with freeways running over each other like spaghetti in a bowl. I nearly panicked.

"Try the CB radio," April said. "Someone will tell us what to do."

I nodded and reached for the mike but with deep uncertainty. I had never bothered to read the CB handbook. Helplessly I looked at the dials. "Turn it to channel nineteen, Mother," April said.

I did so, then picked up the mike and said, "I'm driving to South Dakota and missed my turn. Can someone help me get onto highway 35W?"

April shook her head as I listened to a confusion of talk and static on the set. "Mother, you're going at it wrong. You're not talking to a ladies' luncheon. They're truckers out there. You gotta talk their language. May I try it?"

I gave her the mike, and she took a deep breath. "Breaker nineteen for a radio check."

A deep booming voice came back, "Radio check. How mucha puttin' down?"

"'Bout seven—maybe ten."

"What's your ten-twenty?" the deep voice asked.

"We're lost. We've got a horse trailer, and the horses are goin' *crazy*. How about some help gettin' to 35W?" I stared at April in amazement. Was this my sweet, gentle twelve-year-old?

She communicated a few landmarks and the booming bass came back with directions. He concluded with, "This here's the Black Panther from the Texas Panhandle. Whatcher handle, good buddy?"

"This here's the Dakota Kid," returned April.

"Ten-four, Dakota Kid. Good luck, little buddy. Over and out."

When we were back on course, I asked her, "April Dawn, where did you learn that kind of talk?"

"Mother, Dad tried to get you to read the CB handbook before we left on this trip. When you know the words, you can get the help."

As we drove on the parallel hit me. God has given us a handbook. We need to use it every day to stay spiritually in tune.

Thanks, Lord, I thought. *Or make that, Ten-four, over and out.*

Relationships are essential to identity. If a young man lives alone on an island alone, who is he? He is not a friend, because he has none. He is not a lover; he is not an employee; he is not a boss; he is not a husband; he is not a father. If he does not know God, then he is not a Christian.

We are only someone in relationship to others. After God created Adam He said, "It is not good that man should be alone" (Genesis 2:18).

Relationships, in fact, are vital to survival.

Miles from Sun Valley, a deer hunter came upon a crude cabin in a remote mountain area. It gave off a horrid stench. The Board of Health investigated and found an eight-year-old girl crawling on her hands and knees, lapping milk from a bowl like a dog. The mother had confined this child to a dark room for eight years so no one would learn of her illegitimate birth. She could not walk or talk.

The mother was arrested, and the child taken to the children's hospital. For days, they tried to communicate with the weak, anemic child. The charts were marked the same day after day, "No emotions." She did not cry or smile. Her eyes finally adjusted to the light, but the windows of her soul were dead and expressionless.

Finally the nurses gave her sugar and said to her, "Sugar." She liked it and said, "Sooookah." It was a breakthrough. Later she responded to hugs, to being held, to music, to singing and began to smile.

"None of us lives to himself, and no one dies to himself" (Romans 14:7). Jesus had two simple rules for mankind to survive. First, love God, second love other people. We have complicated our lives.

As we go through life we must sing harmony with others. We need each other. We need God.

The road to success is always under construction. Some people are just "born good." For the rest of us, it seems we are always in reform school. God never gives up on us, He just keeps working on us. Great men like Paul, David, Samson and Peter had to keep returning to the Lord for renovation, reconstruction, revision and even complete overhaul.

I paused momentarily at the door of a seminar for "men only," and heard the speaker drop this one, "Guys, we're the steady ones. You know that across the forehead of every woman is an invisible sign that reads, 'Subject to Change Without Notice.' It's the female prerogative to change her mind [pause . . . laughter].

"I asked my wife, 'What's wrong with you, woman?' She answered, 'Guess I'm going through the change.' 'Thank God,' I retorted, 'I'm sick of you the way you've been!' [raucous laughter].

I almost "hung up" on him at that point; I could hardly believe my ears. But I am glad I listened. He had gotten his audience's attention, then he hit them between the eyes. "The biggest room in your house is the room for improvement," he said. "And know what? You are the carpenter." His message was, you cannot change other people, but you can change yourself.

I re-read Mona Johnian's book, *Renewing Your Mind*. They purchased a house that was in dismal shape. They called it "the black hole." There was nothing to do but plunge in and begin to work it over.

It is the same with "mental and spiritual" renewal. "Be renewed in the spirit of your mind" (Ephesians 4:23). Admit your need to change. Get a fresh mental attitude. The first step is an honest assessment.

"A friend may well be reckoned the masterpiece of nature," said Ralph Waldo Emerson "Things do not change; we must change," said Henry David Thoreau.

If you are willing to forgive seventy-times-seven times, then you can feel free to keep returning to the Lord for pardon and renewal. "If we say that we have no sin, we deceive ourselves, and the truth is not in us. If we confess our sins, He is faithful and just to forgive us our sins and to cleanse us from all unrighteousness" (1 John 1:7–8).

I believe in eternal security. And to keep it that way I do not lean against the tailgate; I try to sit up close to the cab of the truck! To put it another way, Jesus has promised to keep us in the hollow of His hand. He will never dump us out, but we may jump out.

When I was a small girl, many times I disobeyed my dad. Sometimes I behaved like British royalty. Sometimes I acted like an ugly stepchild. During those times he did not throw me out of the family. He did not change my last name. I was still his daughter.

The illustration from the book of Hosea is that God is married to the backslider. It speaks of God's mercy, pardon and faithfulness to the faithless one. "I will heal their backsliding. I will love them freely, for My anger has turned away" (Hosea 14:4).

No matter how rebellious you have become, God will not divorce you. You are the only party in that relationship who can file for divorce.

But don't press your luck. You may skim through this world in His good graces, but a Judgment Day is coming.

Traveling through Texas you will see repeatedly two road signs. I love them both. The first is "Don't Mess with Texas!" I believe God wants us to clean up our act and keep the road clear of rubble and litter so that we have a pure path for our feet to walk toward heaven. The second sign is "Hurry Back, Y'all Hear?" The heart of God is tender and His ear is eternally tuned in, ever listening for our footsteps to return and our hearts to repent. He promised, "I will give them a heart to know Me, that I am the Lord; and they shall be My people, and I will be their God, for they shall return to Me with their whole heart" (Jeremiah 24:7).

The security is sustained by staying close.

We exercise a lot of talent rehearsing the resurrection music for this holiday. We expend a lot of work and time preparing the traditional ham, and coloring, hiding and hunting Easter eggs. Many spend excessive amounts of money for an Easter outfit to wear that particular Sunday in the spring season. This can all be symbolic and meaningful, but I remember when I searched for the largest, most decorated hat in order to impress on people that I knew how to dress.

I was a prisoner of impressions. I spent a great deal of time and energy trying to impress people, and I was impressed *by* people . . . by their addresses, their degrees, their looks, their spirituality, size, salary.

One morning just before Easter, two women came to my door. I could not let them in. I was not dressed, the baby did not have her pink ruffled panties on, nor her pink bow atop her little blonde head. My house was not orderly enough to impress my female visitors. As they pulled out of the driveway, I hated myself and the chains of pride that bound me, forcing me to worry about how I looked and be stressed by what people thought.

Falling across the bed weeping, my limp arms and hands dangled and fell upon the soft, furry coat of our old, sable collie. We called her "Mother Superior," Old Missy. She wore the same thing every day, never had a change of clothes, but was so happy, wagging her tail and content with what she did have to wear. Of course, her coat *was* sable!

I prayed that day for deliverance from pride. The spirit of resurrection brought me out. I emerged to walk "in newness of life." That practical parable learned from a dog at Easter has not left me. Our witness is not our appearance or costumes. People forget what we wear, but remember if they were welcomed or if our love was real.

"A man who has friends must himself be friendly" (Proverbs 18:24). The greatest Easter gift is love.

In the fairy tale "Pinocchio," each time the little fellow told a lie his nose grew a little longer. At our house we never call each other a "liar." The Bible says that anyone who calls his brother a liar is in danger of the fires of hell. We do have a friendly, family signal when the truth is becoming elastic: "Your nose is growing!"

Along with ugly jokes, we like liar jokes, like: He makes his bed and then tries to lie out of it, or, He's a second-story man; no one ever believes his first story.

In a book called *The Day America Told the Truth* the researchers claimed that 91 percent of Americans admit that they lie on a regular basis; 86 percent lie to parents, 75 percent lie to friends, 73 percent to siblings, 69 percent to spouses, and 81 percent lie about their own personal feelings.

To what extent are we faced with a crisis of integrity and the tendency to save our skin by telling a falsehood?

When the Bible says that love covers a multitude of sins, it does not suggest that we should lie for our brother, but "cover for him," that is, surround his transgression with our love. Telling negative things that will hurt others is not the same as "speaking the truth in love."

Remember that God knows the inside story. He sees us inside out so we need not try to put on false faces and airs. God loves us like we can become. Jesus is merciful. "Whoever confesses and forsakes [his sins] will have mercy" (Proverbs 28:13).

I get letters almost every day from people who say, "I want to be a writer. How do I start?" I always reply, "There is only one way to start and that is to begin. Just *do* it. *Write!*" My career was actually launched when I realized I liked to write letters to encourage people. That is writing already.

If you want to be a minister, start ministering. I know a television ministry that is still raising funds for a ministry that has quit ministering. If you visit several doctors and one of them gets results, he is the one who will have better business.

Gravitate toward the needs of people and God will call you. Then, you will not have to go poking around looking for His will. At the point when you love people, God's will has found you! During my brief 28-minute encounter with death, the one eternal "take home" benefit I learned was that you cannot take it with you—except for people. People are the only commodity that transfers from this life to the next.

If you want to swim, go near the water. If you want to be a prayer warrior, start praying. We talk too much. We read too much. We need to stop, look and listen. The Holy Spirit will reveal people's needs to us. This is His job. Success is finding a need and filling it.

Have you known bachelors who read romance novels, but do not have the nerve to say, "I do"? Do you know little ladies who collect recipes, but do not know where the kitchen is? They are clouds without rain (see Jude 12).

We know too much. We attend seminars to learn compassion. On the road to learn more, we pass hundreds of needy people. We do not have time to meet their need, for we are hurrying on to where we will get more knowledge of how to help them.

Do not get so busy learning that you cannot put to practice what you have been taught. People do not care how much you know until they know how much you care!

I have four frequent flyer cards. I have been flying steadily for sixteen years now, since my first book. I never have to look at the card in the seat pocket in front of me; I have it memorized. I can quote the flight attendant's speech without a single mistake. But my last trip was different.

Shortly after takeoff we heard a jolly, mellow voice, "I'm Ursula. I am your flight attendant on this thirty-minute flight from Chicago to Detroit. On this brief flight, as soon as we level off, you will be allowed one drink, one trip to the bathroom and no smoking and no talking [a lovely chuckle]. From Tupelo to Tokyo, from Austin to Boston, we hope that in the future when your travel plans call for flying you will think of us, Northwest, and remember me, Ursula." It was just another flight, but her humor shortened the journey.

My brother Jim has a pretty daughter. In public, so as not to call attention to the fact that she may be nicer looking than other girls, he calls her "funk ball" and "toad." She knows that these are loving expressions that mean, "I love you."

We tell our collie, "Ole Miss, You're simply ugly, lovely, homely." She does not care what we are saying because the tone we use is warm and loving. She thumps the floor, wagging her old tail with joyful glee at our silly humor.

Carl and I have developed stress signals. When I have angered him, he starts singing (and he cannot sing), "If I had the wings of an angel, over these prison bars I would fly!" I insert, "I wish you would." Reprimand can be easily tolerated when mingled with humor. When he is overbearing with me, the signal to "back off" is when I starting whistling, "What a fellowship, what a joy divine! Leaning on the everlasting arms."

Let humor make the journey lighter.

What's this?

It came to our mailbox, a colorful brochure promising, "You'll never be alone in an emergency! Help is available when you're in need. Just press one tiny button and help is on the way." It went on to describe a monitoring system hung around the neck by which you could press a button and talk with a communication center. Even if you cannot talk, the staff member on the other end is alerted to your address and will send help.

The brochure went on to promise peace of mind: "You will never be alone again!" It was a masterpiece of advertising, probably because it touched a need deep in our souls, a need truly met by only one Person.

Jesus said, "I will never leave you nor forsake you" (Hebrews 13:5). He will be with us in trouble. He will be with us even to the end of the world. God neither slumbers nor sleeps (see Psalm 121:3–4).

God's emergency number is always in operation. "Call to Me," He says, "and I will answer you" (Jeremiah 33:3). He does not have an answering machine. He answers His own calls, day or night. He even has millions of secretaries, recording angels, that can travel to your aid faster than the speed of the sound of your praying. "Call to Me, and I will . . . show you great and mighty things,which you do not know."

"My God shall supply all your need according to His riches in glory by Christ Jesus" (Philippians 4:19). "Be strong and of good courage; do not be afraid, nor be dismayed, for the Lord your God is with you wherever you go" (Joshua 1:9).

When Treva's young husband died, she was left with twin baby boys, and a great deal of debt. She met and fell in love with a handsome young man who had a well-paying position. Only a few days after their marriage, however, she learned that he had misrepresented himself to her; he had not told her that he had homosexual tendencies. What a disappointment! Realizing he was not able emotionally to satisfy her needs, they agreed to annul the marriage.

Treva's husband had died in Florida, her mother had died here and now this nightmare had occurred here. After a few years passed, she decided to move to a different state. There she met and married a fine man who had children of his own. He became the godly lover she desired and supplied the fatherly stability her boys needed. It seemed like a happy dream until her new spouse took a business position in the same Florida county of her wounded memories.

With much dread, Treva "faced the music" and returned to her native Florida to start over again. God had "wiped away her tears" and she had been able to get on with living.

Once she encountered a "gossipy old lady" who seemed to enjoy knocking the scab off an old wound and she nearly ran again. It was during the Persian Gulf crisis, Desert Storm. Getting into her car in a parking lot she spotted a red, white and blue bumper sticker displaying Old Glory and the words, "These colors won't run."

She knew she would never run again, but would stand her ground. Safely at home, she grabbed the Bible, her comfort source, and read the story of Joseph. He was misunderstood, sold, imprisoned, but God showed him favor and he became second in command to Pharaoh in Egypt. He blessed the nation of Egypt and that nation preserved his family. These words spoke to her heart: "God has caused me to be fruitful in the land of my affliction" (Genesis 41:52).

Treva's little shop is prospering, her husband has had good success and those twin boys are thriving in Florida sunshine!

Contrary to the belief of many, Clearwater Beach is not heaven. Last February while mowing my grass, I ran over and killed two poisonous snakes in twenty minutes. One was a coral snake, the other a pigmy rattler. Both are deadly. I understand that after the coral snake strikes, you are "out of here" in twenty short minutes. I know what you are thinking if you live up north: "Poor Baby. She had to mow her grass in February." But warm sunshine does not make it heaven. I read in the St. Petersburg *Times* that Florida has the seventh highest suicide rate in the nation. The old are disillusioned; the young are in debt.

There are no perfect situations. The money people up north spend on heat bills in winter we spend on air conditioning.

Vail, Colorado, is not heaven either. While visiting my step-daughter and her family who live near the Vail ski slope, I stopped in a grocery store. There were sixteen different brands of caviar on one shelf. I have never even tasted caviar.

It is expensive living there. There are hidden messages: Vail is for the healthy, wealthy and young. There is not a single cemetery in Vail, suggesting, if you are going to die, don't do it here. No, Vail and Colorado's mountains are not heaven either.

God brought down a sample of Paradise from heaven to earth and called it Eden. But even there Satan deceived Adam and Eve, inflated their pride and ruined it for them (see 2 Corinthians 11:3).

In heaven there is no more, sickness, sorrow, death. Let's talk about heaven's "no more's." No more divorce, no more hurricanes, no more war, no more AIDS, no more drugs, no more pain, no more misunderstanding, no more jealousy, no more friction, tension, stress, anxiety, competition, no more prejudice, no more complexes, crying or quarreling, no more death, only victory! "The Lord will wipe away tears from all faces" (Isaiah 25:8).

Mona Johnian shared the following thoughts with me.

"God is in direct control of our everyday lives, just as He is in control of this universe. He was the Creator, is the Creator and will keep on creating! When God said to Moses, 'I Am,' He was saying that He is the past, the present and the future.

"'The Lord by wisdom founded the earth' (Proverbs 3:19). God could have chosen any number of ways to bring about creation. He could have set nature on her course and stood back to watch her develop. He could have spoken her into existence and then retired. But God is actively involved in exercising His creation powers in the personal lives of those who know Him. God is not nature. He created nature.

"God is an artist of many talents. If nature is just one expression of the Creator then how foolish we are to spend all our energies speculating about a painting while the Artist stands silently beside the canvas!

"As the Creator, God has certain 'legal' rights to His creation. Not everyone wants God to be in control of our everyday lives, however. Some may argue, 'What right does God have to tell me what to do?' And we can respond, 'He has every right. We live on His property, eat His food, even breathe His breath.'"

You never go so far but that your "tale" follows you. I watched a baby squirrel the other day through the window in my writing studio. He jumped from branch to branch in the holly bushes, then, like a trapeze artist, balanced himself gracefully until he found the sunflower seeds I had put out for him.

As the squirrel's bushy tail followed his quick movements, so does an individual's "tale" follow along with him. "Even a child is known by his deeds, by whether what he does is pure and right" (Proverbs 20:11). Sooner or later every man sits down to his own private banquet of consequences.

God did not write rules in the "Guidebook" to hinder us from being free to frolic, but to spare us the consequences of wrong behavior. He suggests lovingly that you read the rules, follow the directions. When you disobey the guidelines, you will have "trouble in the flesh." Jesus forgives the sins of the flesh, He remembers *no more*, but most folks will not let transgressions be forgotten. They whisper, "Let me tell you what I heard."

Take a smooth, new board. Hammer two nails into it. You can pull the nails out, but they leave two holes, two wounds, two scars. The board has been delivered from the nails, but the wounds remain as reminders. Forgiveness is the restoration of a relationship with God, not the removal or absence of consequences.

I love the old song, "Jesus paid it all, all to Him I owe. Sin had left a crimson stain, He washed it white as snow." And these words from Isaiah are like a healing balm: "Put away the evil of your doings. . . . Though your sins are like scarlet, they shall be as white as snow" (Isaiah 1: 16, 18). Jesus paid in full for your sin; your soul *is* saved. God will be with you *through* the consequences, and He is still your God *after* the consequences.

Have you heard the expression, "It's the Pits!" Well, Satan is the accuser of your past and *that's* the pits! When Satan accuses you, reminds you of failures in your past, then say what Michael the archangel said when he contended with Satan about the body of Moses: "The Lord rebuke you!" (Jude 9).

"Resist the devil and he will flee from you" (James 4:7).

A "clique" is a disease that can break out in a church, family, club, choir, softball team or business. It will *infect* those inside the group, and it will *affect*, hurt and injure those outside the group. It is most commonly found among youth groups and immature adults. A man is youthful once, but may remain immature forever. Church groups should be vaccinated against this horrible plague. It is an offense to visitors and the tenderhearted "lambs." It is God's vote that really counts! We need His approval.

In Jesus' day the scribes and Pharisees formed the religious clubs that excluded substandards. Jesus called them "whitewashed tombs" (Matthew 23:27). Winston Churchill said he never let cliques get to him. If an "exclusive" group eyed him disdainfully while he was speaking, he just "saw them all naked." We bring nothing into this world and take nothing out.

God hates snobbishness. He does not show partiality among His children, has no pets. He loves his kids all the same.

Five minutes into a conversation with a clique, you can tell their prime interest, their motives, what makes them laugh and what they hate.

I had an experience with one. As a young eligible widow, a newcomer in town ("The new broom sweeps the cleanest"), I got a phone call from a well-known area businessman. He had hardly given me his name when he started boasting about "his" ministry, "his" contribution to "his" organization. When "his" church wanted something done, they always said, "Pass the ball to Ed. He gets more done in less time than anyone you know!" He went on to let me know how lucky I was that he wanted to take me to dinner. He informed me of how many women wanted to go out with him, but he was asking me. When he started name dropping I gave him a taste of my type of "clique." In the middle of one of his self-centered sentences I clicked the phone receiver down quietly.

If you want God to "hang up" on you, trying pulling rank on Him! "All our righteousnesses are like filthy rags" (Isaiah 64:6).

Growing up, my brothers and I looked forward to the annual Burns family reunion. It was held the first Sunday in August each year. My mother, Fern Burns Perkins, was a direct descendant of Robert Burns, the poet. Ours was a closely knit family. I lived most of my life within one mile of all four grandparents, two great-grandparents, aunts, uncles and cousins.

The reunion was held at Deming Park in the east woodlands of Terre Haute. We loved the monkey cages, throwing rocks in the lake and the loving hugs of relatives. We expected to hear the usual "My how you've grown!" and "You're so tall you could pass for eighteen." (I was eleven at the time I first heard that one!)

I looked forward most of all to my grandmother's fruit salad because it had pineapple. This was a special treat. Actually it had only four ingredients: pineapple, cut-up oranges, sliced bananas and sugar.

There was another fruit salad that was a favorite with the older folks. "Five Cup Salad" consisted of: 1 cup crushed pineapple, drained; 1 cup sour cream; 1 cup coconut; 1 small can mandarin oranges; 1 cup miniature marshmallows. It was especially good if they added 1 cup of English walnuts. Wow!

Now here is the recipe for another fruit salad with nutrients that produce amazing, lasting results and strength both for the person who consumes it and those with whom he comes into contact. The more you partake, the more it multiplies and the more others are blessed by and want to taste it.

This recipe has nine ingredients, all essential to spiritual growth and maturity. "Fruit of the Spirit Salad" consists of love, joy, peace, patience, kindness, goodness, faithfulness, gentleness and self-control (see Galatians 5:22).

Junior high school instructors of literature and English, take heart. Your students do not forget everything you tell them. Strangely enough just this morning as I sat down to start today's devotional, I recalled something that Blanche Wellman, one of my teachers, taught us. I don't know the author and may not recall all of the lines, but it went something like this:

Don't Quit

When things go wrong as they sometimes will,
    When the road you're trudging seems all uphill,
When the funds are low and the debts are high,
    And you want to smile, but you have to sigh,
When care is pressing you down a bit,
    Rest if you must—but don't you quit.
Success is failure turned inside out,
    The silver tint of the clouds of doubt.
You never can tell how close you are—
    It may be near when it seems afar.
So, stick to the fight when you're hardest hit—
    It's when things go wrong that you mustn't quit!

I remember also a book she read us about the Gold Rush. We sat spellbound as we listened to the stories about Americans who, with a pioneer spirit of imagination or a tinge of greed, went west to California to pan for gold in the streams or dig in the mountains.

One young bachelor promised his fiancée that he would "strike it rich" and send for her in the new land of opportunity. He was out of money and losing his drive as he watched instant wealth happen to others, but not to him.

Finally, in utter despair, physically and mentally drained, starving, he drove his pick into the ground and attached to its handle a note with his final words: "I quit."

Before long, passersby found him. And they also found one of the richest gold veins in all of California—not a dozen feet from where he died.

"He who endures to the end will be saved" (Matthew 10:22).

I want to share these words from Tammy Cardwell of Baytown, Texas, with you.

"Do not give up. That is backsliding. Do not keep looking back or you will run into something. Look ahead!

"Do you ever think about how long a baby bird works away inside that eggshell before it finally cracks it open and manages to break out? Only God knows what it might be thinking, if it thinks. Suppose it decided that the whole thing was worthless, futile, no hope. Perhaps, if it were moved by reason instead of instinct, it would decide that there really was no breaking through. It could determine that there was nothing on the other side and decide to take the way of least resistance and stay where it was—and die in ease and comfort.

"Yet, the little bird is driven. And after 'banging its head against the wall' for who knows how long, finally breaks through to—What's this? A world nothing like the one it just came from. It is big, bright, filled with responsibilities and dangers. But it has been driven by an inner need, and now, continues to survive and grow. It learns to 'fly the good flight of faith.' And one day, in due season, the grown eagle will soar above the clouds. It was well worth the struggle in the end.

"'I have fought the good fight, I have finished the race, I have kept the faith. Finally, there is laid up for me the crown of righteousness, which the Lord, the righteous Judge, will give to me on that Day'" (2 Timothy 4:7–8).

Sue is a terrific cook, and Bill is a terrific eater.

Sue to Bill: "I'm giving you thirty days to lose ten pounds."

Bill to Sue: "I can't do it. It's your good cooking that's at fault."

Sue to Bill: "You can do it. Inch by inch, anything's a cinch."

Bill to Sue (later): "You gave me thirty days to lose ten pounds. So far, all I've lost is twenty-one days!"

Losing weight is the battle where the loser wins and the winner loses. It takes perseverance and endurance, two biblical injunctions. I think the story of the two frogs says it all on that subject:

Two frogs were playing in the rafters of a dairy barn one night, and they fell into adjoining pails of cream. Both frogs kicked and scrambled for survival, but one fought harder and longer.

When the farmer came in the next morning, he found one frog dead in the pail, drowned. The other frog was sitting on a cake of butter, exhausted but happy.

Moral: When we let problems overwhelm us, when we give up, stop jumping and hopping and scrambling for survival, we stop living. But, when we hang in there and fight the good fight of faith, we will have the means to stand our ground (paraphrase of 2 Timothy 4:7!).

Here are various and sundry thoughts on patience:

Ed Howe: "A woman who has never seen her husband fishing, hasn't seen patience."

Arnold Glasow: "The key to everything is patience. You get the chicken by hatching the egg, not by smashing or eating it." (On the other hand, patience will never help a rooster lay an egg!)

Ambrose Bierce: "Patience is a minor form of despair disguised as virtue." (In other words, if you're too lazy to start anything, you may get a reputation for patience.)

John Dryden: "Beware the fury of a patient man."

By the use of gigantic lenses, plus long exposures of photographic plates, man has peered into what seems to be the gateway to the Kingdom of heaven.

I have read of the immense wonder discovered in the far, far reaches of space, so brilliantly beautiful that words cannot describe it adequately. Those who have seen it describe river masses and glittering columns, clear walls seemingly of ivory and pearl, and reflections like millions of diamonds and shining stars. One professor said it was like glimpsing "the vastness of infinity itself."

Sunday morning as I played the organ, I listened closely to the words of the chorus, "The Kingdom of God Is Within Me." Because of Him I know no defeat, only strength and power.

And I nearly came off the organ bench with gleeful excitement, for only this week I got a small pamphlet written by my friend, Dr. Mona Johnian. She was describing the awesome order of the "microcosmic" world of our human bloodstream. Seen through powerful microscopes, one blood cell appears to contain a string of beads. In each bead is a pattern that looks like a mosaic, the kind you might see on the walls of an old Byzantine church. Imagine that! Our blood cells may look like so many stained glass windows of a majestic cathedral.

Paul said, "The temple of God is holy, which temple you are" (1 Corinthians 3:17) and "You are the temple of the living God" (2 Corinthians 6:16).

No wonder when Jesus' blood was poured out on the ground at Calvary, the very foundations of creation trembled as more than 25 trillion divine, living cathedrals cried out within that blood, "It is finished!"

When Carl took a missions assignment in Rhode Island, he boasted quite a bit about the fresh Maine lobsters available to him.

Many states have tried to receive shipments of Maine lobsters—tankfuls are flown daily to Florida and California. Many of them die on the way, and one dead lobster ruins the taste of the whole shipment. Marine biologists learned that lobsters are afraid and will try to get away from catfish because of their horn-like feelers on front. So in order to keep the lobsters alive and alert, some companies send one catfish along in each shipment to chase the lobsters. Those lobsters put up a fight. They arrive alive.

I thought of this Sunday morning when Pastor Casey prefaced his sermon with these verses: "Think it not strange concerning the fiery darts of the enemy" (Eph. 6:16). Satan will buffet you, chase you, but, "Behold, the former things are come to pass, and new things do I declare: before they spring forth I tell you of them. . . . The Lord . . . shall prevail against his enemies" (Isaiah 42:9, 13, KJV).

Don't lose Jesus. Keep running in the race, stay fresh in your looking for Him. We have "a lively hope" (1 Peter 1:3). We are not going to die in the flight. We shall arrive there alive.

John calls Jesus "The sent one" 43 times. We are *His* sent ones. "You are My daughter in whom I am well-pleased. You are My son in whom I am well-pleased." David sinned miserably, but he repented and lived to declare the glory of his God, and God called him a man after His own heart.

Don't announce to your soul: "This is a season on heaviness or weakness." God is your strength. God is your joy. When the enemy chases you, runs you down, the Lord will build you up. He will minister to you from His throne room! The incomparable Jesus is God the Son—and the Son of God. God has anointed Him "with the oil of gladness" (Hebrews 1:9) and He will cover you with it. His "years will not fail" (verse 12) and neither will yours.

"For we have become partakers of Christ if we hold the beginning of our confidence steadfast to the end" (Hebrews 3:14).

This is not an appeal for funds. . . . Don't need them. Carl is getting a handsome salary of $100 a week now. This is a love letter, a true report!

We were walking quietly together along the waterfront on Honeymoon Island near Caladesi Causeway. Carl broke the silence with, "I'm a missionary, Betty. I want to be in missions when Jesus comes."

"Carl, you're a dreamer," I responded. "Most mission boards will not even take an application from a person over the age fifty. You are sixty-nine. You're a dreamer."

"Then, what do I do with my heart?" he quickly retorted. And right there at the tip of the island on the beach, my husband prayed aloud, "Lord, you know what I can do. You know what you have gifted Betty to do. Put us both where *You know* that we can do the most good for the most people, to win the most souls to Jesus before He comes again, Amen." Two days later, Benjamin Crandall, president of Zion Bible Institute, shared his vision to go to Latvia, Russia, and especially to establish a Bible School in Siberia. He told us of students ready to graduate from Zion whom God, in His practical providence, had brought from Russia to Zion to study the English language and the Bible.

On our twentieth wedding anniversary, Carl was on his way, on God's newest assignment for his ministry. The same week I signed a two-book contract. God arranged it thus, so I would be neither be lonely nor bored. Until my Carl returned, I kept the home fires burning here in our little retirement home, spending ten to fourteen hours a day doing what I have been called to do—write.

The first week he was in Latvia, one thousand souls were saved and they gave away seven thousand copies of the Book of Life. In Cherkassy, Ukraine, they rented the opera house and had to put up a sign saying, "Sinners may enter first, then if there are seats available Christians may come in." An average of 56 percent of every audience went forward to receive Jesus. Thousands let Jesus' blood cleanse their sins. A young boy born deaf can now hear! A woman who was blind in one eye can see out of it now!

Satan is a dream breaker, but Jesus is a dream maker.

Hold onto your dream.

My first husband never went shopping with me. He thought it was "sissy." One Saturday night before Mother's Day, John resigned himself to it and announced, "Tonight I'm taking you to town to buy you a Mother's Day gift!"

We were coming down the escalator in Root's Department Store. Halfway down I caught the breath of a fragrance. "That's it! That scent is *me*!"

"Let's get it, no matter what it costs. I'm tired of you wearing that cheap stuff. You never have selected a fragrance that you really wanted."

The clerk helped us discover Germaine Monteil's "Royal Secret" and I have been wearing it for 31 years now. If I cannot afford it, or live in a community where I cannot get it, I do without.

When Peter and Doris Glanoukas moved here from Pennsylvania, I learned that he distributes "my" fragrance. I told him that I had only one complaint: It does not last very long. Sometimes by the time I leave home and reach my destination, either I am used to the scent or it evaporates. Peter suggested (and gave me one) that I keep a tiny compact of the cream Royal Secret in my purse and apply it when needed.

My friend Karen Siddle suggested that one fragrance has lasted for 2,000 years. She told me that Jesus appreciated perfume, too.

Once when the chief priests and scribes were hunting Jesus down and plotting to kill Him, He stayed in the town of Bethany at the home of Simon, a leper He had previously healed.

An anonymous woman appeared and with loving compassion for Jesus, poured spikenard ointment on His head worth 300 denarii. (One denarius represented a day's wages.) Jesus commended her, "You have wrought a good work on Me. I won't be with you much longer and you have cheered Me before my death." Then He told the disciples who had protested her gift, "Wherever this gospel is preached in the whole world, what this woman has done will also be told as a memorial to her" (Mark 14:9).

That fragrance *has* lasted 2,000 years!

The gifts that you give to God and others are "a sweet-smelling aroma, an acceptable sacrifice, well pleasing to God" (Philippians 4:18).

When Carl left once for an extended session abroad, our neighbors assured him, "Don't you worry one minute about Betty while you're gone. We're here. If she has a need, all she has to do is pick up the phone and call us." Most of them forgot to verbalize the p.s. in their minds: "That is, if it's convenient."

Not long after Carl left, my car overheated, had to be towed in and I had no transportation for three days. When I called one man on Wednesday night to ask for a ride to church because I needed to play the organ, he informed me that he was retired and only went to church on Sundays. I found a woman who was very busy who graciously came to pick me up.

On Friday I called a gent to see if he would be willing to take me to the Tampa airport. He was kind but said, "Oh, this is my day off. I'd rather not spend the time going to and from the airport." The second fellow I called could not take me because he had an appointment to get his hair cut.

When the shuttle bus delivered me to the airport two hours early, I pulled out my mail to kill some time. Thank God for Lowell Lundstrom's "Front Line Report"! I almost laughed out loud when I read the scriptural introductions to his message: "It is better to trust the Lord than to put confidence in men. It is better to take refuge in Him than in the mightiest king!" (Psalm 118:8–9, TLB). "As a reward for trusting me, I will preserve your life and keep you safe" (Jeremiah 39:18, TLB). "Commit your way to the Lord, trust also in Him, and He shall bring it to pass" (Psalm 37:5).

His message was a breath of fresh air to a discouraged heart. It was like the scent of gardenias wafting into the heart's room. Don't look to men, for "God shall supply all your need according to His riches in glory by Christ Jesus" (Philippians 4:19).

Disappointment, sickness, wayward children, financial pressures, old age . . . these rob you of the *joy* of the Lord. But if you turn them over to Him, you can trust God through all the stress that daily living brings.

Being depressed is not a sin, but staying distressed is wrong. *It is easy to become discouraged.* Physical pain and stress, combined with fear, can create an unbelief that will put you in bondage. When you praise God in faith, however, He will break the fetters. The antidote is the "zeal of the Lord." An antidote can prevent or counteract the effects of poison.

The truth is that you are as big as your dreams and as small as your fears. Your attitude toward life determines how much you really live. There are no "great" people in this world, just great opportunities waiting to be discovered by ordinary people with determination to make the most of them.

Pastor Casey says that God is organizing the elite 2,000 club. He has been calling people, an ecclesiastical group for 2,000 years to be conformed to the image of God's Son: His Church. No weapon that is formed against you will prosper. You are a royal priesthood, a royal nation, called out of darkness into His marvelous light.

When you are up against a struggle, remember that our God will do valiantly. He will win, not just a skirmish, but the final, total victory over the enemy. "Your adversary the devil walks about like a roaring lion, seeking whom he may devour" (1 Peter 5:8). But God has a people that "rises like a lioness, and lifts itself up like a lion" (Numbers 23:24).

"If the Son makes you free, you shall be free indeed" (John 8:36).

"For God so loved the world" . . . and we should love it, too (John 3:16). We must not worship nature, but the Creator who made it. A man was walking through an art museum and, stopping at a masterpiece, grunted, "Ridiculous."

The guide set him straight: "Sir, you do not judge that painting. That painting judges you."

Carl just received a letter in the mail, "You're expired!" It came the day he had flown back from Russia and arrived half-dead. It informed him that his YMCA membership had run out, but it was a good reminder. "We're all terminal." But the good news is that we shall all live again somewhere.

I got a letter from Bryan E. His friend was dying with liver failure in Apple Valley, Minnesota. Relatives begged God to let her live. Just before she died, she quoted this Scripture peacefully: "He must increase. I must decrease" (John 3:30).

Carl's daughter, Carol, and her husband, Jack, have a teenaged son named Colm. When he was five, we gave him a children's illustrated Bible with pictures. His mother sat with her mother's Bible, and Colm held his children's Bible while she explained to him Jesus' death on the cross, the Easter story, and the walk He had on the road to Emmaus with His friends. She read Acts 1:9–11, how Jesus went back to heaven and when He began to rise into a cloud He lifted His hands and told them that He would come again.

Colm at five was a smart little boy. Carol wondered if he got the story. She asked him to repeat the story to her in his own words. He did a good job. At the close he told her, "Jesus looked at His friends, told them that He loved them and His last words were, 'Well, see you guys later!'" Not a bad interpretation!

One thing that makes music delightful is that between the beat, rhythm, thump, tempo and swing, there comes *the rest*. The half notes and quarter notes are necessary for variety in time and rhythm; sharps and flats are essential for range and key change; legato, pp. forte and the crescendos make music interesting, but *the rest* is the pause that refreshes, prepares, teases the listener, makes him ready for what's next, for more music.

My first husband worked sixteen hours a day some days, but Tuesday was declared a weekly holiday, our rest and boating day. We left just before daylight with our small cabin cruiser, headed for Catarack Lake near Rockville, Indiana. We would set up a grill on the back deck and fry bacon and eggs in the early morning sunrise. Then the rest of the day we enjoyed the sun, fishing and waterskiing. Returning, we retired early in the evening, and slept like innocent babies, ready for work the next day, having had some relaxation and fun.

John used to say he believed that if Jesus had been rich He would have owned a great speedboat. Jesus must have loved the water—check it out in the Scriptures. He walked along the shore, preached along the shore, talked about boats, water, weather, and when people crowded in on Him, He pushed offshore to continue preaching or, after dismissing them, to cross over to the other side of a lake. I personally believe that if He were walking among us today He would enjoy waterskiing. He was strong. He climbed mountains. He didn't own a Leer jet, even though He was royalty, so He walked everywhere He went. His legs must have been firm and muscular.

On one occasion after He and the disciples were weary, having met the needs of multitudes of people, suffering from "compassion fatigue," He gave those twelve a little pep talk. "'Come aside by yourselves to a deserted place and rest a while.' For there were many coming and going, and they did not even have time to eat. So they departed to a deserted place in the boat by themselves" (Mark 6:31–32).

In other words, "Boys, you gotta either come apart or fall apart. The music is going to lose its charm if we don't compose a little rest in it. Don't just teach it, don't just preach it, but *do it!*"

I have a friend in Raleigh, North Carolina, who has a prayer ministry to parents of autistic and retarded children. You may contact her at the address below this wonderful article, which she gives to these special parents she counsels:

This year nearly 100,000 women will become mothers of handicapped children. Did you ever wonder how these mothers are chosen? Somehow I visualize God hovering over earth selecting his instruments for propagation with great care and deliberation. As He observes, He instructs His angels to take notes in a giant ledger.

"Armstrong, Beth, son. Patron saint, Matthew. Forest, Marjorie, daughter. Patron saint, Cecilia.

Then He passes a name to an angel and smiles. "Give her a handicapped child."

The angel is curious. "Why this one, God? She's so happy."

"Exactly. Could I give a handicapped child a mother who doesn't know laughter? That would be cruel."

"But does she have patience?" asks the angel.

"I don't want her to have too much patience or she'll drown in a sea of self-pity and despair. Once the shock and resentment wear off, she'll handle it fine. She has a sense of self and independence so rare in a mother. You see, the child I'm going to give her has his own world. She has to make him live in her world, and that's not going to be easy."

"But, Lord. I don't think she even believes in you."

God smiles. "No matter, I can fix that. This one is perfect. She has just enough selfishness."

The angel gasps. "Selfishness? Is that a virtue?"

God nods. "If she can't separate herself from the child occasionally, she'll never survive. Yes, here is a woman whom I will bless with a child less than perfect. She doesn't realize it yet, but she is to be envied. She will never take for granted a spoken word. She will never consider a step, ordinary. I will permit her to see clearly the things I see—ignorance, cruelty, prejudice—and allow her to rise above them. She will never be alone. I will be at her side every minute of every day of her life because she is doing My work as surely as she is here by my side."

"And what about her patron saint?" asks the angel, his pen poised.

God smiles. "A mirror will suffice."

Used by permission of Jackie Ransdell. You may contact her at 3333 Ocotea St., Raleigh, NC 27607.

Sometimes I buy generic brand coffee filters, a hundred at a time, at a price I can afford. Occasionally when I am hurrying, I buy the first pack on the front of the shelf—just so it is size #4 to fit my Braun Coffee Maker.

I responded once to an offer in an in-flight magazine and ordered Gevalia Coffee, the "coffee of kings," a special Stockholm blend, according to the ad. Now that I was a connoisseur of fine java, I deserved and so purchased a package of those brown, natural fiber coffee filters—the ones that brag about filtering out bitterness and distasteful oils and the grounds that are embarrassing to your guests.

One day not long after that, I was driving and my car began to chug, and the temperature elevated to a dangerous level. After a quick servicing I learned that the mechanic I had gone to earlier that week had used an oil that was too lightweight—and the wrong filter.

That weekend, while entertaining company, I felt bad. During the most humid weather in August, our air conditioner kept running but the house simply would not cool down to a comfortable level. When I had it serviced and the freon checked, I found out what I should have expected all along. My filter was filthy. I needed either to clean or replace it!

All of this attention to filters started me thinking. When we were children, Dad would pray with us briefly every morning before we got onto the school bus, then quote this verse: "Let the words of my mouth, and the meditation of my heart, be acceptable in Thy sight, O Lord, my strength, and my redeemer" (Psalm 19:14). When he said table grace, he always, without fail, quoted the same Scripture. He never used profanity. In fact, I have never even heard him use slang, like "Shoot" or "Doggone."

I know now that he was introducing us to the filtering system that had worked down through the years, insulating the Perkins children from society's poison and bitter tastes.

I believe one reason our prayers are not being answered is the fact that our message is switching from "What man can do for God" to "What God can do for man." Old-fashioned appreciation moves the heart of God, and thanksgiving for what He has already done should precede our requests.

The Church has many organizers, but few agonizers; many who pay, but few who pray; many resters, but few wrestlers; many who are players but not pray*ers;* many who are enterprising, but few who are interceding.

Two prerequisites of dynamic Christian living are vision and passion. Both of these are generated in the prayer closet. The ministry of preaching is open to a few. The ministry of praying is open to all, to every child of God. Don't mistake action for anointing, or function for unction, commotion for creation, and rattles for revivals. On life's railway to heaven, the empty boxcar sometimes makes the most noise. Charisma without character produces chaos. The Holy Spirit is a comfort to the dedicated, but to the lukewarm, He is a source of discomfort.

The secret of praying is praying in secret. A worldy Christian will stop praying and a praying Chrisian will stop worldliness.

When we pray, God listens to our heartbeat. Hannah's "lips" moved, but her voice was not heard (1 Samuel 1:12–13). When we pray in the Spirit there are groanings that cannot be uttered (Romans 8:26). It is better to have a heart without words than words without heart.

Tithes may build a church, but tears will give it life. That is the difference between modern churches and the early Church. Our emphasis is on paying, theirs was on praying. When we have paid and paid, the place can still be taken. When they had prayed, the place was shaken (Acts 4:31).

In the matter of effective praying, never have so many left so much to so few. Commit yourself to effectual, fervent prayer. "Lord, teach us to pray."

A pediatrician with four tots of his own said, "It's a good thing kids are cute. If they weren't we'd kill them!"

Richard Exley gave me a packet of greeting cards he designed with this prayer:

Lord, kids are so neat! Sometimes they are bundles of energy gift-wrapped in hand-me-downs. Other times they are pajamaed packages of sleepy sweetness. Always they are a miracle. I love the way they chase butterflies, and the attention they give to mud puddles and rain-drops on a window. I envy their freedom from clocks and calendars, their immunity to pressure.

Oh, they have their moments, skinned knees and nap time, but they recover quickly. They don't nurse their disappointments or make a career out of suffering.

Lord, kids are so neat! Let me be converted and become as a little child. Let me know again the sheer joy of being alive, the pure plea-sure of living one day at a time, fully savoring each solitary moment. Free me from past disappointments and the little hurts I have kept so carefully. Restore to me a childlike anticipation for life, a sense of wonder, which makes each day new and my life truly abundant. Amen.

Every time I use one of these cards to write a letter, I remember a song from the past: "Lord, please bring back the springtime. . . . Take away the cold and dark of sin; May I warm and tender be again!"

Over and over in Scripture, the Lord admonishes us to be like little children in our enthusiasm and in our believing, trusting faith.

Let's anticipate His coming again as kids anticipate Christmas morning! Let's look for answers to prayer as kids look for Easter eggs! Let's celebrate His goodness the way kids celebrate birthdays! Let's love God our Father like little children!

My mother tells me that I was born a seven-months premie and came into this world, poor, skinny and wrinkled. Looking in the mirror one morning at six A.M., I decided that I am going out the same way I came in. We're all terminal.

You know you are getting old when your little black book only contains men's names ending in M.D.

Here are some thoughts by Jenny Joseph entitled, "Warning":

When I am an old lady, I shall wear purple, with a red hat, which doesn't go and doesn't suit me. I shall spend my pension on caviar, candy and summer gloves. And satin sandals. And say we have no money for butter. I shall sit down on the pavement curb when I am tired . . . and gobble up samples in shops and press alarm bells. I want to run my stick along the public railings and make up for the sobriety of my youth.

I shall go out in the rain in my slippers, and pick flowers from other people's gardens, and I'm going to learn to spit.

Maybe I ought to practice a little now, so people who know me are not shocked and surprised when suddenly I am old and start to wear purple.

My sister-in-law sent me a hideous birthday card. It said: "Happy Birthday, Betty. So you're going to be 62! Well, we're all in this together; you're just in a little deeper!"

And here is a birthday poem:

> First you crawl and then you walk,
> Eventually you learn to talk.
> Pretty soon you start to stoop . . .
> Getting old is pigeon poop!

I spoke at a Mother's Day banquet at a church in Watertown, South Dakota. At the speaker's table sitting beside me was the pastor's wife, who also is a fourth grade school teacher. She gave her pupils the assignment of writing an essay in their own words on this subject, "What Is a Grandmother?" Here is a copy of her favorite. The author is a little boy nine years old.

A grandmother is a lady who has no children of her own. She likes other people's little girls and boys. A grandfather is a man grand-mother. He goes for walks with boys and they talk about fishing and stuff like that. Grandmothers don't have to do anything except to be there. They're old so they shouldn't play hard or run. It is enough if they take us shopping where the pretend horse is, and have plenty of dimes ready. When they take us for walks, they always slow down past things like pretty leaves and caterpillars. Grandmothers never say, "hurry up."

Usually grandmothers are fat, but not too fat to tie your shoes. They wear glasses and funny underwear. They can take their teeth and gums off. Grandmothers don't have to be smart, only answer ques-tions like, "Why isn't God married?" and "How come dogs always chase cats?" Grandmothers don't talk baby talk like visitors do, because it is too hard for them to understand. When they read to us they don't skip pages or mind if it is the same story over again.

Everybody should try to have a grandmother, especially if you don't have television. They are the only grown-ups who have time.

I read this child's view of retirement in a mobile home park:

Grandma and Grandpa used to live up north in a brick house, but they got retarded and moved to Florida. They all live in tin huts, and ride big three-wheel tricycles. They play in a building called the wreck hall. They stand in the water at the swimming pool with their big hats on. I wish they would come back north, but I guess the man in the doll house at the gate won't let them out.

Just minutes ago I came in the door from conducting a two-day retreat. I ran immediately to my computer to tell this story.

During the final session of the seminar, a young minister preached our Communion message. He looked more like a motorcyclist than a pastor, with his bronzed face and strong build.

His message was "Commune with God." It is hard to get away from God, he said. You cannot escape His mercy and love. "Life here is not fair, not in looks, not in wealth, and for me, not in health." He explained to the audience that though he was only 36 he had bone marrow cancer and that it was difficult to get adequate health care in the remote part of Florida in which he lived. "This is not heaven," he said. "But, there is a land that is *fairer* than any we know, both fair to look upon and where we all get a fair deal!"

As he was talking I thought for some reason about how a football survives a ballgame because of the simple law of physics. The internal pressure of that small ball is much greater than all the pressure that 22 men can kick, throw, pounce or fumble on it externally.

And suddenly the Word became alive! "He who is *in you* is greater than he who is in the world" (1 John 4:4). The power of the Holy Spirit residing in our hearts and lives is greater than the pressure the external world can place upon us.

List your personal opponents who come against you to impede or block your forward progress. Satan's strategy is to deflate you, but the Holy Ghost, that Supernatural Buoyancy, is *in* you. Greater is the power within you than the pressure upon you. Hang in there, teammate. We're winning.

My Aunt Pearl (Pib) can make a rich, robust cup of coffee guaranteed to "heal the sick and raise the dead"—almost. We also have a very "rich" heritage. Though she is my aunt, my mother's youngest sister, we are the same age and grew up together as the fires of the Azuza Street Pentecostal revival moved east and warmed Indiana.

In the "suburb" of West Terre Haute, called Toad Hop, lived "Grandaddy Horton." All the senior citizens called him "Daddy Horton" and every kid in every town and hamlet called him "Grandaddy."

Living alone, he made his living collecting rags, papers and bottles. His was a "one horse" operation, only the horse died, and he, himself, bent bodily between two planks of wood and pulled a two-wheeled, previously horse-drawn cart. Mounted on the back was a scale. He whistled and sang to announce his coming. Children who had saved rags, papers and bottles waited while he weighed and paid for them by the pound.

Wednesday night prayer meeting was an adventurous night in our little home church. My great uncle Arch Brown was one of the few preachers there who had the courage to open the service to the public for "testimony night." You never knew what to expect.

One Wednesday night Pib and I were eating raisins when Uncle Arch asked, "Anyone got a witness for the Lord tonight?"

Down the aisle came a joyous elderly man.

"I'm probably the richest man here," he said. "I have my own private doctor that travels with me daily on my routes. I have never known serious illness. God knows I have no money for medicine or hospitals. If I feel a little down, I talk to my personal, alongside doctor Jesus, and He touches and heals me on the spot.

Pib and I elbowed each other and laughed. "That old, fool! Who's he kidding? Everyone here knows he's the rag picker."

Looking back now over the years I realize he was right. He was probably the happiest, healthiest, heartiest man we knew as children.

Pearl's mother, my grandmother, explained it this way as she misquoted 1 Timothy 6:6: "The happiest people I know don't have palatial residences, but live in *tents*. Godliness with con*tent*ment is great gain."

My neighbor Christine did two days of substitute teaching in a Largo elementary school with third graders. She tried hard to help them understand portions and fractions. It was the week before Thanksgiving, so she sketched a pumpkin pie on the blackboard and called upon her best math student, Jimmie, to help her.

"Jimmie, how many people are in your family?" she asked him.

"Five people: Mother, Daddy, two sisters and me."

"If I cut this pie in equal portions for your family, what fraction would *you* get?" she questioned.

Jimmie thought, then answered, "One-fourth."

"But, Jimmie, you told me there are five members in your family, right?"

He replied, "Miss Christine, you may know fractions, but you don't know Mother. She would say she didn't want any."

Mothers are like that.

And God's love is even greater than a mother's love. Many women are mothers by love's accident and a few are merely incubators for nine months, but thank God for loving mothers!

Most women tell me they love the embryo upon conception and pray daily for their unborn child.

God's love is greater still. He knew us before the foundations of the world were formed. King David states: "Your eyes saw my substance, being yet unformed, and in Your book they all were written, the days fashioned for me, when as yet there were none of them" (Psalm 139:16). Isaiah proclaims divine love on the unborn child: "the Lord . . . made you and formed you from the womb" (Isaiah 44:2).

I was riding my bicycle down Gulf Drive in Crystal Beach not long ago and rounded the corner at the boat dock. I spotted an old fisherman with a cane pole in hand, back against a big rock, lazily sunning himself, and atop his nodding head was a purple cap. Printed on the front was this message: *I am not brilliant. It's just that my friends are all stupid.* I recalled immediately one of our U.S. Presidents who made a statement about himself, a total reversal of the one above. He said, "I do not even consider myself intelligent, but I am smart enough to surround myself with people who are much smarter than I am." That's genius!

I thought of this when I received a letter in the mail from a writer friend up north. She had been driving long miles to hear a minister who was eloquent in his delivery.

On more than one occasion she asked him to give her a copy of a poem or source of a quote he had used. Spoken words are forgotten, but words written are preserved and passed on. Not once did the man respond.

The smooth speaker was a pulpiteer, but apparently flawed in his motives. He could speak with the tongues of men and angels but did not have love. He never asked another person to pray in public who could pray more effectively than he, nor ask a singer for a solo who had a better voice than his own.

Perhaps he harbored a restless fear of loss or decline of his personal rating? The Word warns us to "beware of secret sins" and tells us that "jealousy is cruel as the grave." A private cache of jealousy will eventually develop into a seething fester. Those who embrace or harbor it will lose the reward from the promise in Luke 6:38: "Give, and it will be given to you."

Give credit to whom credit is due. Paul exhorts us to "be kindly affectionate to one another with brotherly love, in honor giving preference to one another" (Romans 12:10).

I have always liked pelicans; now I love them. I have pelican nap-kins, pelican coasters, pelican salt and pepper shakers, pelican tooth pick holders, pelican T-shirts, pelicans on the porch and pelicans on the mantle.

Late one afternoon, around four o'clock, I was driving north on19A and saw a cloud of pelicans overhead, I mean thousands. I turned quickly onto Caladesi Causeway and stopped in the south cove near the bridge. Two men in a refrigerated truck were feeding minnows and small fish to the pelicans at the water's edge. They told me that many times they feed from two thousand to four thousand in an hour each evening. Some that swooped near us had a wing span of seven feet and must have weighed forty pounds. There were many tiny baby pelicans scurrying around their mothers' feet trying to pick a bit of seafood snack, too.

I stayed until the two men began to load their gear back into the truck and the pelicans flew away. One man lingered behind and was making notes in a ledger.

He explained to me that when the temperature drops into the thir-ties or forties the fish go down so deep that the pelicans cannot dive down far enough to get them. Pelicans are clean and they refuse to eat junk, so many of them starve. The brown pelican especially has become almost extinct. So environmentalists feed them in cold weather. He said this happens only every five or six years here in Florida, and I happened to experience it. What a sight it was!

Then the man said, "Since you like pelicans I'll tell you a won-derful story. When a mother pelican cannot find food for her young, rather see them starve, she gives her life for their preservation. She will, as last resort, plunge her beak deep into her own breast that the babies might drink her life's blood."

Driving home I wept when I thought of Jesus' love for you and for me. He was willing to hang on a cross and permitted a soldier to plunge a sword deep into His side, shedding His pure and sinless blood, to bring us eternal life. He gave His life that we might live.

Young soldiers can learn so much by listening to old warriors. I sat on the front porch listening to two "old timey Texas preachers" in dispute. The older one had run a stop sign he did not see and struck a car. The man whose car he hit was accusing him of drunken driving. Everyone in that cowboy community knew the old man was a "tee-totaler." He had never had a drop in his life.

His friend ranted, "Retaliate! Avenge yourself!"

The older man responded, "Aww. I've jest turned that over to my attorney." Everyone in that community also knew that he could not afford a legal attorney, but counted on the Lord to be his defense, his Wonderful Counsellor. And if it goes to court, God will be the judge.

"The battle is not yours, but God's" (2 Chronicles 20:15). We are soldiers in the battle of life to the finish. The final victory, the outcome of that warfare is predetermined, for God omnipotent reigns. We shall win, and reign with Him forever (Revelation 22:5).

We have our own individual skirmishes, those private battles with misunderstanding, coping with disappointment and false accusations, pride, lust, anger, fear, loss and a host of other opponents. Because He has overcome, we can overcome too (Revelation 12:11). In extreme cases, if necessary, the angel of the Lord can fight for you (Psalm 35:5). The battle is the Lord's—His truth against Satan's lie, His light versus the enemy's darkness. This warfare pits health against sickness, faith against fear, prosperity against poverty, godliness against iniquity. We fight, but it is the Lord who gives the victory. You may feel outnumbered and outmatched, but take courage from the knowledge that we are on the side of ultimate triumph.

With the Lord on your side, you can say, "The battle is the Lord's! The victory is the Lord's!" Just turn it over to your attorney. Blessed assurance!

Carl was invited back to Bangalore, India, to speak at the silver anniversary of the Southern Asia Bible College, where he was president some years ago. To enjoy a ride down memory lane, he boarded the same old rickety bus and took the old, familiar, scenic route of years before, from Kerula to Kodi Kani.

The women in that country still carry large, heavy, nearly impossible loads, on their heads in boxes and baskets. One bent old woman boarded the bus and, long after it took off, still sat holding her heavy load on top of her head, wrestling with it as the bus bounced up the mountainside.

Looking in the rearview mirror, the driver applied the squeaky brakes. Turning to look at the woman he said, "*Ahmah* ["Mother" in Hindi], put your load down and let the bus carry it for you." Her expression was one of relief coupled with embarrassment as she set it down.

Carl leaned his head back on the head rest of the old seat and wept. What a lesson he had just heard! How many times in recent years, during some very hard trials and private storms of life, had he tried to keep control? He had continued carrying his own loads, keeping control, when he could have rolled them over on Jesus, the great burdenbearer. He could have lain down his burdens and let the Lord carry them for him.

Then and there he determined to do so.

As Isaiah prophesied, Jesus "has borne our griefs and carried our sorrows" (Isaiah 53:4). "Humble yourselves under the mighty hand of God, . . . casting all your care upon Him, for He cares for you" (1 Peter 5:6–7). Remember the words set to music, "Just turn it over to Jesus, and you can smile the rest of the day."

May 15   *We Am (This Is an English Lesson)**

When an individual speaks of himself he says, "I am," but when God speaks of Himself, He says, "We am."

Used by anyone else it would be bad grammar, but God can get by with it because He is God. *Elohim* is a plural noun, but is always followed by a singular verb. God says, "We am" because even though God is "plural," a triune God, our God is one God (Deuteronomy 6:4). Three family members—Father, Son and Holy Spirit—sharing one universal, eternal throne. He is the rewarder of those who diligently seek Him. He is the God of Genesis 1: In the beginning, God created. He was then, is now and will always be. He is, and can say, "We am"!

Jesus did not begin in the manger. He came from fullness past, is present with us now and projects eternity! His earth birth was only God's introductory form of Jesus, His Son, to us earthlings. Christmas was our rich inheritance to receive Him as Deity, loving shepherd and servant to mankind's need. By Him and through Him all things were created (John 1:3; Colossians 1:16).

Do not be taken in by the evolutionary nonsense taught as fact. There was not a "big bang" when Uncle Amoeba slithered from a marshy swamp and developed legs, sired a family and went to college. It would be easier to believe that there was an explosion in a print shop, and when the papers, letters and ink settled, it miraculously became Webster's *Dictionary*, than to believe in evolution.

Jesus does not struggle for equality with God. Jesus is not God's shadow. A shadow is inferior to substance. He said, "He who has seen me, has seen the Father." He is equal with God and shares the eternal throne of the invisible Kingdom to come!

"Jesus Christ is the same yesterday, today and forever." I am so glad we serve a permanent God! When you get to heaven and see Jesus then you will be satisfied.

Remember the old song:

It will be worth it all when we see Jesus,
Life's trials will seem so small, when we see Christ.
One glimpse of His dear face, all sorrows will erase,
So bravely run the race . . . till we see Christ!

*By Betty Malz with a lot of help from Pastor Roger Casey

Many feel certain that miracles ended when Jesus left the earth. Gwen Lanning in Reedsport, Oregon, can tell you that this is not true.

For four years she suffered from reticulum cell sarcoma, a rare malignant bone cancer. Tumors had ravaged 75 percent of her body. It affected her blood stream, and had spread to her spinal column and vital organs, including the liver and spleen. Tumors made elimination almost impossible, and food would not stay down. Her body was so swollen and the pain so severe, she was treated like a baby for months.

Gwen's treatment bankrupted the family funds and their oldest son, a music major, had to drop out of college—but not before he asked two new-found friends to pray for his mother. One of the young men built a "bridgework" of hope when he called her the morning of May 17, 1971, and said, "The Lord directed me to call and tell you not to worry, that you are not going to die." Her reply was, "I want to die and get out of this life."

Eleven days later accompanied by two friends and a nurse, Gwen was "packed" in mountains of pillows to make a 400-mile trip to Portland, Oregon, where Miss Kathryn Kuhlman would speak and pray for the sick in the Civic Auditorium. Her husband bade her good-bye, certain that the trip would kill her, that it was "come what may," the best way for her to terminate her terminal illness.

Outside, the cold, chilling rain caused her body to shudder, but later when Miss Kuhlman introduced a radiant girl healed of an incurable rare blood disease, Gwen prayed, "Lord you can heal my fatal bone cancer." As Miss Kuhlman prayed she explained, "My hands are human, with no magical power. God heals. He is here for you."

Warmth in her body increased to intense heat, burning out the cancer. Gwen's swelling went down. She made the trip home without the pillow packs, and now does not even take aspirin. One of the first people she talked to was a doctor who had lost three patients with the disease she had been healed of.

Jesus heals!

"He said, 'The things which are impossible with men are possible with God'" (Luke 18:27).

"Mother?" It was the voice of my youngest, April, calling from Emory University. "I just talked to our travel agent. You can't believe how the price of flights has gone up since I came home last."

I could. I had just talked to the same agent to learn that my flight to Sacramento would be $1,303.00 next Tuesday.

April talked on, "Aren't you glad that our one-way ticket to heaven was bought and paid for two thousand years ago, free and clear? No price changes there!" I recalled the old song,

Jesus paid it all,
All to Him I owe;
Sin had left a crimson stain,
He washed it white as snow.

Whatever happened to words like *price freeze* and *fair-trade*?

We chatted a little longer. I remember when we first moved to Florida in 1961, the admission to Busch Gardens was free. You purchased food, souvenirs and tickets only if you wanted to enjoy the rides.

The pass to get into "Dismal World and the Tragic Kingdom," (a quite negative dub for Disney World by parents who are weary with the kids' haven), was only $7.50 per person. I believe it is between $25 and $30 now for a day.

I am glad the ticket admission to heaven is not negotiable, but set by the Authority. I meet people who think they can get in at a discount fare, but there are no cheap rates.

It is free to us because the cost has already been established and paid by Jesus, our travel agent, at a great personal cost to Him. He had to fight off sin, death, hell and the grave. He paid for our ticket in advance with His life's blood, which flowed from Calvary's mountain. We must forsake all to follow him, laying aside our sins, asking forgiveness. He has arranged our passports.

Call Him today. The one who calls on the name of the Lord shall be saved, receive eternal life, and hold a ticket to eternity.

We look too little and talk too much. It is like the difference between chickens and turkeys. If you are a farmer you know that turkeys gobble and chortle all day long. Chicks look and pick.

Now, chickens are dumb, but turkeys are dumber. I always wondered what the quote "Chickens always come home to roost" meant until we children helped raise them. They would crawl under or fly over the fence to pick grass and eat grasshoppers on the other side, but when the sun went down, they were smart enough to find their way back to the brooder house and jump up on the long poles strung inside called roosts, tuck their heads under their wings and sleep.

Not turkeys. I have seen turkeys stay outside in a storm, look straight up into the rainy sky and drown. They actually died from letting the rain run up their nostrils.

Are you a chicken or a turkey? When trouble comes, the storm strikes or an evil person imposes hurt on you, do you let it "get to you"? Do you drown from letting the situation consume you? Or, do you run for shelter and tuck your head under God's almighty care?

Jesus said to the city of Jerusalem, "How often I wanted to gather your children together, as a hen gathers her chicks under her wings!" (Matthew 23:37).

Guard your insides, your heart, for out of it are the issues of life. "It is He who shall tread down our enemies" (Psalm 60:12). "Vengeance is mine, saith the Lord. I will repay." Don't try to pay people back in kind. God is an awesome, fearful God and He will even the score. You cannot afford to fight. Close your mouth. Open your eyes. Remember this verse: "Set a guard, O Lord, over my mouth; keep watch over the door of my lips" (Psalm 141:3).

The Lord is *your* defense. *You* have an advocate with the Father. The Word tells us that He is ever interceding before the throne for you. Run into the brooder house, His House, to His safety. Put your head under His wings. Let the Lord take care of it!

Remember the old teeter-totter at the city park? Some folks call it a "see-saw." When I grew up at the end of the Great Depression we made them with a one-by-twelve plank of wood balanced over two or three cement blocks. If it got out of balance—if one end was longer than the other or one person outweighed the other—one end would hit the ground and you could bite your tongue and jar your eye balls, even pinch your feet under it.

To be out of tune with yourself, or out of balance with God, is like that. It is is like having dental floss caught between your teeth, or when your underwear doesn't fit. The Bible asks a question, "How long halt ye between two opinions?" Some people are like the Word further describes, "clouds without rain." One of my granddads was a small man with a tinge of a "foul mouth." He spoke thus of fence riders: "Either have a b.m. or get out of the toilet." He was a carpenter who built houses, and would dismiss an employee who was weak inside and could not make decisions on the job.

Psalm 62:3–4 describes them "like a leaning wall and a tottering fence. . . . They bless with their mouth, but they curse inwardly."

Ellen Goodman has written a book that asks the question, "When will my insides match my outsides?" I have known people who look strong, talk tough, but have shaky innards. On the other hand I have known frail looking folks who were a tower of strength, steadfast and unshakable. St. Francis of Assissi said of himself, "I am small, frail and insecure in myself. Thus God gets all the glory for miracles that result from my faith and my praying."

The key to receiving answers to prayer and the miraculous is being sure in our asking, firm in our statements in prayer. "He who doubts is like a wave of the sea driven and tossed by the wind. For let not that man suppose that he will receive anything from the Lord; he is a double-minded man, unstable in all his ways" (James 1:6–8).

"Let us hold fast our faith without wavering, for He who promised is faithful" (Hebrews 10:23).

In June of 1971 I met "Big Rose."

It was three weeks after Carl and I were married that he took me to Cleveland and introduced me to his mother, Rose Malz. I found her to be a large-framed German woman with a big heart, charitable but outspoken, and with strong preferences. Her first words to me were, "You are very lucky. You could look the world over and never found a finer man than my Carl." Her next words were, "I was married to Carl's father for 56 years. You can always tell a German, but you can't tell him much!" Then she roared with laughter.

I have used her quote frequently in the past twenty years during family "debates." Carl always retaliates with, "Betty is a true 'Brit' with grit, a 'Limey, Johnny Bull.' She sinks her teeth in and holds on like a determined bulldog for what she thinks is right and what she wants." When we do marriage seminars, we tell the younger couples, "We are still fighting the German-English war. If we can make it, anyone can make it."

Most people are strongly opinionated. It is just that all do not always show it. I was crossing a busy street in Johannesburg, South Africa. Ruth North grabbed the back of my blouse—and saved my life. She kept me from being struck down by a fast car coming from the right. Catching my breath I said, "I'll never get used to people driving on the wrong side of the road."

She replied, "Not the *wrong* side, the *left* side." Most of us find it hard to consider that we just might be in error sometimes.

Determination and firm opinions are not always bad. Remember the persistent widow? Scripture coaches us to "be strong in the Lord, and the power of His might." "My soul silently waits for God . . . I shall not be greatly moved" (Psalm 62:1–2). "Be steadfast, immovable, always abounding in the work of the Lord" (1 Corinthians 15:58). "God . . . confirmed it by an oath, that . . . we might have strong consolation, who have fled for refuge to lay hold of the hope set before us. This hope we have as an anchor of the soul, both sure and steadfast, and which enters the Presence behind the veil, where the forerunner has entered for us, even Jesus" (Hebrews 6:17–20).

I was a junior in high school and so much wanted a copy of the yearbook. They were $22, but I had only saved $12, so I approached my dad about the $10 deficit, and he came up with a solution. He always had one, it seemed.

In the side yard, he had planted Gem Everbearing strawberries. Mother had canned them, frozen them, given them away, made jam and ice cream topping, and we had eaten them until they almost ran out our ears. Dad suggested, "Do the best you can to sell some, and I'll make up the difference."

I picked strawberries, stacked the quarts in the front basket of my bicycle and pedaled them to neighbors for 40 cents. (I wish I could buy them for that now!) Yet, on Monday morning, the last day to order the 1947 edition of the Otter Creek High School yearbook, I still lacked $4.

When I went out the door to catch the school bus Dad inquired how much I lacked. When I told him he remarked, "Why didn't you say so? I told you I would make up the difference"—and he did!

James 4:2 describes this situation. "You . . . covet and cannot obtain. . . . Yet you do not have because you do not ask." We have access to God's supply. God is willing to back us, to underwrite our attempts in life, but we must ask.

Jeanette McFarlin in her book *God and the Little Blue Bear* tells the story of how she stole a pack of Dentyne chewing gum. Her father spanked her, then sent her to the old man who owned the corner grocery store to confess. The grocer replied kindly, "Why didn't you tell me you wanted the gum but couldn't afford it? I would have gladly given it to you."

In Luke 15:18, a prodigal son learned through poor management and self-indulgence that he could not make it on his own. Sorry for his sinning, he wised up and said, "I'm sorry. I've sinned. I'll ask my dad! I'll go to my father."

Will you be big enough to say, "Jesus, forgive me. I have learned I can't make it on my own. Help!" You have access to His forgiveness and the Source who will always make up the difference you lack.

Athletes and entertainers are always looking for a "quick fix," that shortcut to an adrenal flow to get them through the next performance.

David said, "My heart is fixed, O God, my heart is fixed: I will sing and give praise" (Psalm 57:7, KJV). I am amazed at the multi-use of this verse. I know a young man who had a heart murmur and misquoted this Scripture about a steadfast heart, using it this way: "My heart is fixed, *repaired!* I praise God!" To the amazement of the man's family and his physician, he actually received a miraculous healing.

God does not change the rules of nature to accommodate even the best of us. Sooner or later it will become necessary to eat, sleep and think right in order to keep on going. One woman, who travels widely, singing and giving her testimony, told me how she drank strong coffee and ate lots of candy bars to keep going longer. It finally caught up with her. She collapsed and wound up in the emergency room of a hospital.

Christians are dependent upon the Lord Jesus, our sole supply. This is not the mark of weakness, but of intelligence. Our reliance is upon the only absolutely dependable thing in the universe. David states, "The righteous will be in everlasting remembrance. He will not be afraid of evil tidings; his heart is steadfast, trusting in the Lord" (Psalm 112:6–7).

April, who is working toward her master's degree in physical therapy, preaches nutrition to her dad. She says that the quick fix of junk food is cheap and not lasting. She ranted as she came through the door last November. "Dad told me not to worry about him, he was 'being good' with his diet. I found a doughnut box and two candy wrappers in his van!"

We "fixed" him. For Christmas we bought him a talking scale. He was not aware of the talking element. When he opened it, he said, "Now don't look when I get on this. Go in the other room." We did, but heard the booming recorded voice say, "Two hundred and twenty-two pounds"! There is a recompense of reward for the deeds done in the flesh!

I am glad God doesn't just order a quick fix, but "He restoreth my soul." God doesn't rehabilitate people, He makes them *new*.

"Create in me a clean heart, O Lord." Make me better than new.

I stood in the early morning sun, leaning on the fence between our backyards, complaining to my neighbor: "John's mother is a nib nose."

"Hold steady," she coached me. "Give it time. When you become a grandmother you'll perhaps understand her better."

"Hmph," I responded. "This morning she tried to straighten out my grapefruit knife with a pair of pliers. I've had it with her. She tries to straighten out my knife, my life, my kid, my housekeeping, my philosophy, my parenting views on her first grandchild. Does she think that her God-given calling in life is to straighten everybody out?"

John, our little daughter and I, had just moved to Florida from Indiana, and his parents had come for their first visit in our new home. He loved them dearly, and I wanted him to love me dearly, so I didn't complain to him, but to my neighbor. That night after everyone had fallen asleep but me, I lay awake thinking about our wedding.

I had written my own vows based on the words of Ruth to her mother-in-law, Naomi: "Entreat me not to leave thee, or to return from following after thee: for wither thou goest, I will go" (Ruth 1:16).

I wondered why I couldn't have a mother-in-law worthy of that kind of loyalty. It did not occur to me that just maybe I didn't deserve one like that, or that I had one but was too immature to recognize that fact.

They stayed most of the winter. As days of adjustment came, we walked the beach together, exchanged recipes, and my father-in-law helped tremendously with the landscaping. I missed them when they left. Now that I am a grandmother, I have great respect for the woman I criticized and misunderstood during those early maturing years.

A word to the daughter-in-law: Respect the older woman. Guard against jealousy. Pray for her and learn from her. She can give you pointers, instruction, short-cuts and detours around some pitfalls of life.

A word to the mother-in-law: Take it easy on the young wife of your son. Give her time to learn and to respect you at her own pace, on her own timing and terms. Don't hurry or push her. Be patient.

"The aged women [should] be in behavior as becometh holiness . . . that they may teach the young women" (Titus 2:3–5, KJV).

Ignorance isn't always bliss, and innocence doesn't always count.

Shortly after Carl and I were married, he pastored a small church in a German Lutheran community in the Dakotas. He scheduled a choir from Bismarck to perform a Christmas concert, then realized that our small sanctuary would not hold the crowd. An idea came on like a light in his brain.

He spoke with the pastor of the Seventh Day Adventist church. It was large, and since they worship on Saturday, they would not be using it on Sunday. He offered a sizeable donation and was permitted to rent their facility for the concert.

The arrangements were nearly completed when Carl was called to Ohio for a funeral and left me in charge. All that was left was lunch arrangements and I joined the women of our church in making ham sandwiches, finger pastries and coffee for the choir members.

The concert was a great success, but I made a mental note that Carl should register a complaint to the pastor of that church. The custodian mowed grass all during the service. Just because they did not consider it their Sabbath, it was still a rude expression.

Early Monday morning the tall, red-haired pastor knocked at our front door. He let me know that he had found scraps of ham and coffee grounds in their trash can. Now my husband is as smart as a tree full of owls, but I majored in kids and minored in quarterhorses. I got my education the hard way, by experience.

I pled innocence. I did not know they don't eat meat, especially pork, and abstain from coffee. ("At least we didn't do it on *your* Sabbath," I said brightly. "Wasn't that good?") That conversation was a real experience. We concluded, "Let's talk about how we are alike, not how we're different."

Fools fight one another. Wise men agree together. Jesus said, "I am the way, the truth and the life. No one comes to the Father, except by Me."

North Florida Christian Center near O'Brien has a unique pastor.

When Dr. Roxanne Brant, the founder, died, she commissioned this church-missions outreach to her associate and director, Retha Garten. "I'm a business woman and would not have chosen this mantle," Retha told me.

The auditorium and worship center is nestled in a 240-acre setting of pine trees, birds, sheep, squirrels. They have remodeled a small barn into a very attractive, two story guest cottage for their speakers. The grounds are a mini-sample of how the Garden of Eden must have looked.

Looking out the window of the cottage, I spotted a rather modest, homely attempt at gardening: a few rows of vegetables and a small hand-printed sign: "This is the Garten of Eaten." I thought, *Retha Garten has an imagination*, and it hit me. The practical definition of faith is *sanctified imagination*.

I believe in "different strokes for different folks." The Bible tells us that each person is given a measure of faith. I believe that the variety of faith is as unique and diversified as the mind and heart that house the power of faith. Hebrews 11:1 tells us that faith is "the substance of things hoped for, the evidence of things not seen." Faith is the promise in hand of things hoped for. It is like the title deed to an inherited piece of land you are traveling to see for the first time.

Another variety of faith is the gift of faith. This faith is not saving faith, not natural faith, but supernatural faith, a special demonstration of faith of the Spirit.

This faith is characterized by authority and surety. It is invincible, unwavering faith, usually given, dropped down from God above, and distributed during crises.

Joshua experienced this kind of faith when he was winning a battle for the armies of God, but needed a few more daylight hours. He prayed then commanded the sun to stand still. "So the sun stood still, and the moon stopped" (Joshua 10:13). Historic records bear evidence that this indeed happened.

Karen Siddle is visiting from Belleville, Illinois, just across the river from Saint Louis. One noon last week while eating freshly caught fish at Nett's Dock, a tiny restaurant in Ozona that boasts four tables alongside the creek and a great seafood menu, Karen confessed, "Betty, I've read all your books and honestly wondered, 'Can all these things happen to one person? Are they really real, or is this poetic license?'"

Since she has been here, I opened the garage door and found a 30-inch diamondback rattlesnake. I killed it with a shovel. Coming up the steps, shaking with relief, I popped a chocolate chip cookie into my mouth. I thought I bit down on a large pecan shell and threw it into the trash. Minutes later I realized my front tooth was missing. I had flipped out the cap that had been put on six years before. I scrambled into the garbage among used kleenex, popcorn and toothpicks, found it and rushed to Dr. Crim, my dentist. He made another, and put it in for only $620!

Karen shook her head in disbelief. But that wasn't all.

Yesterday I asked her to run a couple of errands while I sat down at my computer. "Then," I asked her, "will you stop by the seafood place and pick up a pound of extra large, fresh shrimp? And don't forget to get a lemon, too." Later when I went to boil the shrimp for the required three minutes, I looked for the lemon. She had forgotten to get it.

But when you say "yes" to God, He works for you. *Before we sat down to eat* I heard the honking of a horn. Looking out the kitchen window I saw my friends, Ed and Joyce Settle. I went down to meet them and Joyce handed me a sack. Peeping inside I found a fresh papaya and *two* lemons! You would have thought I had seen that snake again.

As a bonus, in the back of their little pick up truck they had brought me a papaya tree, which Ed set out for me in minutes.

"What kind is it?" I asked. Ed grinned and quoted, "By their fruits ye shall know them." Three tiny papayas were hanging from the branches.

"By this shall all men know that ye are my disciples, if ye have love one to another" (John 13:35, KJV). They not only have love *for* one another, but they get it *to* one another. And doing so can mean that little miracles happen every day.

"Delight yourself also in the Lord, and He shall give you the desires of your heart" (Psalm 37:4). But, what if your desires are extremely extreme?

I left my home here in Florida, and went to Wasilla, *Alaska*, to conduct a women's retreat in *February*.

During the first session there, I told the women to write down their deepest personal need, the most secret desire of their heart, and ask God to do something that was impossible for them to do for themselves.

Today, nine months later, I received the following letter:

Dear Betty,

As I wrote out my secret request, I felt a Divine impulse, *It's time* now, *Nancy*. I didn't know exactly what it meant, but. . . .

My little written note to the Lord expressed the fact that my husband and three children had been dissatisfied with living in Alaska. For eighteen years, my husband, Henry, had worked at the Chevron Refinery in Nikiski, long hours, a week on and a week off, night and days with a lot of overtime. The three children were growing up with this hectic lifestyle and the long, cold winters were starting to "get to us." I petitioned the Lord to let us move to a warmer climate with a job for Henry with sensible hours where he could be with his family nights.

Shortly after, at an employee meeting, the announcement was made that the plant was being closed, either sold or disassembled. What a shock. Henry's boss offered to let him stay and work on a pipeline, same hours, but less pay, or move to a plant in either Utah, New Guinea, or Waianae, Hawaii!

Two weeks later, we were on our way from Alaska to Hawaii. The company paid for our moving, our living expenses for a month, gave my husband a promotion, and no more night shifts. All the answers to our extreme prayers, and more plus. My husband loves his new job. The kids have settled into and are enjoying their new school and we have a wonderful church home. "God is able to do the exceeding, abundant above our asking."

"The steps of a good man are ordered by the Lord" (Psalm 37:23). One of my daughter Brenda's favorite verses is, "In all your ways acknowledge Him, and He shall direct your paths" (Proverbs 3:6).

When I moved to our sleepy fishing village, some of my metropolitan friends said, "You will be bored to death there!" They were wrong. I have never been bored since moving to this small community. The phone calls, the letters I receive and the tourists I meet challenge me, inspire me, and I am exhilarated with opportunity.

Monday morning I pulled perhaps 32 letters from my post office box. The top letter was in a square, blue envelope, postmarked and return addressed from Boring, Oregon. I showed it to the post office manager, Miriam Blohm. She joked, "That's got to be the most *boring* letter you've ever received." We both laughed. We were both wrong. The content was almost unbelievably exciting.

Dear Betty,

Thanks for your husband Carl's tape which you mailed me, "Healing the Wounded Spirit." After listening to it, I felt impressed that I should be sensitive to the needs of people I work with here in Boring, Oregon, instead of just being a teammate, fellow worker and employee.

A college-aged girl came by my station here at the work place and asked me to pray. She suffered severe back pains. She received immediate relief. Another woman heard about this and we together prayed for her. The cyst from her tail bone has since disappeared. After hearing your message when you were here in Oregon, on saying "yes" to God, I have not been bored. I say "yes" each A.M. and the code word on my computer at work is "yes!"

Carl tore a Timex ad from his *Outside* magazine: "It takes a licking and keeps on ticking."

"Sounds like Connie. Don't you agree?" he asked.

Our daughter Connie at sixteen fell in love with the lifeguard at the swimming pool in our little hometown. After high school and his college graduation they had a beautiful, outdoor, garden wedding beside a little waterfall and fountain at our home. They moved to Texas for employment and bought a lovely home and produced three children, a son first, then twins, a boy and a girl.

Connie has undergone laser surgery and the successful removal of three brain tumors. Shortly after the final surgery, she was called upon to survive the very painful experience of divorce.

Last week in the mail we received a 8 1/2 x 11-inch document on parchment paper: "This is to certify that Connie Malz Bobzien has been elected to Who's Who Among Students in American Universities and Colleges in recognition of outstanding merit and accomplishment as a student at Northern State University."

We are proud of her. Connie has come through the surgeries fine, is a single mother taking care of three teenage children, drives ninety miles round trip per day to study, and is making *A*s and *B*s in college working toward a degree in sociology, with a business and gerontology emphasis.

She is making it and *you can make it, too!* Like a Timex watch, if you've taken a licking, you can keep on ticking.

"But we have this treasure in earthen vessels, that the excellence of the power may be of God and not of us. We are hard pressed on every side, yet not crushed; we are perplexed, but not in despair; persecuted, but not forsaken; struck down, but not destroyed" (2 Corinthians 4:7–9).

We may be knocked down, but we are not knocked out.

If you have ever been diminished or snubbed, had a job application turned down or a manuscript rejected, proceed to the next paragraph.

I was sitting in a church cafeteria with my friend Retha Garten eating an utterly sinful piece of blueberry pie. The berries were picked at nearby Cross Creek, the wilderness site where Marjorie Kinnan Rawlings found sanctuary from the elite jungles of New York life to hide while writing her two bestselling novels, *Cross Creek* and *The Yearling*.

The Gainesville *Sun* carried a most curious story on Friday, August 16, 1991. David Wilkening, a magazine reporter, purchased a book *American Psycho* for his own personal reading pleasure. He later said, "I immediately regretted purchasing such a bloody novel." He was driven to make a literary experiment, wondering if this generation could still recognize quality.

Marjorie Rawlings' Pulitzer Prize-winning novel, *The Yearling*, written in 1938, also became an immensely popular movie in 1946 starring Gregory Peck. Mr. Wilkening decided to submit the first three chapters of *The Yearling* under a tongue-in-cheek title, to 22 publishers including Doubleday and Scribners. In all, thirteen of the publishers rejected it, eight did not respond at all, and only *one* small publisher, Pineapple Press in Sarasota, recognized the book and its top-seller quality.

If Jesus returned to the earth today, would this generation recognize Him, or fail to realize who He is? Scripture says "He came to His own, and His own received Him not." Because Jesus was born in a stable many thought Him only a carpenter, someone leading fools astray. But the stone that the builders rejected has become the chief cornerstone, the only Son and sole heir of God.

Pharisees in Bible days rejected Jesus, and they still do so today. Pharisees will criticize and scrutinize you, too. But have heart! Take courage! The Editor-in-Chief has endorsed you!

Carl and I were leading a marriage retreat for Lowell Lundstrom Ministries in Iowa. Sitting in the motel restaurant for an early breakfast, we overheard some entertaining talk from the couple in the next booth and their waitress.

"Morning, Mollie." It was the woman's voice addressing the waitress. The husband chimed in, "That's not Mollie, that's Miss Piggy!" The waitress grinned, setting down hot biscuits and a bowl of homemade gravy.

After Mollie left, the wife chastised her husband. "Don't call her Miss Piggy. Why did you do that? Shh! Here she comes again."

This time he said to Mollie, "Tell my wife why I call you Miss Piggy."

So Mollie explained. "My husband and I own a hog farm. The reason I look so blurry-eyed this morning is that I was up almost all night farrowing pigs. We had lots of piglets born and the weather's too cold. I had to keep taking them into the barns."

"Where was your husband?" asked the wife.

"He was sound asleep. I don't think he knew how serious it was."

"How'd you get roped into this kind of life?"

"Wasn't paying attention when the deal was made, I guess!"

We all laughed. Mollie (Miss Piggy) was not complaining, just functioning—farrowing pigs all night, then waiting tables at breakfast.

What a lesson! How many of us have been "sweet talked" into some deal? Many a man has taken on the debt of a new car without counting the cost of monthly payments. Many a young woman wanting a wedding not a marriage has not counted the cost of what it means to be a wife.

I sat with my father counseling an unhappy wife who admitted, "I was impressed by his position. My motive was wrong. I wouldn't have even considered going out with him had he not been a medical doctor."

She was not paying attention when the deal was made. It must have hurt her mate. I wonder if Jesus doesn't grieve that many people use Him as a fire escape, leaning on Him only when they face a problem.

Pay close attention when you make a deal with the Lord. Jesus said, "Whoever does not bear his cross and come after Me cannot be My disciple. For which of you, intending to build a tower, does not sit down first and count the cost, whether he has enough to finish it" (Luke 14:27–32).

As I pulled a hot, steaming pan of Texas spoon corn from the oven (cornbread with jalapeno peppers and sharp cheddar cheese), a shabby old van squealed its tires speeding out of our driveway.

During dinner, we detected a "meow." The following morning we detected four extra, faint baby "meows." A mother cat had chosen the insulation in the ceiling of our garage below the living room for her maternity ward.

Eight days later we discovered fleas in the carpeting, fleas in the floor mats of the cars, fleas in our pants cuffs. Sitting in church on Sunday night listening to Carl preach, I looked across the aisle to see two small children scratching their little ankles furiously.

At the close of the service the head usher suggested that we fog the building during the night hours, since several people had complained of mosquitoes during the evening service. "Betty and I would like to donate this project to the church. We will call and pay for an exterminator." We did not tell them that we had likely transferred the plague of our fleas from the carpeting in our house to the lovely orange carpeting in God's.

Eight days later, we again called the exterminator. He explained to us, "You can kill the fleas, but the eggs previously laid will continue to hatch." It took three applications to terminate our misery.

A saintly old gent in our neighborhood shared a story with me. "I struggled with profanity all my life. Months after I became a Christian, I had to drop on my knees, or bow my head and ask God's help with this habit, because before I realized it, my brash tongue would slip. Years after I quit cussing, my grandchildren were using words they had heard me say beforehand." The eggs continued to hatch long after he had killed the culprit.

Don't give up if you are struggling with alcohol, smoking, profanity. Call out again to the exterminator, Jesus. "If we confess our sins, He is faithful and just to forgive us our sins and to cleanse us from all unrighteousness" (1 John 1:9).

Jesus makes return calls, and never gives up on us. When we call Him, ask Him, He makes yet another application.

Self-pity can kill you. Read on.

It was Saturday night. My two little girls were tucked into bed and I sat so long in the bathtub, bathing in self-pity, that the water became cold and I shivered with chills. I didn't even care, my misery was so deep. My husband was dead. The past two days my nursing baby had cried almost constantly. I didn't realize that she was nursing my discontent. My restlessness and depression were being transferred directly into her little being.

When I finally crawled into bed, I decided that I would not go to church in the morning. I didn't want people to see me this way.

Next morning, my good habit of waking early kicked in, and my childhood training surfaced. I could almost hear my father say, "God gives us six days to do *our* thing, and asks for only one day to do *His* thing. 'Not forsaking the assembling of ourselves together, as the manner of some is; but exhorting one another: and so much the more, as ye see the day approaching'" (Hebrews 10:25, KJV). I recalled a sermon I had heard. If you love your heavenly Dad, you will want to go see Him at His house.

During church my mind wandered until Pastor Chapin announced his sermon topic: "Self-Pity Is Sin." He based his sermon on the book of Job. Now, Job had cause to be depressed. He lost his property, his children died and his wife refused to comfort him. Job suffered sores and sat on an ash heap scraping himself to relieve the itching and burning. God spoke to him and said, "Job, get up!" When Job didn't rise, God sent a whirlwind that blew the ashes of burned-out hope from beneath him, and when Job did not have anything to sit on, he got up. After the message, after church people hugged me and admired my children, I went home exhorted, cheered and having repented of self-pity.

Years later, as I was speaking at a church in California, down the aisle came a young man wearing a back pack. We learned that his wife had left, taking their baby. He had lost his job and was atop the Golden Gate Bridge. Self-pity told him to jump. A passerby stopped his car, got the man inside and brought him to the meeting. Brent knelt at the altar. Jesus saved his soul, saved his life and cured his self-pity.

My friend Tina Marie Kazmierczak is a very creative designer and distributor of jewelry. (She also makes a marvelous hot artichoke dip.) She established the unique little "Tina's Gift Haus" in her Frankfort, Illinois, home, and displays and sells jewelry made by other artists as well. This past year she and others worked hard for one full year to ensure plenty of wares for sale at a large Chicago arts and crafts show. One of Tina's specialties is a lovely seed pearl and rhinestone creation. A friend in North Carolina with arthritis in her hands turned on her kiln and made hand-molded earrings and pins from the native clay, a difficult but rewarding process.

Tina came away from the festival disheartened. The few people who got some of her things had not bought them but stolen them while she turned her back. She told me, "What was really popular at the fair was what I call 'flash and trash.' Women, young and old, bypassed pieces that required expensive materials, creative artistry and hard work, and bought baubles, trinkets, glitzy stuff made from broken mirrors, chains, faded denim and junk."

It is a change from seeking the beautiful, to accepting the mediocre.

Jesus said that in the last days before He came again to the earth that people's taste for the things of God would change, too. They would prefer fortune-telling and palm reading to digging out God's truth for themselves by reading His Word. They would become pipe dreamers and idle schemers rather than preferring the authentic revelation of God's eternal plan. They would have itching ears, wanting to hear doctrines of devils. They would be "sounding brass" and "tinkling cymbals."

But there are those who have their eyes on the prize, things of eternal value. Let the Word of God abide in you so that you may overcome the wicked one. The lust of the flesh, the lust of the eye, the pride of life pass away, but the one who does the will of God will abide forever.

My father pastored as long as nine years in one church. People were amazed that he always had a fresh prescription, and new telegram each Lord's Day morning, rarely ever repeating an illustration.

As I grew a little older I understood at least two reasons why. An elderly saint, Nova Clark, would quietly slip out just before my father's sermon and go to the furnace room alone, kneel and pray for him until he finished his message. When my dad stepped to the pulpit, opened his Bible and took his text, my mother closed her eyes, slightly bowed her head and, without looking up unless one of the Perkins' kids misbehaved, never stopped praying until he gave the altar call and she slipped to the piano to play the closing hymn.

He had others, I am sure, but these two especially were the pastor's friends. Prayer can develop a good pastor out of a poor one. Scripture warns us, "Do not touch My anointed ones, and do My prophets no harm" (see 1 Chronicles 16:22 and Psalm 105:15). There is a penalty for persecuting them, even when they deserve it. God will reward you personally for respecting their position.

Carl gets angry at the way Hollywood portrays ministers as stupid or idiots, often making them the "heavy" of the plot. True, some ministers have blundered big time, but let's not penalize the good guys with ridicule and preacher bashing. They are human beings with needs of their own, sometimes getting lonely, discouraged, weary, isolated and afraid.

Be your pastor's friend. In Paul's second letter to Timothy he wrote: "The Lord grant mercy to the household of Onesiphorus, for he often refreshed me, and was not ashamed of my chains; but when he arrived in Rome, he sought me out very zealously and found me. The Lord grant to him that he may find mercy from the Lord in that Day—and you know very well how many ways he ministered to me at Ephesus" (2 Timothy l:16–18).

Pray for your pastor's personal needs, for his family, his prosperity, and his safety and protection as he engages in spiritual warfare. He is Satan's target because he is warning the lambs and the sheep. Avoid criticism, private and public. Be faithful in attendance and giving.

"Either change jobs, or change your attitude toward your job. You are making yourself sick." The doctor was straightforward with me.

"But I don't want to be a pastor's wife. I was a pastor's daughter. I know the sacrifices my mother made. She died when she was fifty-one," I replied.

Sometimes in self-sacrifice for others, we sacrifice ourselves, even our health. Even feeders need to be fed. Juvenal asked, "Who shall guard the guardians themselves?" And the Lord spoke through Micah, "What does the Lord require of you but to do justly, to love mercy, and to walk humbly with your God?" (Micah 6:8). The doctor was right. When I changed my attitude, my health improved.

I began to study what others had learned about the power of attitude. Marie Curie said, "Nothing in life is to be feared. It is only to be understood." Attitudes can affect your health, your life, your future. Ethel Barrymore said, "You grow up the day you have the first real laugh at yourself."

Maturity is when we change from cocksureness into thoughtful uncertainty. Growing old is mandatory, but growing up is optional!

I talked to Connie Lundstrom about her busy life riding a bus for 31 years, sharing her evangelist husband with the public in rallies and on television. She said, "I would rather have ten percent of a one-hundred-percent man, than to have one hundred percent of a ten-percent man." She has learned to like her lifestyle. Before Marcia Kendall founded Flame Fellowship, she shared her concept with her husband. She told him, "I want the ministry of helps . . . to be a door opener. I want to rekindle the lost art of hospitality. If God would give us a bigger house, I would do just that."

He replied, "You don't use the little house you already have."

So she became hospitable, a door opener. She developed her ministry of helps. That organization has grown now from Texas to other states—and she does have a larger home.

Charles Swindoll says, "Life is ten percent of what happens to me and ninety percent how I react to it. We are in charge of our attitudes!"

We go to bed early in the P.M. and we wake up early in the A.M. Our bedroom faces the sunny east morning side of our house. Every morning is like Easter at my house. Since my death experience in 1959, I greet, salute and anticipate each morn. I love God's alarm clock, sunrise!

After saying "yes" to the Lord and having a brief time of prayer, I prop up in bed with a cup of my rich, dark Stockholm-blend coffee, listen to the birds' first song, watch them nibble the bird seed I put in the feeder on the rail of the sun deck by the bedroom window, then I am up and working hard all day.

This morning, the first customer at the bird feeder (a plastic lid tacked to the rail) was a gray dove. She was enjoying the seeds, but a wide-eyed, bushy-tailed squirrel arrived and decided to take over. He flashed his tail, chattered his fine teeth and shook himself trying to frighten the quiet, solemn dove. She was not impressed or intimidated, but kept pecking, picking and enjoying her breakfast. Then a blue jay swooped down, flapping his wings. Neither his high plume atop his sharp pointed head nor his bright blue feathers impressed the plainly dressed gray dove. The jay warned, chattered and squawked, but she just set that small oval head solidly and remained unmovable.

A Florida red-winged blackbird stole a few grains, then flew away. Next came a bright red, male cardinal. She neither welcomed him, nor attempted to fight him off, but merely ignored his gorgeous, red uniform and his calls of "cheeeet, cheeeet." She was not cheating; she was there first and remained steadfast, unmovable, waging her silent battle until the redbird, disheartened and losing courage, moved on. Without a fight and with that quiet, peaceful quality of low-key determination, the dove set her heart on her goal, focused on her food. The tempter threatens and raves. Charisma without character produces chaos. The dove, plain but powerful, was victor. She won, and ate the good. No wonder the Scriptures type the Holy Spirit as a gentle dove. The one who is faithful and endures to the end with quiet consistency shall be saved (see Matthew 10:22).

I love ethnic jokes as long as they don't poke at "limeys," those of us of English descent! Probably the oldest "cop-out" is an ethnic joke: "Of course I have a temper; I'm Irish." Canadians tell "Newfie" (Newfoundland) jokes. The Swedes ask, "Is there anything dumber than a dumb Swede? Yes, an intelligent Norwegian." Yanks take shots at Rebels; Rebels poke fun at Yanks. And Pollock jokes are here again.

I slipped into Jack's chair to get my hair styled and was thoroughly entertained by the newest P.M.S. jokes. "What's the only difference between a woman with P.M.S. and a pit bull? Lipstick." Or, "The difference between a woman with P.M.S. and a terrorist? You can reason with a terrorist." I played dumb and asked, "What really is P.M.S.?" The girl answered, "Putting up with men, silly."

The cover up for an "air head" is, "She's a dumb blonde." What is a brunette between two blondes? She's an interpreter. It goes on and on. I wonder if Eve was a blonde? Did she have P.M.S.? What was her excuse for being tricked by the serpent? It couldn't have been her mother's fault, because she had no mother. It wasn't bad blood, poor potty training or child abuse. She couldn't blame it on sibling rivalry because she had no brothers or sisters, no family at all. She couldn't plead rejection, for Adam, her husband, loved her and wanted her.

It is hard to spiritualize nonsense, but I want to remind myself that God said, "Come let us reason together. If your sins are scarlet, they can be as white as snow."

At the Last Supper, the disciples did not pass the buck. They asked, "Lord, is it I?" X-ray yourself, judge your own motives. Answer your own why. Don't kid yourself. Paul said to speak the truth in love (see Ephesians 4:15). You can be better than you are.

My husband says of my dad, "He is the only living saint I know." He was my role model of reaction under pressure. He was not only good with the Bible, but excellent with tools. Without the help of another person he built an addition onto our home, two bedrooms and a bath. While hammering a heavy 2 x 12, it slipped and struck his knee with a terrible thud. I watched him wince and react with, "Praise the Lord!"

A few years after that I was working as a secretary and clerk for the jeweler in New Castle, Indiana. At the day's end, I put a stack of letters I had typed on my boss's desk. I had learned to copy Mr. Edwards' signature and signed them, but he always reviewed the letters before I mailed them. He returned one of them and, though he was not an outwardly religious person, surprised me with a quote from the Bible: "Out of the abundance of the heart the mouth speaketh" (Matthew 12:34, KJV).

Whatever did Mr. Edwards mean? I looked at the letter he handed me. His official signature was "H. Ray Edwards." Not paying attention I had signed it "H. Rat Edwards." Horrors!

I liked the man! It was not indicative of how I felt, not intentional. Fortunately, we had a good laugh and he quoted yet another Scripture, "How can bitter and sweet come out of the same fountain?" What we are usually comes through under pressure.

David Carlson, a young husband and father, dove from a pier into water that was too shallow and broke his neck. David told me, "Waiting on the dock for the paramedics to arrive I wasn't thinking, *My God, I'm a paraplegic.* My first and only thought was, *We have never taken our children to Sunday school.*"

A man phoned me once and said, "My wife left and took our two daughters." He asked me for $200 to cover an overdraft in his bank account. I declined and later learned that he was a professional parasite and had "hit" several other people for $200.

Under pressure "a good man out of the good treasure of his heart brings forth good things; and an evil man out of his evil treasure brings forth evil things."

A little church near Apple Valley, California, is pastored by Doris Eddy. When her husband died she became the shepherdess. We drove by Dale Evans and Roy Rogers' home near the church, on the edge of the desert.

"Stop!" I called out. "What are those curious, funny-looking trees?" They looked almost bare, no leaves, but the covering on the surface of the branches had the appearance of short, fuzz, almost like fur.

She explained to me that these were Joshua trees. They are ugly, but durable. This is one classic case where looks and beauty do not count, but durability does. (Reminds me of some women I know. They are classic clothes racks—pretty, but not practical; fancy but not functional.)

You cannot kill the Joshua tree. They have been stuck by lightning. The highway department has bulldozed them into a heap and burned them. There is no moisture for them; in fact, it had hardly rained in that part of California for almost six years. They not only survive, but thrive. *The only way a Joshua tree dies, is from within.*

This is a good parable for the Christian's survival. Satan doesn't care much about surface sins that only hurt you or aggravate others. But if he can target your heart, kill the spirit of your inner person, your soul, hit you dead center, he can finish you off. No wonder Jesus warned, "Guard your heart (your insides), for out of it are the issues of life."

You can make it through life limping, but a dead spirit first paralyzes then kills. We must be inoculated by the Word and prayer against inner death caused by bitterness, jealousy, envy, strife, malice resentment. Lick your wounds if necessary, but shield your center from them. In a hockey game, the puck can bounce around, but the goalie is intent on keeping it from entering that central area where games are lost.

Be a Joshua tree. Read the book of Joshua in the Bible. It is powerful! I love the old song, "The kingdom of God is *within* me; I know no defeat, only strength and power."

It was one of those days in early June, forever spring climate, slight breeze, and the water in the bay on the south side of Caladesi Causeway was smooth as glass . . . what our family calls a perfect "SeaDoo" day. We had to sell that wonderfully fun water-toy to help with April's college bill, but we sure had a lot of fun the two summers we had it.

I was circling the small island south of the causeway when I spotted a young man sitting out there all alone, strumming a guitar and singing. Could he have had boat trouble, marooned out there, stranded alone? I pushed the choke button and killed my motor.

"Don't tell me, let me guess. Your music is so bad they sentenced you to this remote island."

"Wrong," he replied.

I recognized him. I have heard him do concerts in the area and sing on television. He promised to reveal his reason for being there if I would not reveal his name. His concept is a powerful one.

Once a month he comes there alone with God, a free spirit, free admission, no audience, no offering, no applause, no honorarium, no microphone, no back-up music. "This is my sacrifice of praise to God, an unselfish performance for no other reason but to worship Him who gave me the gift of music and the ability to make a wonderful living doing what I do best and love most—sing. I spend an hour alone with God, offering my concert to Him. I return to the mainland renewed and my battery charged to keep going."

When I returned home, I went into the house and sat down at my white spinet Kawai piano and tried it—just ministering to the Lord. My husband was not there to tell me it sounded good. My children were not there listening. It was simply my gift to Him.

If you're a musician, try it. You'll like it. God likes it, too. "Sing (not to an audience) but unto the Lord" (see Exodus 15:1, Judges 5:3; Psalm 9:11; Psalm 101:1; and Jeremiah 20:13).

Ministers minister, yet sometimes they acutely need ministry. It is tough being a shepherd today. Many reverends have set poor examples, having built for themselves a shrine or magic kingdom. By comparison, the humble servant of God feels intimidated or like a failure. But those who are setting up their own kingdoms have forgotten that the church is not theirs, but God's. It is not their ministry but His.

You ministers: Pray before starting any project. Avoid any deceptive thoughts that you must work or perform any duty before prayer. When a man quits prayer for business, it will entangle him and he will not pray the whole day long.

Lean on Jesus. Ask for His strength to perform your duties.

St. Richard of Chichester prayed three things: To see Thee more clearly, love Thee more dearly, to follow Thee more nearly, day by day. Abraham Lincoln said, "I have been driven many times to my knees by the overwhelming conviction that I had nowhere else to go. My own wisdom, and that of all about me, seemed insufficient for the day."

Karen Siddle has letterhead that would be wonderful for ministers. It is a drawing of three young lambs. One little fellow is flat on his back and the other two are looking down on him with pity. I didn't know it, but a sheep, like the turtle, flat on his back cannot turn himself over. It could die without help. One little lamb leans forward and asks, "Do you want me to go get the shepherd?" It touched my heart.

Many times like David, the minister must "encourage himself in the Lord." Pastor, find yourself a prayer partner, maybe someone out of town with whom you can share your deeperst personal need, who will pray and keep your confidence. One pastor showed me a letter he received from a fellow minister. "I have no magic formula, but I do have a genuine concern and a deep love for the Lord and His faithfulness to answer prayer. I'll pray for you as long as you need me." God will reward that kind of concern and prayer commitment.

Thank the Lord for the privilege of serving God and His people. Ask him to equip you with joy, and "tarry . . . until you are endued with power from on high" (Luke 24:49). "You will be strengthened with all might according to His glorious power, with joyfulness!"

Jesus was perfect and they pulled out His beard and killed Him. Do not be astonished if people "split hairs" with you.

The Pharisees had just witnessed a marvelous healing miracle, but they couldn't see the forest for the trees. They complained of Jesus, "He did it on the Sabbath!"

Have you ever been criticized because you did not go through proper channels? They criticized Jesus because He didn't follow their religious rules. He cut the red tape and, in an emergency, healed a man.

I did a writer's workshop on the East Coast. An author with a Master's in journalism picked a quarrel with the director of the convention because he was not asked to lecture instead of me. If you have ever been the victim of criticism or jealousy, you know the "sting."

April had a boating accident just off the causeway to Honeymoon Island. She nearly bled to death while some "Dollie Do-Good" in the emergency room did her proper paperwork, went through proper channels and prissy procedures. I wanted to shout, "Cut the red tape; save her blood!" Paul said, "The letter kills, but the Spirit gives life" (2 Corinthians 3:6).

If you have ever been lacerated by a legal eagle, hair splitting or a misunderstanding, take courage. If they did it to a green tree (Jesus), then what will they do to a dry one (us)?

Before we moved to Florida, we advertised our house for sale. A man offered us cash in hand if we could move out in days. We did it and moved into a miserably small mobile home. Someone started a rumor that we had moved into the trailer because we lost our home and our business. We didn't care, for we headed for Florida.

Jesus kept His mind on His Father's throne business. Let the accusers accuse. Ignore them. You are headed for heaven.

Kathy Hamon says, "Anything that is over *my* head is under *His* feet!"

"Thus says the Lord: 'Heaven is My throne, and earth is My footstool" (Isaiah 66:1). "It shall come to pass that before they call, I will answer; and while they are still speaking, I will hear" (Isaiah 65:24).

The earth is the Lord's and the fulness thereof, so ask largely that your joy may be full. That is a big order, so think big, pray big, expect big, act big, love big and live big. If you think little, you will get little results.

Madame Chiang Kai-shek, who has an undefeatable spirit, has told how she survived the war-torn years in China by praying two hours a day. Jesus said, "In the world you will have tribulation; but be of good cheer, I have overcome the world" (John 16:33). And He has prayed for you. You have heard the expression "I'm in over my head." Remember that the Holy Spirit is "the one called alongside to help." Even if you are head over heels in debt, God pays all bills He authorizes. Delight yourself in the Law of the Lord, meditate on Him day and night, and whatever you do will prosper.

Anything over your head is under His feet. "Many are the afflictions of the righteous, but the Lord delivers him out of them all" (Psalm 34:19).

We are on an uphill journey of life, an obstacle course. Every turn in the road is a pressure point. But, the Lord delivers us out of them all and we keep going. Do not major on the pressure points of life, rather major on Jesus' power and ability to deliver.

Let the power of God within you trample underfoot your enemies—the enemies of sickness, depression, discouragement, financial reversal, misunderstanding, debt and doubt.

It was where we aired views, solved problems, healed wounds, joked, ate popcorn and peanut butter fudge, debated, bossed, quarreled very little, watched roosters fight, first heard the facts of life, talked about dating and mating, watched cars go by, waved at the drivers, philosophized, stroked kittens, listened to them purr, patted puppies, drank our first cups of coffee, watched the sunrise and exclaimed over the sunset.

After dinner dishes were done, Mother and Grandmother removed their aprons and joined us, resting in the porch swing while we played "May I?" and tag and caught fireflies until bedtime. Then, in the living room we, as a family, read a daily devotional much like this one, prayed together, we children were tucked lovingly into bed, where we slept peacefully for nine hours. No baby should ever be deprived of a rocking chair or falling asleep in the porch swing on Grandma's lap.

What has happened to the back porch? It was the place where neighbors left surprises, returned the borrowed, shared woes and good news. There was either a note box by the door knob, or a note pad with a string dangling and a pencil at the end where you could scribble a mini letter. First thing when we arrived home, we looked for those friendly notes. There was a worn spot in the paint on the door from friendly knuckles knocking. We have become sophisticated with our bells and chimes, but mostly we are lonely and depressed.

Where are our porches? People who have them don't use them. They are curios, antiques attached to the front of the house for display. Before architects eliminated this necessity from their sketches, and builders cut the front porches off our houses, we had homes. I had never heard of tranquilizers. A drug store was a place where you bought ice cream cones. And we could not even spell *stress*.

How long since you walked at sunrise or viewed the sunset from your porch and talked aloud to God?

I believe there is an Rx for every complex. Some people don't have an inferiority complex, they truly are inferior. By that I mean that most people are well below par of what they could be with God's help.

Jesus said, "In the last days before I come again there will be perilous times." *Peril* means exposed to danger. We surely do need a *calm*plex.

"You will keep him in perfect peace, whose mind is stayed on You" (Isaiah 26:3). The prescription for spiritual vertigo (confusion and disorientation) is Isaiah 41:10: "Fear not, for I am with you; be not dismayed, for I am your God. I will strengthen you, yes, I will help you, I will uphold you with My righteous right hand." What hope! What a promise! That would give anyone a calmplex!

Do not make decisions when you are in the valley. You will make them out of self-pity. Do not make decisions when you are on the mountain top. You will make them out of self-confidence. Be steady, level and calm in your God.

I remember a chorus from my children's church days. I could not have been more than five. It was, "When we all pull together, together, together, When we all pull together how happy we'll be. For your work is my work, and my work is God's work, When we all pull together how happy we'll be!" We, the Body of Christ, really do need each other.

"And let us consider one another in order to stir up love and good works, not forsaking the assembling of ourselves together, as is the manner of some, but exhorting one another, and so much the more as you see the day approaching" (Hebrews 10: 24–25).

One old saint said, "I don't know how many more Sundays God may give me. It would be poor preparation for my first Sunday in heaven to have slighted my last day on earth."

Basically there are two kinds of Christians, the tooters and the root-ers—the talkers and the doers.

In one parable Jesus said that those who arrive at the banquet should not be tooters and take a front seat to be seen in a place of honor, for the host might ask them to move down and make room for others. 'Tis better, He told us, to take a back seat and have the host of the feast invite us to come up front. A promotion is better than a public demotion.

A certain man had two sons. He came to the first and said, "Son, go work today in my vineyard." He answered and said, "I will not," but afterward he repented and went. (That's a rooter.) The man approached the second son and said likewise. He answered, "I will go, sir," but he didn't. (That's a typical tooter, only a braggard.) Which son did the father's will? Mere tooters do not pray effectively. Their brand of praying has no more effect than putting a Band-Aid on a broken leg.

A rooter has character. Even when he knows he will not get caught, he still does that which is right. When no one is around, even if God was not looking, he would still choose the straight way. Rooters are pray*ers*. Satan is afraid of rooters.

In the book of Acts, Sceva had a bunch of boys, seven sons who were mere boasters, just tooters, not fortified with the armor of the Holy Ghost. They decided that they would put on an act like rooters. They tried to exorcise some evil spirits from a man. The demons from hell said, "We know Jesus and we have heard of Paul, but 'who in hell' are you?"

What kind of reputation do you have in hell? Is your praying so effective that demons know who you are and tremble and flee? Do you root out the invisible enemy? Does Satan oppose you, and feel you are such a threat to his kingdom that he finds it necessary to rally his evil forces against you? Rooters win in this kind of invisible warfare.

Have you ever heard anyone called a "dipstick"? I never could understand what that word meant. My brother and I think we have it figured out. This one brother was, and still is, "smarter than the average bear." He would get bored in church if the speaker was not especially interesting. On one such occasion he told Mother he really, honestly needed to go to the men's room. When he overstayed his reasonable term in there, she asked me to go check on him.

I found him in the furnace room trying to hide from Deacon Jones. Now we grew up when deacons really deaconed. They felt especially inspired to keep the preacher's kids in line. Big Ben, as we called him, had found him. I stood "afar off" and listened to the dialogue.

Big Deacon: "What are you doing down here? You should be listening to the preaching. After church I'm telling your dad."

Little Brother: "The Bible says to work out *your own* salvation with fear and trembling. You take care of yours and I'll take care of mine!"

I have heard the Word used to advantage in various ways, but this was indeed a different application!

Now that we are grown and are trying to teach our children to apply the Word in our daily lives, the above incident has become a traditional family joke.

A dipstick is a person who is always going around judging, poking under everyone's hood but his or her own, examining everyone else's cars, checking everyone else's oil.

Check your own oil, and let your brother check his. Let God be judge.

Don't be a dipstick!

When we first moved to Florida in 1961, we purchased two wooded acres of land just one block from what is now Countryside Mall for $5,000. Don't I wish I could buy it for that now!

It was full of weeds and one morning one of our neighbors turned out of his driveway and ran over several times a five-and-a-half-foot diamondback rattlesnake.

We learned that the man doubled-wrapped that poisonous thing in glad bags and tucked it deep in his freezer. It was his trophy and conversation piece anytime northerners ("snow birds") or relatives came for a visit. He loved to have them count the eight rattlers and show its deadly fangs.

One day when they visited the veterinarian to have a family kitten vaccinated, their vet warned them to bury it, and bury it deep. "What if someday when you are away, your kids should decide to show it off? Those poisonous fangs are still deadly."

The man hurriedly buried the snake. But he did not bury it deep enough. Later that week he noticed a stray dog lying dead beside the shallow grave. He had snagged his mouth against those deadly fangs.

Know someone with a poisonous past? Bury it and bury it deep. Don't dig the deadly thing up. "I had great bitterness; but You have lovingly delivered my soul from the pit of corruption, for You have cast all my sins behind Your back" (Isaiah 38:17). "As far as the east is from the west, so far has He removed our transgressions from us" (Psalm 103:12).

God has forgiven and forgotten our sins, but sometimes people will not. Have mercy. He who refuses to forgive, breaks the bridge over which he himself must pass to get to God.

Do you own a pencil? If you have a pen, a tablet, a typewriter or a computer, you are a writer—you just have not turned on your equipment yet.

Writing is merely talking on paper. "My tongue is the pen of a ready writer" (Psalm 45:1). Some of the best things I write are done quickly on the impulse—scribbled on napkins or toilet tissue in the bathroom, while the thought is sharp and the description fresh on my mind.

You can find my notes on scraps of paper stuffed in the ash tray (*cash* tray in our car), jotted while I cook dinner, or on the clipboard I keep on the floor by my bed with a pen and flashlight so I do not awaken Carl. I even write notes to myself during church. The easiest flow of mind and spirit is when God is moving, people are singing and believers are praying.

I was a writer before I knew it! When I saw a person who needed encouragement or exhortation, I scribbled a positive note, saturated it with prayer, licked a postage stamp back when first class was ten cents and sent it through the mail. My letters helped because I cared.

A book is a bunch of letters connected by bridges called chapter headings. When you care more about communicating than selling books or making money, you are a mature writer. If you want to be an inspirational writer you must love the readers more than the book.

Writing is not a lazy means to make a living. Believe me, there are easier ways. You have to be disciplined. Many of my friends are at the beach with their grandchildren or playing golf while I sit ten hours at this Macintosh. Writing is not for the fainthearted. You must have a hide like an elephant. When I finished my first manuscript my editor told me that it had potential, but that, as it was, it "would sell about thirty copies to your relatives. It rings with triumphalism."

He explained that people read about those who have rebounded from situations like their own. Mine was a narrative, a story, but it lacked a strong theme, the element that would help the reader identify with me. People don't read books for entertainment these days; they watch TV. They usually read a book when they are searching for an answer to life's questions.

I followed his guidance and rewrote that book. It became a bestseller.

Do you want to write? The way to start is to begin.

Sonja Shryer sang a song at church with the words, "Will those who come behind us find us faithful?" Her lovely singing voice, combined with that challenge, set my brain to clicking.

I was so very fortunate growing up with a rich, godly heritage. I read Gene Stratton Porter and Catherine Marshall. I idolized my grandmothers and my mother was a loving Christian example with a creative imagination that would not quit. She was a one-woman enter- tainment center. Guess where I am headed? I am soliciting mentors.

Plugging my Wollensak tape duplicator into the wall socket, I saw something I had not noticed before. A small brass plate with this printed instruction: "Dirty heads make poor copies. Clean heads peri- odically. Follow instruction booklet."

What a message for life and living! Our daughters, our sons, even acquaintances are following us. You may be a choice mentor. Is your head clean? Would you make a good, clear copy? Are you using the instruction Book God gave us? On the spot, I determined to obey Philippians 4:8, thinking about virtuous, pure, true, clean and lovely things that are of good report.

The apostle Paul was not afraid to say, "Follow me as I follow Christ. Follow us for we have tried to imitate responsibility. We have worked that we be not chargeable to any of you. We want to make ourselves an example for you to follow" (see 2 Thessalonians 3:1–18).

Where are the heroes? This generation needs mentors. If you want your family tree climbed and traced, get into politics or become a Christian leader. The media has dug out and pulled down the dirty. We need some good examples.

When I was attending Main Jr. High in Mishawaka, Indiana, in 1941, there was a life-sized cardboard statue of Uncle Sam dressed in red, white and blue in front of the post office. With his finger pointed he said, "I want YOU. Be a soldier, be a sailor, be a marine! Protect America!"

I believe God is saying, "I want you to be a mentor. Protect our next generation by setting a good, godly, praying example."

Berdie did not have a childhood. She was not blessed with stability, but at the age of ten, she found Jesus Christ at a small Hungarian Assemblies of God church in Milwaukee, Wisconsin.

Growing up she did not have a job, but a caring pastor and his wife encouraged her to develop her love for music. At the age of 21 she married a talented violinist named Steve Kovacs, and it seemed that finally Berdie would find the happiness for which she had searched. Seven years later he was killed in a tragic automobile wreck. Now she is alone, again.

Now she did not have a family. She had no children and no other living relatives.

Berdie looked at her hands. She *did* have hands. "Whatever your hand finds to do, do it with your might" (Ecclesiastes 9:10). She did just that. She put her hands and her heart into her piano and organ playing.

For 46 years she taught music at Great Lakes Bible Institute in Zion, Illinois; Central Bible College in Springfield, Missouri; Southeastern College in Lakeland, Florida; and Trinity College in Ellendale, North Dakota.

God was her father, Jesus was her brother and her husband, and the students were her children. She had hundreds, even thousands of them who became her family. As she traveled with choir members around the country she counseled them, loved them, let them cry on her shoulder, prayed with them, encouraged and mothered them.

She laughed readily, sang with glee and great gusto, shopped fervently, loved to taste new food and buy beautiful things. I lived near her. She showed me her red and black lace "nightie," and dressed up with fine jewelry and high heels twenty years after other women her age were too old.

On May 19, 1991, she went to heaven. I am sure she is teaching music to people who were too poor or too busy while they were here on earth.

Now Berdie has it all.

I did a writer's workshop for *Decision* Magazine at Northwest College near Minneapolis. One of the other workshop leaders was Jill Briscoe from Liverpool, now living near Milwaukee. In one of her sessions she cheered the writers on by challenging them to "push past push." She explained that when she jogs and starts to wind down, she has a talk with herself, telling herself to persevere, push past push, get her second wind. Then she is off and running again.

There are times in life when we must push past push, when we do not feel like praying, going to work, getting up on Sunday morning to celebrate Jesus at the Lord's House. The race is not to the swift, but to the runner who completes his assignment. "He who endures to the end will be saved" (Matthew 10:22).

This morning, early, I had a fresh peach with my whole wheat toast. I put the peach pit in the feeder for "Clifford," Carl's favorite squirrel. He gnawed (the squirrel, not Carl), he chewed, he turned it with his little sharp claws and kept at it, until, pushing past push, not giving up, he cracked that hard shell and went crazy with joy for the kernel inside.

My Scottish grandad, Pearl Burns, had a terrible illustration of importunity—but I'll tell it to you anyway.

A middle-aged woman in a backwoods, mountainous area was seen running for her life down a winding road with a young man of perhaps seventeen chasing hard on her heels. A policeman happened by and stopped the young man to question him. "Oh, he's not a criminal," the woman explained, panting. "He's my son. I'm either going to wean him or run him to death!"

Don't give up. Remember Jacob's prayer of perserverance: "I will not let You go unless You bless me!" (Genesis 32:26).

I sat in the front seat of Eileen's car while she told me, "My husband shocked me when he suddenly walked out and moved in with a young woman. She's not much older than our oldest child. I followed him to her house and begged him to come away with me and start all over again. He just sat on her bed and said, 'I'm staying.' I left feeling absolute futility."

Eileen went directly to her pastor's office. He was shocked and hurt too, but then he spoke calmly and said, "Invite Jesus into this situation and, for your own sake, forgive your husband and this woman. Don't act like them. Counteract what they have done by acting like Jesus. Show His mercy and His forgiveness."

Eileen said at first that she did not feel they deserved forgiveness. She wanted to hate them, to hurt them as much as they had hurt her. But, miraculously, ten years later she had a visit from her husband's new wife and was able to forgive her and pray with her to accept Jesus.

Sooner or later it happens to all of us: We get hurt, cheated, lied about or abused. It is painful. We are unprepared and in our outrage we cry to God against the one who wronged us. We ask for justice and vengeance.

This is because we mistakenly identify our enemy as the person who hurt us. But in Ephesians 6:12 Paul informs us that we wrestle "against the rulers of the darkness of this age." Don't waste energy ranting and scheming against the people who cause you pain. Aim your ammunition at the right target—the devil. Go after him!

Hit Satan with the Word of God. Let him know you are not going to give up your rights as a child of God. Serve him notice that he will restore to you seven times what has been stolen from you (Proverbs 6:31). Then bind the devil from doing any further harm (Matthew 18:18).

Next, pray for your enemies. Bless them that curse you, pray for those who wrong you (Matthew 5:44–45). When Moses asked God to show him His glory, the biggest, weightiest, grandest thing about Himself, God showed Moses His mercy (Exodus 34:6). Look at your situation with spiritual eyes.

When you pray for, not against, your oppressor, when you go against the devil on your enemy's behalf, that is pure intercession. Let God give recompense to your enemy (see Isaiah 59:17–19).

Next time someone does you wrong, fight the devil on that person's behalf. Show mercy and Satan will think twice before he bothers *you* again!

You never get a second chance to make a first impression. I walked down the aisle at the "animal orphanage" (S.P.C.A.) between the cages of cats and kittens. One little character reached his small paw between the wires and slapped at me. I hurried to the office and stated my choice. "I want that one."

"That was quick," she commented. "How did you choose so fast?"

"I didn't choose. He did. I must have impressed him, for he chose me." While she filled out the papers I picked up several kittens. I knew I had made the right choice. He was the only one who purred for me immediately.

At home, I put him down in the living room. He shot up the drapes to the top, and jumped off—onto my back. Ouch! That did it! His first impression on us named him. We call him Sinner Man because he is so bad. My husband and I volley back and forth with, "When he's cute, he's *my* kitty. When he's bad, he's *your* kitty." He looks like he's wearing a black tuxedo with a white shirt in front.

That little twelve-ounce kitty is now a full-blown 21-pound cat! We have weighed him so many times, he thinks the scales in the kitchen corner are his personal property.

He has a pattern. First thing after we let him out of the bathroom early each morning (where he sleeps) he goes directly to the scales to be weighed. Next he goes to the breakfast bar and stops in front of the coffee maker. Then he proceeds through the doorway into the computer corner of our bedroom. One of us has undoubtedly impressed the other: This is the same pattern I follow! I weigh myself, get a cup of coffee, then proceed to the computer to write.

On my last birthday two of my four brothers told me, "The older you get, the more you look like our mother." She impressed me, from the womb and delivery room to the hospital room where she died years later.

You, too, are impressing someone. You will never get a second chance to make a first—or a last—impression.

This could well be named a dance step!

Pastor Casey has taught us a song he learned in England based on Psalm 37. It says, "Rejoice, for your steps are ordered of God!" Our congregation sings it frequently as our call to worship on Sunday. It is true, it is practical, it still works today. "I will be glad and rejoice in You; I will sing paraise to Your name, O Most High" (Psalm 9:2).

Eighty years ago, Daniel Berg and Gunnar Vingren were both sitting in a church service in Chicago. They listened intently to a prophetic message that included the word *Para* several times. Researching, they discovered that Para was the name of a state in northern Brazil. Their missionary hearts were strangely warmed, and their steps were ordered of God. They made their way from Chicago to New York where by miraculous provision they received their fare for passage on a freighter. Upon arrival in the city of Belem in Para, Brazil, they went to a park, sat on a bench, first rejoicing, then waiting, waiting for God to lead their steps further.

Lead them He did! Recently at the anniversary celebration of the Assemblies of God church there, a great parade of believers marched in jubilation through that city. They stopped at the same park to dedicate a monument in honor of these two obedient servants of Jesus Christ, who allowed Him to order their steps. Now, thousands of congregations minister to millions of people.

Carl believes that Russia may well be the last frontier before Jesus comes again. Let God lead your steps. Whether He leads you to step next door to help and love someone, or to go to Russia, it will bring rejoicing!

This week I received the following from an old family friend, Art Lindsay. The source is unknown.

Blessed are the husband and wife who continue to be affectionate, considerate and loving after the wedding bells have ceased ringing.

Blessed are the husband and wife who are as polite and courteous to one another as they are to their friends.

Blessed are they who have a sense of humor, for this attitude will be a handy shock absorber.

Blessed are the married couples who abstain from alcoholic beverages. They impose undue expense and a lot of social friction in marriage.

Blessed are they who love their mates more than any other person in the world, and who joyfully fulfill their marriage vow of a lifetime of fidelity and mutual helpfulness.

Blessed are they who remember to thank God for their food before they partake of it, and who set aside some time each day for the reading of the Bible and prayer, who humbly dedicate their lives and homes to the Lord.

Blessed are they who remember that children are a heritage of the Lord.

Blessed are the couples who have a complete understanding about fiancial matters and who have worked out perfect partnershp with all the money under control of both.

Blessed are those mates who never speak loudly to each other and who make their home a place "where seldom is heard a discouraging word."

Blessed are the husband and wife who faithfully attend worship services together, for the advancement of Christ's Kingdom.

Blessed are the husband and wife who can work out their problems of adjustment without interference from relatives.

Be "heirs together of the grace of life, that your prayers may not be hindered. . . . Be of one mind, having compassion for one another; . . . be tenderhearted, be courteous; . . . knowing that you were called to this, that you may inherit a blessing" (1 Peter 3:7–9).

If at first you don't succeed, try, try again! The Scriptures put it this way, "Go to the ant, you sluggard! Consider her ways and be wise" (Proverbs 6:6). She does not give up easily.

It happened in Southwest Asia in the fourteenth century. The Emperor Tamerlane's army had been routed, dispersed by a powerful enemy. Tamerlane himself lay hidden in a large old feeding trough while enemy troops scoured the countryside looking for him.

As he lay there, desperate and dejected, Tamerlane watched an ant try to carry a grain of corn over a wall. The kernel was larger than the ant itself. The emperor counted and counted. Sixty-nine times the ant tried to carry it up the wall. Sixty-nine times he fell back. On the seventieth try he pushed the grain of corn over the top.

Tamerlane leaped to his feet with a shout! He, too, would triumph in the end! He would try again. And he did, reorganizing his forces and putting the enemy to flight.

Perhaps you are struggling with a habit—overeating, smoking, drinking. I know a man who lost 1,200 pounds, gaining and losing, gaining and losing, then finally he kept it off after trying so long. He has been his desired weight now for more than fourteen years.

Perhaps your business is failing. Don't give up, keep pushing. Perhaps the next new concept you try will put your business over the top.

You may be locked into a dead marriage. Try again.

With gentle perserverance and patience you can help that hyper, nervous child.

Perhaps you are pastoring a small church and wonder if it will ever have the outreach you dream of. Don't give up. Keep being friendly, preach the Word and pray.

Jesus never gave up on Peter. He said, "I have prayed for you, that your faith should not fail; and when you have returned to Me, strengthen your brethren" (Luke 22:32). Peter slipped some, but he kept trying, went over the top, received the Holy Spirit, and preached one sermon in which three thousand were saved.

The Lord will not give up on you. Don't you give up. Try!

"I was glad when they said to me, 'Let us go into the house of the Lord. . . . Jerusalem is built as a city that is compact together" (Psalm 122:1, 3). No wonder Jerusalem was a compact city, had it together. It was built around the church. My ancestors came from near Middlewich, Nantwich, in England on the Cheshire border. My people are proud Americans, proud to be here in the land of the free and the home of the brave, to worship according to the dictates of our own hearts.

Early settlers built the community around the church. Churches were the center of activity and the heart of every family, the glue that bound them together. No wonder there were few divorces then. They prayed together, they played together and they stayed together.

Now, our churches are more among the elite, far removed from the needy. It used to be that people gladly worshiped the Lord on the Sabbath, giving God one-seventh of their time.

My friend Patty Polce works at a religious book and gift shop. For my birthday, she gave me a coffee mug. On it is inscribed: "*Betty* means consecrated to God. I will dwell in the house of the Lord forever." David was a happy, singing man and declares this latter part in Psalm 23.

For some of us this seems literally true now! I went to church long before I was born. If God had not surprised my parents by causing me to be born early, I think they would have planned for me to be birthed on the front pew of the West Terre Haute church. My parents loved to go to the house of the Lord and to pray. Jesus was their resting nest.

I could not have been more than five years old. The scene is still vivid in my mind. I was leaning against the chimney in the corner of the hallway, my head against my folded arms, whining, half-crying. My tired little mother with other small babies to look after, passed by. I thought she would feel sorry for me, sympathize and "baby" me a little.

Wrong! She swatted my south side and said, "Straighten up. Stop pouting." Then she turned aboutface and asked, "What's wrong with you?"

"Aunt Lillian brought Donnie a present and not me," I sniffed.

"Why didn't you tell me? I would have given you a present," she assured me.

Recently in time of great need, I found this verse: "Ask Me of things to come . . . ; and concerning the work of My hands, you command Me" (Isaiah 45:11).

Me? Command Him? No, I could not do that. It seemed wrong even to suggest that God would invite us to direct the work of His almighty hands. Yet He does.

I reflected on this. God's hands are creative hands . . . hands that supply. All that He created was for us to enjoy. Jesus is like God His Father. Jesus offered His hands, too. They were nail-scarred to heal us.

Light came into my thinking. I am not Jesus' slave and He is not mine. He is my Lord and Savior, but in another sense we are partners working together for the Kingdom to come. Because of Jesus' sacrifice I am an heir of God and joint-heir with Christ (Romans 8:16–17).

If any of my daughters should stand on the porch and cry because they needed something in my house, I would be angry. Don't they know how much I love them? Where they are concerned, my door is never locked.

Everything I have is theirs. I would give my life for them.

So I began claiming His help. True friendship with God implied my right to appropriate. In God's service I have perfect freedom in this partnership. I picked up the devotional book *God Calling* and found this: "Use your right. A beggar supplicates. A son or daughter, appropriates."

If you are born again into God's family, you qualify to start claiming results. It is an undying law.

Dr. Dayton Kingsriter preached a sermon on "cleaning out the corners in your life." We have the choice, he said. We can cut corners, or we can clean the corners. It is by cleaning out corners that we can then "turn the corner" toward maturity in our lives.

Our young daughter was running the vacuum cleaner. Mom said, "Be sure to clean the corners." It takes longer to clean a corner because you have to use the proper attachment. It was hard work but she had the satisfaction of knowing she did it right, a good job. If she had cut the corners, she would have ended up with dirty corners and an unclean conscience. Now, she was ready to "turn the corner"! On now to new challenges, new responsibilities and more new corners.

Whether it is mowing a yard or ruling a kingdom, if you let the little corners go, they will catch up with you.

Eve tried to cut the corner to knowledge and was banned from Eden. Jonah tried to cut a corner instead of going the longer route to Nineveh and eneded up in the belly of the whale. He repented, cleaned out that corner, and God sent a great revival. The rich young ruler would not, could not turn the corner, the final turn. Something else was more important.

David wanted Bathsheba. He refused to clean out the corner of coveteousness and lust and had her husband killed. Later, he repented and God helped David clean that corner. He became the man after God's own heart.

Judas should have cleaned out that secret corner of greed. He refused and committed suicide.

In contrast, the three Hebrew children refused to cut corners, stuck to their diet, served the true God. They had better health, were saved from the firey furnace and were heralded as heroes. Elisha did not cut any corners but waited until he saw the mantle fall and got the double portion of Elijah's miracle-working power.

Keep the corners clean. And don't argue with God when He reveals an untidy, dark corner of your life. The best corner cleaner in the world is the Word. It pierces, and its fire burns out the dross. Do your homework. Don't fight back. Your arms are too short to box with God.

I drove hurriedly to pick up my mail. The parking lot was full. In front of the house across the street from the P.O. someone had thoughtfully leveled a load of smooth white sand. I swung into a spot. Bad choice.

Now, that white, soft sand is wonderful on the beach, but it is not a good foundation for a parking lot. My car sank down and would not budge. I tried to pull out slowly. I got angry and tried to gun it . . . but went deeper and deeper until the frame of my car was hung up. I was hot and sweaty by now, and didn't look presentable to go to work, and didn't feel presentable either. Several people looked on. Anyone could have applied a little pressure on the back of my car and it would have pulled itself out. No one offered.

I closed my eyes, leaned my head back and suddenly—I couldn't believe it!—a Scripture surfaced in my mind. "Train up a child in the way he should go, and when he is old [now, I'm getting old] he will not depart from it" (Proverbs 22:6). The old story from Sunday school about the foolish man who built his house upon the sand, and the wise man who built his house upon the rock Christ Jesus, came to my mind.

I began humming the song we sang in Children's Church: "The foolish man built his house upon the sand. The rains came down and the flood came up and the house on the sand went [we would blow] whoosh! But the wise man built his house upon the rock. The rains came down and the flood came up, but the house on the rock stood fast." That was it! I had it! I needed a rock, a rock foundation. All I had was a little canvas beach bag in my trunk, but I filled it with rocks from the hiking trail nearby, chucked the rocks behind my wheels and in the ruts, and I was out of there!

I sang all the way to work: "On Christ the solid rock I stand, all other ground is sinking sand." I believe music and the words of songs, are engraved and engrained in the grooves of our spirit, and surface in times of need, distress and crisis. Thank God for those good old songs!

A newborn baby's head has a soft spot that is vulnerable and needs to be protected. You can even detect a heartbeat there if you look closely. People are careless here in this hot climate and take young babies into the hot sun, without a head covering, and wonder why they are slow learners in elementary school.

Several weeks ago a praying friend of mine called. She asked if I would help her in prayer "to bear the infirmities of the weak" (Romans 15:l, KJV). Anything that is infirm is not solid, but has a soft spot. Hebrews 4:15 says that Jesus is touched with the feeling of our infirmities, our soft spots, places where we are weak.

The object of our concern, the soft spot of our loving prayers was a "baby Christian," Alexis. She is a young working mother with two small, active boys. Her husband is a high-strung music teacher. Funds were low, tempers high and Alexis said, "I have dug for myself a ten-foot hole and only have a nine-foot ladder. I'm in a deep, dark pit of depression, and the lid of circumstances has closed tightly over my head, sealing me in. I have tried, but can't climb out of this darkness into light. Please pray."

Her friend and I agreed and started praying at eight A.M. for Alexis and her little family. We introduced her to young people and they prayed. We mailed material to her daily. She set a faith-filled picture in her mind and held fast, climbing one rung of the ladder at a time, until she did reach the top and come out with a song in her heart.

Jesus told Peter, "I've prayed for you. When you come out, pray for your infirm soft brothers." God will give you a miracle if He knows that when you receive yours you will pray for others with the need you had before deliverance came to you. Alexis is now a strong lifter!

They're worthless, yet every one of us has a story, "and it all began when" No, I am not going to tell you my life's story, and no, I do not want to hear your life's story.

God walked down the stairway of heaven with a *baby* in his arms. Jesus did not begin on earth, but ruled in heaven before this introduction to us. The all-powerful God, in His overruling Providence, devised a very fragile plot for His son's earthly beginning. God entrusted the babe to a young woman, Mary. Jesus rested helplessly in her arms.

God did not inoculate or vaccinate His son against reality. Jesus ate, slept, went to school, was made a fool and misunderstood as we are. At His bar mitzvah, he was the typical adolescent who wandered from His parents and got lost. But when they found Him, He was talking with priests about heaven.

Jesus lived on earth as a human so He could empathize with us. He spurned temptation to enable us to resist evil. When Satan tempted Him, He didn't escape reality by parachuting out, nor did He pull rank on God by telling the devil who His Dad was. Satan tempted Him with the miraculous—"Turn these stones into bread, prove yourself." Jesus' debate and rebuttal was *quoting the Word*. His was a manly answer, "Man shall not live by bread alone" (Luke 4:4).

He was tempted with politics and popularity. They waved palm branches and wanted to take Him off the donkey and enthrone Him. Later He was rejected so that He could understand you when you are either exalted or abased. Jesus was compelled/propelled by the Holy Spirit. You can make it by the same Holy Spirit within you.

Have you gone to hear a speaker, introduced as a celebrity, and the intro was longer than the theme and benefit of the speaker's message? I drove a long distance, heart-searching for a telegram or prescription, hoping for prayer. The speaker's appeal for the offering to supply one person's needs (his) was twenty minutes, and he prayed only two minutes to meet the needs of his audience of 600 waiting listeners. That's unbalanced.

When Carl was a missionary in Egypt he once walked across a dusty intersection near the city and saw eight men huddled together, looking at him and whispering. He knew the men and went over to them and asked, "What are you talking about?"

Now, Egyptians are not shy. They replied boldly. "We talk about you, Sahib. The last missionary had air-conditioned automobile. We recognized his auto when he come to city. You have no auto, we know your face."

Walking back to the mission complex he wept and prayed, "Lord Jesus, help me like You, always to gravitate toward these people's needs. Let Your face shine through mine, and keep my face and heart always readily available to the needs of these searching people."

There were trade-offs to his sacrifice. He said those Egyptian men were the healthiest he had met in any nation where he had been. They were lean and strong. They taught him to eat fish, cheese, nuts, raw fruit and raw vegetables and to walk. He lost 66 pounds and has remained healthy.

Jesus walked this earth as the Son of God, but He never impressed the masses with a colorful monthly magazine, imposing on people to help Him pay for it or an expensive promotional packet that He sent ahead of His meeting. He merely met people where they were. Some Christians have an illusion of grandeur, but He did not call us to be stars. He called us to serve, to love and relieve mankind. He did not call us to impress people, but to invest in their needs, to comfort them in their sorrow.

Paul said that if we suffer with Jesus, we shall also reign with Jesus (2 Timothy 2:12). This does not mean that He inflicts pain to purge you. This is not heaven, but it is not purgatory either. If you are going to sit on the throne in the Kingdom to come, you may be inconvenienced for others in the name of and for the sake of Jesus here in this world.

Dry toast again this morning. If I just had some jelly, jam or honey . . . but dry, dry toast for four days in a row now. I'm pushing a deadline, listening to people's prayer requests on the phone, no time to go to the store, money just for the basics . . . I'm in a "jam."

Quickly tying my running shoes, I sprinted off the sun deck and into the street to jog the two and a half blocks toward the post office to pick up my daily mail. Passing by her house, I spotted Carolyn V. on the porch. "Carolyn, am I glad to see you! I'll give you the last five dollar bill I have in my mail envelope for a jar of your homemade citris marmalade!"

"Didn't make it this year," she called back. "I'm gettin' too old, arthritis, my back hurts, hands ache."

I turned the key in my post office box and found a small parcel from Rethea Schaden, Longview, Texas. I opened the box on the spot. It contained a jar of homemade apple butter and another of wild plum jelly! There was a little blue note. "This is the fruit of my hands. I'm so excited, I had to share the good news and a sample with you. They won first place ribbons in the Texas State Fair this year!"

"It shall come to pass that before they call, I will answer; and while they are still speaking, I will hear" (Isaiah 65:24). That wild plum jelly and apple butter were mailed even before I expressed my complaint and my desire. *I must write and try to express to her my jubilation.* I grew up as a kid in the middle of an apple orchard. My brothers and I climbed the apple trees; built tree houses in them; picked them to eat and play with; threw them for hand grenades; used them for weapons; and being poor, my mother knew how to prepare apples in a thousand and one ways. What a flood of fond memories from the taste of apple butter!

Dear Rethea,
God shall not soon forget your work and labor of love (Hebrews 6:10). Nor shall I. I'm plum grateful.
Loving thoughts and fond memories,

B.M.

Hot and sweaty, I pulled my old MGA into the garage and cut across the yard toward the steps and a good, and much needed, warm shower. Ooops, dropped my old favorite pelican beach towel. Grabbing it up, it stuck to my swim suit tightly. What's this? Oh, no! Stick tights! They jump; they're alive; they're electric; they're committed. Stick tights are patient, have a great holding pattern, hanging on there. You can't get rid of them.

Finally into the shower I thought, *A good marriage is like that, two people committed to each other as those stick tights were attached to my towel.* At a couple's retreat one old Texas boy told me jokingly that he and "his woman" were compatible: "I'm common and she's pattable. That's compatability." Ha! Hardly.

A person's character is the most important thing to evaluate before a marriage. It will come through long after the sex factor has lost its lustre. It is not enough to claim to be a Christian: Does he or she live like one in difficult circumstances or when around difficult people?

William Coleman makes this statement in his book, *Before the Ring:* "Spouses are the greatest human influence on our spiritual lives. They have the unique ability to motivate us to new heights or drag us down to spiritual despair. Faith isn't like kitchen linoleum. Couples can compromise about floor covering to keep each other reasonably happy. But religious convictions are not so easily adjusted. When one partner feels a call to discipleship and the other is a Christmas Christian, both will be uncomfortable."

What is the adhesive that holds couples together, that common bond that glues lovers together on that permanent basis called marriage? It must be the Wonderful Counselor, the Prince of Peace. First is their personal and corporate relationship with Jesus, then their unconditional commitment to each other. Like the wedding card I inserted in a shower gift recently. It showed two bony grey skeletons propped up together, covered with cob webs. Caption: Marriage is forever. That's a long, long time!

Dr. Ben Harrison delivered my first baby, Brenda, on Father's Day at the Henry County Hospital, New Castle, Indiana, June 21, 1953. He and all doctors have had a spot in my heart since that day. Probably a year after she was born, I stuck my head into his office and said, "Good morning, I just wanted to say 'hi.'"

"What a pleasant surprise!" he commented. "I usually just see 'down' people, sick people or those who have a complaint."

I wonder if we forget to look to our Great Physician. He is still the same, yesterday, today and forever.

I was sitting recently on the front row of a small church in Colorado between Denver and Grand Junction, pastored by Bruce and Pam Chambers. Just before Pastor Bruce took prayer requests and prayed for the needy, the congregation sang an old classic hymn of the Church: "The Great Physician now is near, the sympathizing Jesus; He stoops the drooping heart to cheer, Oh, hear the voice of Jesus! Sweetest name in seraph's song, sweetest name on mortal tongue! Sweetest carol ever sung! Jesus, blessed Jesus." Jesus is still the same Great Physician, yesterday, today and forever.

At the close of the hymn, they introduced the soloist, Sue Chrisco. She and I have done retreats together, and it was a joy to see Gary and Sue Chrisco and their sons three again.

She sang, by my request, a song she wrote, the modern version of "The Great Physician." In the song she says, "Dr. Jesus, no one has power like You do." He is *ever* present in your need, 24 hours a day, and still makes house calls.

"O Lord my God, I cried out to You, and You healed me" (Psalm 30:2).

"If some people's testimony for Jesus and salvation was as powerful as their faith in Super Glue, we could save the world."

After Carl made this statement he handed me a newspaper clipping. An unnamed person on the medical staff at a hospital had given the story to a reporter. A woman formerly from Yonkers, New York, fed up with her husband's infidelity, caught him drunk and asleep and punished him. She glued his guilty moving parts together, then sealed his shorts with Super Glue. The emergency room had a hard time repairing the damage.

I have repaired several pairs of earrings with the magic potion, myself. A neighbor's visiting relative told me, "While driving through the Smoky Mountains last summer, the top plate of my dentures fell out and onto a rocky ledge and broke. I didn't know a reputable dentist within seven hundred miles. We had neither the time nor the money to look for one, so I put the dentures back together with Super Glue and they held the last four days until we got back to Florida."

I began to muse. I want to talk about *the* Super Glue that is an all purpose product: By Him all things are held together (Colossians 1:17). "Having made known to us the mystery of His will, according to His good pleasure which He purposed in Himself, that in the dispensation of the fullness of the times He might gather together in one all things in Christ, both which are in heaven and which are on earth—in Him" (Ephesians 1:9–10).

"Your mercy, O Lord, will hold me up" (Psalm 94:18). Four angels hold "the four winds of the earth" (Revelation 7:1). That's powerful cement!

"He puts the solitary together in families." He mends marriages. "What God has joined together, let not man separate" (Mark 10:9).

That glue fixes families. It can turn the heart of the father back to the child, and bind or weld the heart of the child back to the father (Malachi 4:6). David said, "My heart is fixed." The Lord mended David's heart.

God can fix anything if you give Him all the pieces. He's all He said He was, and more!

The popularity of Peter and those with him is recorded in chapter 5 of the book of Acts. The people "were all healed." Even when the shadow of Peter was cast upon the sick lying in the streets, they were healed (verses 15 and 16). The high priest and the sect of the Sadducees rose up, captured Peter and his men, and cast them into the common prison. What a contrast to go from being followed by multitudes for your miracles to being placed in a common prison! That's quite a demotion.

Are you in a "common prison"? The prison of boredom, bland routine, living in "an East of Egypt" remote place? Many young mothers are removed from the marketplace where they have worked with the public and now feel trapped by love to remain home, talking baby talk and wiping runny noses and small "behinds" all day. Sometimes I feel I am a prisoner of the clock or a slave to television.

I talked with a thirty-year-old woman who told me her feelings: "The media wants me informed. Hollywood wants me beautiful, advertisements demand me thin. My husband wants me passionate. The kids want me home. I love who I am, but sometimes I feel as though I'm in prison."

It is not so much the hard trials, the crises or emergencies, but the cares of life that press in on us, that crowd out our time for the Lord and dull the lustre of life.

I heard a joke that encourages us not to give up: "Keep smiling through the rain and the storm. At least you'll have clean teeth."

Peter's story has a good ending. "An angel of the Lord opened the prison doors and brought them out" (Acts 5:19). After beating them for good measure, the council let them go about their joyful business of proclaiming the Gospel.

If you are suffering in some common prison, persevere. It can be done, and you can do it! Survival with God is not hanging on by our thumbs and arriving at the end of our trial all tattered and torn, but thriving in the supernatural power of the Holy Spirit, riding the wind triumphantly and victoriously.

"Through God we will do valiantly" (Psalm 60:12).

July 10   *The 25-Year Dream That Didn't Die*

Marla's grandparents, the Pavliks, immigrated to this country and built a modest cottage on Lake Geneva near Salem, Illinois. Their cooking and hospitality made their home a natural "bed and breakfast."

Marla's parents had a hard time keeping her out of the water. They strapped her into her little chair on the beach. They have her baby picture where she walked into the water with the chair still strapped to her waist.

At six, she won her first blue ribbon for a 25-meter race off the pier in Williams Bay. At age sixteen she worked with the water safety patrol and spent six years lifeguarding and teaching others to swim. The summer of 1960 she and her friend watched the sunset on Lake Geneva. Marla stated her dream: "Some day I'm going to swim the eight and a half miles across this lake, nonstop."

Time moved on, but the dream stuck. She married, went to college, had three children, taught school, and returned to the lakeside to play with her children. A spiritually and physically aware person, Marla often turned to the lake and fond memories to get her through a painful divorce.

She decided to take the plunge and started training the winter of 1981–1982. She visualized herself first coming into the water, becoming almost a part of the water and then, at the end, walking out of the lake.

August 18, 1982, dawned sunny and hot. Her seventy-year-old mother asked, "You're really going to do this?" Her friend Sonia rowed a boat alongside for support. The first part of the 8.5-mile swim went fairly smoothly. Then came the Narrows and the wind. Big whitecaps challenged the swimmer and caused an unexpected case of seasickness. People in boats cheered her on. Schools of minnows swam alongside her. "Suddenly the thrill . . . the sandy bottom . . . and I walked out." It had taken her 6 hours and 25 minutes. On August 11, 1983, her second swim, she finished in 5 minutes less than 6 hours.

Hold onto your dreams. Tuck them easily into your subconscious bed of hope. Let your seed thoughts germinate. Then cultivate them into realities.

I received two letters the same morning. One was asking, the other telling. Consider the contrast with me.

The first letter was scented with a pleasant fragrance and on an impressive letterhead. Inside was the photo of a daintily groomed young man. He was entering a hair styling contest in Paris, France, and wondered if I would be so kind as to donate $1,000 to help make it possible. I turned the letter over, and scribbled a little crazy note: "Let's have some fun at my expense. I have two kids in college and my husband is raising funds to enable him to return to Russia to teach, preach and feed the hungry. I would ask *you* for a donation of $1,000, but I won't. You keep your thousand dollars, and I'll keep mine. O.K.?"

The other letter was from Pearl Beeman Kabanuk. She heard of a student with no family who had dropped out of college because of bone marrow cancer. She wrote to express her availability and willingness to mother that student, and nurse her without charge until she died. (Pearl was a practical nurse). She told me that she had married a fine Canadian minister and he would be willing to father and pastor the girl in their home in Idaho.

I first met "Mom Beeman" sixteen years before, when, as a widow, she applied for the position as dorm mom for freshmen girls at Trinity Bible College. In exchange for this job, she got a modest salary, free meals and housing for herself and her daughter, enabling Sandy to attend the college at no expense. She dedicated her time and love. God has rewarded her faithfulness. One of her daughters married a fine teacher/missionary now serving overseas.

Jesus is saying, "Pearl will not lose her reward for her willingness." "You clothed the naked. You took Me in when I was sick, a stranger, both thirsty and hungry."

They asked Jesus, "When did we do all that?"

He replied, "As you have done it to the least of these, you have done it unto Me. You shall not lose your reward." (See Matthew 25:37–40.)

Our God has all the strength you will ever need for every day and every occasion. "Your God has *commanded* your strength" (Psalm 68:28). To command is to set up a rule of strength for your action. If God has commanded your strength, then why are you weak today?

John Weaver, an elderly minister in England, visited his good friend Mrs. Kriswell. "How are you today?" he inquired of her.

"I'm weak," she informed him.

"But the Word promises that your strength shall be as your day."

"Then I guess I can't expect much as I am past ninety."

"No," he said, "That's not what the Word means. His strength does not depend on your age, but will be ample to meet the demands that your day makes on you, every day, even in the 'every-day' mundane things of life."

At any age, when demands are made on your strength, God's strength will be adequate.

In family. A lot of strength is needed and expended to rear a family, to support it and to train and nurture your children. His strength will help you then. Pray, ask for it.

In fellowship. If you need strength to help you get along with your mate and to get along with others, to be accepted, His strength is adequate. Just fighting for life in this fast-moving world can cause our natural strength to run low. His supply of strength is always ample.

In fruitfulness. Strangely enough you need His strength during prosperity. There is an illusion to success, "Beware and pray for a steady hand not to spill the cup when it is too full."

He increases strength to cope! Pray: "Strengthen, O God, that which You have wrought for us." He commands strength from His source according to your schedule to meet the demands of what He has planned for your life.

Thy God, or Eloihim, is a name used by the blessed Triune God. Father, Son and Holy Spirit represent themselves under oath, to be your ample supply. In your weakness or old age, God is still ample. In any sphere in which there is demand for strength, He will display His strength in anything that He has wrought (planned) for you.

The Christian path is sometimes difficult, even thorny and stoney. Joseph's situation was "the pits." But God's strength was ample and he was delivered from the pit to a position of rulership and prosperity for himself and to the preserving of his family and his nation.

Paul tapped the ample source of God's strength. He said, "I can cope with all things through Christ who enables me." God doesn't want any weaklings. Remember the children of Israel in the wilderness? For forty years, the Bible tells us, there was *not one* weak or feeble among them on that long foot journey. Outside of Christ, you are vulnerable to Satan and you are no match for his evil power, but *you have ample source through the supernatural strength of the creator God.*

"He gives power to the weak, and to those who have no might He increases strength" (Isaiah 40:29). Ask Him, then rely!

July 14   Tough Trio: Nehemiah, Dan and Zeke

When you mention strong men of the Bible, most people think of Samson. I want to talk about three other tough men. These men confirm British John Weaver's comment that "God never prepares the ministry for the man, but prepares the man for the ministry."

Nehemiah, whose name means "Jehovah has comforted," had a job to do and God's strength was sufficient. This man stood on a large wall around the city. With masonry tools in one hand and a sword in the other, God equipped him to build and fight, either, or, sometimes both. He didn't back down, didn't come down, but just kept on going in the power of the Lord and the strength of His might. He told the tempters and those who wanted him to come down and debate intellectual matters, "I am building a wall; therefore, I cannot come down." He stuck to his assignment, steady, unwavering, in God's adequate, ample supply of strength.

Daniel was strong in faith, and God came through for him when he needed mental strength and courage, even protection in the lion's den. His name means, "God is my judge."

Ezekiel means, "My God strengthens." Zeke found himself in a foreign country. He was shaky and afraid. He lay down by the rushing mighty River Kebar, and something more rushing and powerful than that river happened to Ezekiel. The heavens opened and he saw visions of God. The hand of the Lord was upon him. He saw a side view of the messenger, but he got a full view of the message.

God is our very present strength in need. His supply is supernatural, creative, always ample and adequate. His strength is yours.

The babies and old people at Dunedin Assembly love Karen Siddle. She worked with Carl as associate pastor and family counselor. Her sense of humor, love for God and love for people are contagious.

One older lady expressed concern about Karen. "She drives that old Chrysler convertible around with the top down at night. She lives alone, and travels around the country speaking, alone in motels in strange places. I'm afraid for her. Isn't she afraid?"

"She says she's not afraid," I responded. "She has employed four body guards, two who walk in front and two who walk behind her, accompanying her everywhere she goes." Now, we know that she went to college, had a large school bill to pay, taught school for a while, worked with the church for modest wages. How could she afford to pay four body guards?

Two invisible angels, one named Goodness and one named Mercy, walk behind her. As the Twenty-Third Psalm says, "Surely goodness and mercy shall follow me all the days of my life; and I will dwell in the house of the Lord forever." Guess she's right. She practically lives at the church!

Psalm 25:21 describes the two body guards that go before her: "Let integrity and uprightness preserve me."

If our ways please the Lord, we need not be afraid. He can even cause our enemies to be at peace with us. "The angel of the Lord encamps all around those who fear Him, and delivers them" (Psalm 34:7).

The three oldest Perkins kids were a different lot. My brother Jim and I loved to eat. My brother Don hated food, would even hide at meal time. Jim and I arrived early and stayed at the table late. We laughingly told folks, "Our parents pay Don to eat. They pay us to quit."

Don was thin and listless. One year he grew four and a half inches in height, but had leg cramps and was vulnerable to colds and flu. Our mother was a conscientious cook and prepared well-balanced meals, but could not tempt Don to eat properly.

He would whine and beg, and she would eventually give in and let him have what he asked for, instead of what he really needed. His two favorite sandwiches were mayonnaise sandwiches and sugar sandwiches: two slices of white bread with mayonnaise or two slices of white bread, the center fat with butter and lots of sugar. I saw him as a little fellow climb onto the middle of the table and eat dry, gritty sugar with a spoon.

God gave the Israelites in the wilderness "their request, but sent leanness into their soul" (Psalm 106:15). Watch your diet, else your soul will get skinny.

Now that Don is older, he eats what he needs instead of what he wants and has developed into a mature man.

God shall supply all your needs, not your greeds! When you pray, making your requests known to your heavenly Father, add a P.S. to your petition. This is the way Jesus prayed. "Father, I'd rather this cup be taken away from Me. However, not My will but Thine be done."

Father knows best!

Elijah "walked his talk." He trusted His God. He wasn't intimidated by the wicked King Ahab. He refused to denounce the true and living God for political reasons, leaving both Ahab and his witchy wife Jezebel both to God's judgment and their fate.

But at one point on his journey Elijah "hit bottom," was depressed, afraid and wanted to die. When he lay down under his burden and gave up, the Lord spoke to him and told him to go to the Brook Cherith: "I have commanded the ravens to feed you there." Now Elijah could have gone wherever he chose, but God gave the ravens order to deliver Elijah's food *there*, and if he wanted to be sustained, he better find *there*.

Now ravens are filthy foul fowls. I am sure Elijah squirmed, being a Jew and hating that which is unclean. But the ravens brought him two meals a day of meat and bread, and he drank from the brook's fresh running stream. (See 1 Kings 17:4–5.)

You may be seeking direction, wondering, Where is *my* there? Don't strain, just train. People expend too much energy trying to find God's will. Relax. The power of God is not that marginal. His will will find you. God is always aware of your need. When you don't know where God is, you can be sure that He always knows where you are. In the words of the hymn, "Be not dismayed whate'er betide, God will take care of you!"

Later when Elijah was nearly famished, the Lord told him to go to a widow's home. She and her son were nearly starved, but she was making pancakes from her last bit of meal and oil. She fixed pancakes without syrup and served Elijah first. That investment in God's man was a two-way street. The miraculous took over. Her barrel of meal never ran over, but it never ran out, and her cruise of oil never went low. (See 1 Kings 17:9–14.)

This Elijah story is getting better! The first waitress was a raven. The second cook after the brook, was a widow with almost no food. Soon after these two events, during a time when he was hungry and faint and had fallen asleep, God sent an *angel chef* who baked a cake, brought him a jug of water, tapped his shoulder, awakened him. Elijah jumped up, ate the meal, went on that angel food for forty days. (See 1 Kings 19:6–8.)

That's nutrition!

You can go around the world with your praying. I know "little old ladies" who give $15 to God's work out of their Social Security checks each month, and who sit in their little maple rockers, praying, moving the "hand of God," writing the news.

When you hear the bad news on television, don't cluck and grind your teeth. Kings cannot do what they want to do; they must do what God wants. Put your hand on your television set as a gesture of reaching out to the people you see there in need and pray for the nations. God is still in charge of the evening news.

My ninety-year-old mother-in-law, Dorothy Upchurch, has given Carl $20 on two occasions to buy "The book of Life" at $1.50 a copy translated into the Russian language. She sits in her little trailer on Gulf to Bay, yet is a missionary to the Soviet Union, Latvia, Ukraine and Siberia. She prays daily, and sends her energy to searching humanity by that powerful medium—prayer.

When you read the newspaper and the news is doom and gloom, lay your hand on the paper and pray for the parties involved in sorrow and grief. You can make a difference, help write history!

I know of three groups of unknown, ordinary people, with extraordinary hope and faith in the power of prayer, that joined others in praying for the walls in Germany to come down. They prayed each morning at eight A.M. during the Desert Storm conflict. God heard and answered both prayers, turned the tide, brought order out of chaos.

"He makes wars cease to the end of the earth" (Psalm 46:9). God is still in charge of the nations. Charge your heart to pray!

No wonder Mary, Queen of Scotts, said, "I am more afraid of the prayers of John Knox than of all the armies of Europe."

Be *God's* anchor man. Pray!

Shortly before Catherine Marshall's death, I was visiting in their winter home at Boynton Beach, Florida, and spoke at a Methodist church nearby at Del Ray. The pianist was late, so Catherine slipped to the piano and played for the congregation to sing, "Blessed assurance, Jesus is mine!"

In the car on the way home I remarked, "I know you play the typewriter keys, but I didn't know until today that you play the piano keys, too." She told me that "Blessed Assurance" was her favorite of all songs. That assurance is essential when you face death. We had no idea that she would die near St. Patrick's Day some time after that.

She also told me a funny story. I believe it was her little granddaughter, Mary Elizabeth, whom she overheard singing with gusto in the congregation: "Blessed insurance, Jesus is mine. Oh, what a good taste of glory divine." It may have been a misquote, but it certainly was a good quote. The Bible tells us to believe on the Lord Jesus Christ and be baptized in His name. That baptismal certificate is a sort of policy guarantee of eternal life through Christ.

Those certificates have come in handy for other purposes also. I know one woman who had lied so long about her age, that when she wanted to apply for Social Security, she wondered if she really qualified. The first place she checked was that certificate. It was dated and bore her name and age at the time of her baptism.

If you don't have that blessed assurance, stop now and ask Jesus to be your Lord. Perhaps you were so busy when you were baptized or confirmed that you did not get all God intended you to have. Make your salvation secure.

Once you have done so, don't be pushy, but also don't be backward about asking others if they have the blessed assurance of eternal life. They may be waiting for someone to point the way. Christian doctors have told me that many patients linger between life and death, seemingly waiting for someone to lead them through the sinner's prayer, then they die peacefully.

Our friend Paul Priddy in Pasadena, Texas, has given us a guideline that he uses to approach people about life's most important decision. If he doesn't know the person, he asks, "Do you know if anyone has ever prayed for you in your whole life?" If they answer no, then he asks, "Will you let me pray for you, with you, now?" They almost always say yes.

Presidents do it! You can do it. They declare holidays and impose them upon us, depriving us of postal service and banking hours. If they can do it, you may as well do it too. Declare a holiday!

I live an exciting life. Since I first said yes to Jesus and He gave me a second chance at life, and since I started saying yes to Him each morning when I awaken, I have never been bored.

I have found a lustre about life, and love what I do, but most of my waking hours, though filled with thrilling challenges, are spent meeting the demands of my family, the public and publishers. You can actually be "standing dead" from being overstimulated; numb and bored from the whirlwind of too much to do.

I picked up the Bible and found the solution. When Jesus and the disciples were overworked and underpaid, He said to them "Come ye yourselves apart into a desert place *and rest for a while* (Mark 6:31). (Or, as I say, "Either come apart or fall apart!") I decided at that instant to declare a weekly holiday for myself, to come apart and rest, for fun and flavor. I called my dad, "Daddy, what day was I born?"

"Why, November sixth."

"No, I know the date, I'm asking for the *day*."

"Oh. O.K. You were born early on a Wednesday morning."

I announced Wednesday as my weekly break day, my declared, private, personal holiday. Even if only for two hours, I would do something selfish for me, or just for fun. If I am in bad shape, I take the whole day. When I go back to my work it has new meaning, like the rest in the rhythm of music is the pleasing break of anticipation for the next strain of song.

I'm glad that the Great Commission gives permission for an intermission. Take one. Try it. It works. God usually speaks to us in "the *still* small voice." Nothing can so touch our hearts as the power of stillness.

When we cease from our works, God works in us.

Saturation point: That threshold of tolerance, margin of patience, better known, in common language, as that stomach-turning point. I once heard a nurse say, "You may use my husband, you may use my station wagon, but you may not use my comb. That's where I draw the line."

About ten years ago Jack and Carol Acuff attended our family reunion along with their energetic four-year-old son, Colm (an Irish name). He was so cute, and knew how to have fun! If you haven't lived with a four-year-old, you haven't yet lived! They are self-confident, ask a lot of questions, yet know all the answers.

Colm's mother Carol would let him express himself, give him rein and plenty of leash, up to a point. Then she would pull him up short with a secret, coded signal. It was one word: "Enough!" (He knew what she meant.)

Our loving, heavenly Father is kind to his children, but there is a place where the God of mercy draws the line. The Egyptians pressed their luck when they pressed the Israelites, God's children, to produce more work than they were capable of doing. God said, "Enough," and Moses led them out of that place of bondage to a land of plenty, milk and honey.

God created Adam and Eve and put them in a natural paradise. Mankind became perverted, resorted to the unnatural use of the body, and God said to Sodom and Gomorrah, "Enough," and rained down fire and brimstone and destroyed them.

Jannes and Jambres were magicians who withstood Moses, God's leader, by duplicating some of his miraces (2 Timothy 3:8–9). "Enough," God said. Sometimes God cut offenders off "till there was no remedy" (2 Chronicles 36:16).

"Because the sentence against an evil work is not executed speedily, therefore the heart of the sons of men is fully set in them to do evil" (Ecclesiastes 8:11).

I believe that "the cup of iniquity" is about full again in history. The heart of God is sad at the perversion, spiritual wickedness in high places, unholy living. God's mercy will have reached His holy tolerance level.

Jesus will return to the earth to take away those that are looking for Him. God will say, "Enough, come up a little higher." We will be gone, and the wrath of God will be poured out on the unbelievers left behind.

A wealthy oil man in Houston before the oil crisis told Carl and me, "It's truly lonely at the top. Even fellows I graduated from high school with come to visit and I think 'Good. Now here's someone who's genuinely interested in me, not my money.' But not long into the visit, I learn that they came to see my oil fields and my horses, not me. You don't really know who your true friends are. And when you think that you've found one, you find they are interested in what you can do for them, give them or loan them."

One of our relatives was a money making fool. He worked too-long hours and gave his family everything, but they suffered because they didn't have *him*. I overheard a conversation one evening: "Here, darling," he said to his little girl. "Take this ten dollars. Have Mother take you to the mall and buy you something." The daughter threw the money on the floor and screeched, "I don't want your money. I want you."

Once when I was hospitalized briefly and stayed in a four-bed ward I met a woman who told me, "I was unconscious for two weeks with pneumonia. During that time my daughter and son sat in my room, not knowing that comatose people can hear, and quarreled over my money and real estate. My son remarked, 'I don't hope to get as much as you will get when Mother dies. You have always been her favorite.' Well," Ida said, "I fooled them both. I got well and changed my will!" She got the best of the situation, but it was a lonely one for her.

I believe it is lonely at the top for the Lord. Most people only show God love for a handout. But 2 Chronicles 7:14–16 says, "If My people will . . . seek My face . . . I will hear from heaven, and will forgive their sin and heal their land. Now My eyes will be open and my ears attentive." (Let's face up to it: Many people seek God only in a bind, for healing or material gain, not loving His face, but opening His hand.)

Want God to be intimate with you? Seek His face first, then He will open His hand. "At [His] right hand are pleasures forevermore" (Psalm 16:11).

It was the sweet voice of the flight attendant: "Thank you for choosing [better unnamed] airlines." Choosing, did we have a choice? If you wanted to go anywhere from Watertown, South Dakota, you had no choice. After you fastened your seat belt, the elevator music overhead played, "On the Wings of Love." The last song before take off was "I'd Die for You, Girl!" Then that heavy, old, fat-looking plane, which we lovingly called 'The Blue Goose,' shuddered and shook and lifted safely skyward. It sounded like a cement mixer and had the feel of a cheap vibrator.

My air traffic controller brother, Marvin, informed me that that old Army plane was probably the safest old bird in the sky. I still have my doubts.

When you sat in the front row you faced the rest of the passengers and flew backward. It was more of a thrill (make that, chill) than some of the rides at Disney World. One full flight, all the seats were taken and I was compelled to sit by an elderly gent who was very ill and insisted on talking to me non-stop. When I told him I needed to sleep he quarreled with his invisible enemy named Gordon.

Now that I have moved and fly out of Tampa I still prefer that airline because of the perks. You get a free round trip ticket for each 20,000 air miles. Others require 40,000. Why do I keep flying when I hate to dress up and despise travel? The perks. It's rewarding to travel around and tell my story and relieve the fear of death from the hearts of listeners. David killed Goliath in part for the perks. He never had to pay taxes again and got to marry the king's daughter. Jesus endured the cross, despising the shame to save us, then sat with His Father on heaven's throne.

Endure. Heaven is worth it!

I grew up in the state of Indiana and the state of poverty. Mother made our clothes and we rarely took a vacation. I will never forget our first. My brothers and I colored in coloring books and did dot-to-dot in the back of our old Hudson car the whole first day. The second day we watched for road signs indicating how many more miles to the Florida border. In Georgia we spotted a sign: "200 miles ahead . . . Georgia's finest Southern Pecan Pie."

"That's about right," Dad said. "We just had grits for breakfast, a piece of pecan pie would top off a great lunch!"

We were starved, nearly caved in, we waited so long till we found the restaurant advertised all along the highway mile after mile. Sitting down, we ordered the pecan pie even before the entree. "I'm sorry," the waitress informed us. "We don't serve it any more."

"Then you'd better take down your signs," my dad suggested, a bit loudly. What a disappointment!

If you're a singer, then let's hear you sing. If you're an auctioneer, then sound off. People say they are married yet don't act like it. I know parents who have quit parenting. Being a stud does not make you a father. A mother is not merely a baby incubator. Many bear titles without qualifying. Flattery can be a form of false advertising. He who praises everyone, praises no one. When everyone becomes someone, then nobody is really anybody. Jesus said, "Beware when all men speak well of you." It seems that nearly every item marketed today is described in unbelievable superlatives. But all too often it turns out that what is billed as "the world's greatest spot-remover" destroys the fabric as well. After a while, you don't believe anything the "ad techs" say.

Not so with the Bible. It tells us many things we *can* know. It is the greatest "doubt remover" in this world. "You may know that you have eternal life" (1 John 5:13). That blessed assurance carries a "lifetime" guarantee.

Naaman was a great man of valour, an honorable captain of the host of the king of Syria. When it was discovered that he had leprosy, his wife's maid told him about Elisha's gifts of healing.

Naaman approached Elisha, who wasn't impressed by his high-ranking status. Instead of making a royal house call, he merely FAXed a message, "Go and wash in the River Jordan seven times and your flesh will come again to you, and you shall be clean."

"That's ridiculous!" Naaman yelled. He was wroth. "That river is filthy and that prophet is mad. He didn't even have the courtesy to come talk to me."

Years ago people thought that moldy cheese was a ridiculous way to cure infection too, but penicillin changed their minds. If a formula works, don't fix it. Why do you think God instructed Elisha to give the formula to dip 7 times? "Delayal" is not denial. There were seven lessons to be learned.

Don't formulate. Naaman formulated how it should be done. Not the River Jordan, but a cleaner river in Damascus, perhaps the Abana or Pharpar.

Don't designate. He took silver, gold and garments to buy his cure.

Don't dictate. "When you get this letter," he told Elisha, "call on God, strike your hand over the places and cure Naaman's leprosy."

Don't complicate. Naaman complicated the process by reason.

Don't stipulate. When Naaman tried to stipulate which location he preferred, his own servants dared to approach him. "If he had asked you to do something great, you would have done it. Try it his way."

Don't manipulate. Naaman pulled rank on Elisha. He had the King of Syria write a letter to the King of Israel, instead of humbly requesting prayer from the servant Elisha.

Don't speculate. Finally Naaman stopped speculating, followed the formula and dipped himself seven times as he was told by the man of God. His flesh became like the flesh of a little child. He was clean.

If your situation is incurable, know that God has a thousand ways to work. When you cannot see even one, when all your means have reached their end, His have just begun.

Peggy is a single parent living in southern California with her almost three-year-old, Amber. After working hard one day in the hospital insurance office, she picked Amber up from day care, and unlocked the door to their apartment. "I want a Daddy," Amber stated.

"Jesus is our Daddy," Peggy quickly informed her. As Peggy told me, "I thought my answer had satisfied her young searching mind. She was very quiet for only a brief moment, then, looking up at the picture of Jesus on our wall, she called out loudly, "Jesus, *come home!*"

I seized the opportunity to tell Peggy, "He *is* coming here to get us soon, and we are going to go live with Him at His house." He is a father to the fatherless. We are exhorted to comfort one another with these words: He is coming soon! We become disheartened because we keep forgetting to remember the hope: He is coming soon!

Peggy told me that she was glad that she had attended a single's support group at church. Only recently they had been admonished not to further complicate their lives by seeking a new mate prematurely. Loneliness is better than trouble.

She was also grateful that they had just studied Isaiah 54, "Your Maker is your husband, the Lord of hosts is His name. . . . 'With everlasting kindness I will have mercy on you. . . . This is the heritage of the servants of the Lord, and their righteousness is from Me,' says the Lord" (verses 5, 8, 17).

Who you are does not depend on whom you are married to. Let Jesus make up the differences in your emptiness. He is all sufficient and has the supply for all your need.

Our dentist has two curious posters. "We cater to cowards," says one and "Success is finding a need and *filling* it!"

He asked me once, "Do you think I enjoy having my wrists drooled on, my thumbs slobbered on and my knuckles gnawed? The journey is sometimes distasteful, smelling people's foul breath all week. That's why I only work four days a week. You can only take it so many hours and then you get depressed."

"Then, why do you keep doing what you do?" I quizzed him.

"Along the way there are rewards. It is so gratifying to repair a child's smile, or to rebuild and repair an older person's bite so that he can enjoy food. Then, of course, the end result is the good pay."

A creative woman has displayed her ad on benches at bus stops and on billboards in prominent places: "Hate to clean? Call Maureen." I found a most interesting ad hanging on my door knob when I returned home: "Call the odd couple. We do odd jobs that no one else wants to do. Give us a try. We even do windows." Here are two systems that are working and paying off. They do things you don't want to do, get paid for it, and are making a good living in the meantime.

Life is like licking honey from a thorn. If your work is unpleasant and you are rewarded for it in the end, you can count one blessing. If you love your work and get paid for it, too, count your blessings—you have a double reward. If you enjoy your job, are doing a service to mankind on the journey and get paid well for it, your blessing is triple. You are in the minority. Learn to absorb the sunshine and rest in the cool shadows. Swallow the bitter with the sweet. Can you not accept both good and reprimand from God's providential hand?

The Christian's job is to work like Jesus, to deny ourselves, put away selfishness and serve others. Many times ours is a thankless job, but if in this life only we have hope, we are of all men most miserable. Jesus promises us joy for the journey. "'And behold, I am coming quickly, and My reward is with Me, to give to every one according to his work. . . .' Blessed are those who do His commandments, they may have the right to the tree of life, and may enter through the gates into the city" (Revelation 22:12, 14).

Looking at the clock on the dash of my car, I realized how much the "snow bird" traffic coming into Florida from the north country had further complicated bumper to bumper driving conditions on the already hectic Highway 19. I had an appointment in downtown Clearwater. I was nearly late.

I couldn't believe it. An old model Thunderbird had stopped dead still in the middle of six lanes of traffic while Granddad looked at his map. Cars were driving off into the grass on the right side of the highway, horns honked, folks with their windows down verbalized profanities. These senior "cits" are characters! They congest the highways, teach us patience and remind us that we are next. Up the road, there go I.

The old gent's spouse was waiting patiently at the steering wheel for his indication that she should go on when . . . the "imp" of impatience took over. Before I realized it, I heard my own voice yell out the window of my car, "Move that turtle, Myrtle!" Gramps gave me the finger and Myrtle, or whatever her name was, slowly and undisturbed, moseyed on.

If the devil can't get you to be immoral, drunk, profane, backslidden or a cheat at business, he will rally his imp guerillas of impatience and cause you to wound someone's spirit and bring guilt to your own inner control.

"By your patience possess your souls" (Luke 21:19). How many times I had been aggravated when people ride my bumper, and I feel pushed to drive faster. But I can't go anywhere because there are 28 cars between me and the next stop light, which is only two blocks away. I recall one man's definition: "A split second is the amount of time it takes after the light changes until the car behind you honks."

I often recall living in the Dakotas with nostalgia. There are sixty miles between towns; the roads are sparsely sprinkled with cars; fields of sunflowers, purple alfalfa blooms, acres of golden wheatheads nod lazily in the prairie breeze. We had just one stop light in Elendale, and sometimes it didn't work. The "imp" of impatience has not found that place yet.

The best thing to do if you pick up a piece of hot iron is to drop it. If you want a fire to go out, don't fuel it. It will die on its own. If you have experienced hurt, do not keep on reciting your injustices. To rehearse your hurts is like knocking the scab off a wound over and over again, not letting it heal.

I know a wise wife who was married to a quarrelsome, mouthy man. She told me, "For two years I tried to defend myself, speak up and talk back. I don't mind being misunderstood if they will just let explain my side of the story. Give me my day in court."

Silence is golden. She started keeping silent instead of debating with him. He called her later during the day from his job. "Honey, I could only hear my own hateful voice, and it echoed in my ears, and I don't like the sound of it. Your silence emphasized my overbearing nature. I'm sorry. I promise to bite my tongue from now on, before I ever offend you again."

"Look also at ships: although they are so large and are driven by fierce winds, they are turned by a very small rudder wherever the pilot desires. Even so the tongue is a little member and boasts great things. See how great a forest a little fire kindles!" (James 3:4–5).

Perhaps the reward when we get to heaven will be greater, not for being right, but for being quiet. "Blessed are the peacemakers, for they shall be called children of God" (Matthew 5:9).

Do you realize what that means, to be called the children of God? When God is your Father that means you will inherit all His riches.

Jeff Nelson was youth director for the children of Trinity College's staff members. He was of slight build, quiet manner and married to a real sweetheart. One day he shared with me that he was going to the school of missions in June to prepare for a foreign mission overseas. "When were you called?" I inquired of him.

"I wasn't called," he said. "I volunteered. I personally believe that volunteers make better soldiers than men who have to be drafted."

When I was a little girl during World War II, I thought a draft dodger was the quilted roll that Mother stuck around the window frames to keep out winter's cold windy blast. I remember hearing my granddad tell of a draft dodger in the Allegheny Mountains of Kentucky who, when he received his draft call, replied with a brief postcard: "No, thanks, but I'm not coming to the army. I have a good paying job here in Albany, Kentucky."

There are no draft dodgers, no physical rejects and no conscientous objectors in God's army, just the "whosoever wills." I love singing the marching song: "God's got an army marching through the land. Deliverance is His song, there's healing in His hand. Everlasting joy and gladness in His heart, and in this army, I've got a part!"

Fight the good fight of faith! God is raising up an army of believers to reach this generation for Christ, to make a positive impact on our community and beyond. You are a soldier on maneuvers in preparation for that Grand March through the Pearly Gates into the "Kingdom to Come." Volunteer. Endure hardness as a good soldier.

It is hard and going to get harder, but as Daniel saw in night visions, "One like the Son of Man [was] coming with the clouds of heaven! He came to the Ancient of Days, and they brought Him near before Him. Then to Him was given dominion and glory and a kingdom, that all peoples, nations, and languages should serve Him. His dominion is an everlasting dominion, which shall not pass away, and His kingdom the one which shall not be destroyed" (Daniel 7:13–14).

And in this Kingdom, you and I have a part!

Sunday night after I spoke in his church, the pastor was driving me back to the Kansas City airport. He broke the silence, "What's going to happen to these television evangelists who have sinned, 'prime time,' more than once?"

We discussed Romans 11, which tells us that if they do not turn from their wicked ways they will know the severity of God and be turned into hell. But if they abide not in unbelief and turn from their wicked ways, God is able to graft them in again (verse 23). God warns us about being wise in our own conceit! There is an illusion to success. Because a man has one divine impulse does not mean that all his impulses thereafter are divine.

At the airport, waiting for my flight to depart, I opened my Bible and turned to Romans 11:23. In the margin with bold, blue ink, I wrote the name of three fallen leaders and prayed, "Lord, graft them in again!" Each time I thumb through my New Testament, I put my hand on that Scripture and claim their return and restoration, praying that Jesus will heal their minds.

"For who hath known the mind of the Lord? He is the counsellor." "Seek the Lord while He may be found, call upon Him while He is near. Let the wicked forsake his way, and the unrighteous man his thoughts [lust, spiritual pride, self-satisfaction, immorality, greed]; let him return to the Lord, and He will have mercy on him; and to our God, for He will abundantly pardon" (Isaiah 55:6–19).

The Lord has told us, "My thoughts are not your thoughts and My ways are higher than your ways."

"It's no disgrace to be this way, but it sure is unhandy!" That is a quote from Harold Bowden whose job description is: paraplegic and full-time wheelchair driver. He wrote us this letter.

Dear Carl and Betty,

I came home from surgery at the University of North Carolina Medical Center, a fullblown paraplegic, with all the physical problems that are a part of the package. But the beautiful side of it is that my difficulties and weakness have afforded a platform upon which the Lord can display His power. I don't consider myself a para or even think about it. He took all the trauma away and has given me peace of mind. I think my condition bothers others more than it does me.

Now that God has seen fit to deliver me from the terrible burning and spasms, I can sleep at night without ice packs, enabling me to keep busy and enjoy the day. "Do something," I told myself. Then I told the Lord, "I want to leave my mark in life. Guide me. Provide me an assignment to serve you and others. I want to be remembered for my work for you." I have spent full days. I have written four articles and write letters to shut-ins. I make phone calls to the lonely, and mostly let them talk. God has given me a compassion to understand the lonely, sick and suffering.

I go to church on Sunday determined to touch as many people as I can wheel toward. The faces of the elderly light up when I come to them and not expect them to comfort me. Of course all of this would not be possible were it not for my lifeline, my "wife line," Pauline. If anything would happen to her, I'd be in a whole heap of trouble, big time.

I have built a small shop here at home where I do some gun repair, engraving, carving powder horns, and have developed the art of scrimshaw.

Life begins with a cry and ends with a sigh. Our lives are but a vapor that appears for a little time and then vanishes away (James 4:13–17). Have you noticed the dash that appears between the birth date and the death date on tomb stones? What have your done with your in-between?

Thanks Harold, for leaving your mark, making us laugh a little, think a lot.

When St. Francis of Assisi was asked, "How may I acquire the intimacy with God to do miracles as you do?" he replied quickly, "Three things are necessary. The first essential is humility, the second is humility and the third is humility."

Being humble does not mean being a doormat. Only people with dirty feet appreciate doormats. Being humble is not looking dowdy, cast down or frumpy. Phillips Brooks, the nineteenth-century Boston preacher, said, "The true way to be humble is not to stoop until you are lower than yourself, but to stand at your full height against some higher nature that will show you the smallness of your greatness."

"Whoever exalts himself will be humbled" (Matthew 23:12). As Kate Oaks said, "A stiff neck usually supports an empty head. A narrow mind and a wide mouth usually go together. So it is better to be pruned to grow than to be cut to burn." Who was it who said, "I never get lost; someone is always telling me where to go"?

Amos Parrish was thought a proud man. One of his friends described walking with him along the ridge near Tuscon, Arizona, and there learned what real humility was. A. P. said, "Look at those mountains. The sun is setting and the desert is turning from lavender to deep purple. Generations of people have lived and died in the shadow of these ancient mountains. I am humbled and learn how small I really am, and how brief my life is when compared to God's mountains."

The friend told of another time when they walked from the University Club in New York City, across the East Fifties when A. P. said, "Stop and look up at that building." Pointing to a skyscraper on the corner of Park Avenue, A. P. noted that it looked like a tall ladder of windows reaching toward the sky. They couldn't see the top. "Now and then I stop and look at one of those buildings. It gives me a perspective about how big I really am."

It was almost sundown and I should not have gone all the way to the end of the island. I had not allowed for the time change and was caught almost at the tip of Honeymoon Island, with a return trip of a mile and a half, when it dawned on me: *They close the gate at the guard station at sundown. All I need is to be stranded out here all night in a pink bathing suit.*

I sprinted for a shortcut between the sand dunes topped with huge plumes of pampas grass. As I stepped between them, a black figure loomed out of the water! I gasped. No need to scream; there was no one else around to hear or help.

It is strange what runs through your mind in an emergency. Tammy Bakker said that she had been fearful most of her life. One day she decided to attack her fears, and when any lion roared at her, she "ran at the roar." So instead of running from that black shadow, I turned and learned that was exactly what it was—a shadow in the early twilight . . . mine.

Fear hath torment. I had been frightened not by a reality, but by a shadow.

There are good shadows. Peter was so filled with the Holy Spirit that his shadow passed over passersby and they were healed.

Walking back, I thought of Pastor Casey's Wednesday night Bible study. "The fear of man brings a snare" (Proverbs 29:25). He taught two truths: the fear of what man thinks of me, and the fear of what man can do to me.

The shadow at the beach was a mirage. This week another shadow loomed larger, in my path of progress while writing, blocking my creativity. For some time now I have noticed that I bruise easily. I almost panicked. Mother died with liver cancer, and the first symptoms were bruising easily and internal bleeding.

Satan is the author of fear, and I rebuked him in Jesus' name; then I "ran at the roar" to Mease Hospital and had a blood test. The findings: I'm 62. My skin is aging, my arms are thin. The skin on them is thin. It is normal to have bleeding under the skin when I bump them . . . just another shadow.

Avoid hasty conclusions and snap judgments. Things are not always as they seem. Once I had to stay after the Wednesday night prayer service for choir rehearsal. Carl took our five-year-old daughter home to tuck her into bed for an early night's sleep. On the way home he treated her to a piece of French silk chocolate pie.

The following morning I asked her, "Did you and Dad have a good time last night while I practiced?"

"Yes. I liked that good pie, but Daddy flirted with the pretty waitress. I didn't like that. He shouldn't have done that, Mommy."

"What did he say?"

"He said, 'Hi,' and when we left he gave her a dollar."

This was a misunderstanding from an immature mind. Carl and I winked at each other and had a good laugh.

He and I bowled on a league team one season. While our team member Rob was at the lane, he turned to see his new bride, Kendra, leaning close, whispering in the ear of an excellent bowler who happened to be much better looking than Rob. Without hesitation, explanation or even a goodbye, Rob drove home and left Kendra without transportation. Jealousy and misunderstanding had blinded him to the fact that they were planning a surprise birthday party for *him* the following Tuesday night.

The real culprit that caused the devastating damage was not the initial skirmish. The bomb that caused permanent damage to Kendra's sensitive, young, already wounded spirit was the harsh, angry barrage that followed. Rob dug up quotes from in-laws and quarrels from their dating days. He had been saving green stamps and cashed in a whole book that night, at one time.

The Bible says there are three things that cannot be recalled, brought back or returned: a shot arrow, youth, or a sharp word spoken in haste. "Their tongue is an arrow shot out; it speaks deceit; one speaks peaceably to his neighbor with his mouth, but in his heart he lies in wait" (Jeremiah 9:8).

Let's not lie in wait to make snap judgments.

Today we have microwave ovens, the ultimate time-saver. But when I was small, Mother had a pressure-cooker. It cut cooking time in half and made meat twice as tender. They could have been dangerous but for the safety valve.

Every busy man or woman needs a safety valve. Lowell Lundstrom, his wife, Connie, and their four children live and travel on a large bus, evangelizing, preaching and singing at mostly one-night rallies. Lowell says that when he is frustrated and overwhelmed with "stressure and press," when the bus is running a tight schedule and Connie is hard at work compiling another new cookbook, his release or safety valve is to shift his brain into neutral and think of something ridiculous.

If you are suffering from compassion fatigue or leadership burnout, get a grip on yourself. . . . No, better still, *Get a grip on God*. One who walks with God always knows what direction he or she is going. "When the righteous are in authority, the people rejoice; but when a wicked man rules, the people groan" (Proverbs 29:2). "Blessed are those who keep His testimonies, who seek Him with the whole heart. They walk in His ways" (Psalm 119:2–3).

God never leads us to a dead end, but helps us turn a corner. Simon Cameron wisely said, "He would not have taught me to trust in His name, and brought me this far to put me to shame."

In order to be on time, I carried my shoes in one hand, rushed down to the car where Carl was revving his engine, buttoned my blouse and brushed my hair in the car. Carl is obsessed with two great virtues. They are:

1. Integrity. (I personally believe that you can avoid deliberate transgression without becoming a prisoner of impressions.)
2. Punctuality. (He believes that "anything worth doing is worth doing fast," and that "if you can't be pretty, you can be punctual.")

Carl is a natural born preacher. He has a marvelous tone quality and volume to his voice. Driving toward St. Petersburg, he was preaching, teaching, coaching; "Idiots, driving 10 m.p.h. in a 35-mile zone. Don't back up now, he's so slow. The light's red today, it'll be green tomorrow. Look at her use her right turn signal to turn left. Women . . . the only thing you know when they use a signal is that they're going to do *something*." I wish I had brought my recorder. It would have made a hilarious monologue. I was the only one enjoying this one-man entertainment show.

He started to pass a station wagon when suddenly the wagon turned left in front of us and into the turning lane. Carl braked, and just missed the man's back bumper.

"How did you get your license?" he yelled. "Didn't they teach you to use turn signals?"

I was glad the windows were rolled up so the man couldn't hear.

"Maybe his left turn signal is burned out," I suggested.

"Then he could use his left arm for a hand signal; his arm is not burned out," Carl retorted.

A minute later when we did pass him, we saw a sticker on his license, *Disabled Veteran*. Looking in the window we saw that his arm was not burned out, but was indeed amputated at the shoulder. He had no left arm.

Carl's next words were repentance. "God, forgive me. Betty, I apologize for harsh words that you had to hear. This is not kind, not even Christian." He quoted Romans 12:10: 'In honor giving preference to one another.'"

Look before you leap and think before you speak.

The phone rang. I picked up the receiver of my second telephone and heard only a shrill whistling sound. I hung up. It rang again, but the same thing happened.

After four such calls, I had had it with that "new fangled, dangled apparatus"! I unplugged it, that nuisance complete with memory dial and the works. It was too temperamental. Every time it thunders or lightnings, it malfunctions. I disconnected the answering machine attachment, walked down the hallway and trashed it in the garbage bin.

When the phone rang again, I went into the kitchen and picked up my old faithful phone, which is practical but not pretty, functional but not fancy. The call came through loud and clear with no shrill whistling. Good choice. Even if I returned the fancy phone, the process would undoubtedly require explaining, justifying, wrangling, waiting for a claim or, worse yet, applying for a replacement. To save time, I did the right thing by trashing it, it saved me lots of time.

But the following morning as I walked down the street to put out the big black garbage bag for the "sanitation engineer," I thought, *Should I give that phone one more chance? It did cost $79.*

Back up the stairs I went and plugged it in. I called my number from the kitchen, hung up and let it ring through the troublesome phone. This time it was fine and clear. It turned out that the phone installer had been on a pole by my house splicing a new line and finishing just as I gave credit to the old phone for being good.

So don't throw in the towel. In anger I almost lost a good phone by giving up too soon. Both my phones are now functioning beautifully.

"He who is slow to anger is better than the mighty, and he who rules his spirit than he who takes a city" (Proverbs 16:32).

Following a Christmas wedding in Indiana years ago, my brother Marvin carried Sharon, his sweet little blonde Hoosier bride, across the threshold of their blue, four-room house at 310 Pennsylvania Avenue, Crystal Beach, Florida. They painted the interior with bright shades of orange, and landscaped together with a hedge of red, "Turk's Cap" around the front yard and lined the short driveway with palms.

When Marv showered that evening before bed, he noticed his wedding ring was missing. Perhaps he had laid it on the lavatory. No. He called work to see if he had left it on his desk at Honeywell, or even in the men's room. Both he and Sharon, with the aid of a flashlight, searched among the tools in the storage shed, the carport, and even crawled around the driveway and by the hedge on their hands and knees.

The wedding ring was missing. He was still married, of course, and they were still in love, but the token of that love was gone. Perhaps it would be found. Marv had taken an engraving tool and inscribed his name, a brief quote and a phone number inside the gold band.

Five years later a neighbor asked if Marvin would give him a start of those beautifully blooming, bright red Turk's Cap bushes. They were now too thick and needed thinning, so Marv and the neighbor took spades and began digging up every fifth bush. When Marv lifted the third one from the ground, he heard a clinking sound from the shovel, metal against metal, and saw a flash of bright gold in the rich black soil. It had been five years, but his wedding ring had not been lost, just badly misplaced. What a joy, what find!

Don't give up on those who have fallen from grace. They are never out of God's sight (see Psalm 139:7–12). God is married to the backslider. We give up on them too soon. You may not know where God is, but the Lord is always aware of where you are (see Psalm 46:1, Isaiah 41:10 and Matthew 28:20). He is always near and will never leave us.

Wednesday night after prayer meeting, my friend Rena Van Patton asked how this devotional book was coming. "Let the Lord help you write this one," she encouraged me. "Don't forget you are yoked to a strong man and teamed up with a weightlifter."

We pick up unnecessary burdens instead of the prayer burdens God wants us to bear. He will bear the burden and the heat of the day, so our side of the yoke is easy. What a delightful sense of freedom ensues when we realize we have only to keep half of the bargain. He will always keep His half.

God neither slumbers nor sleeps, so we need not lie awake nights trying to figure out "how." My side of the yoke is to commit; then I can go serenely on with my other business, knowing that my weightlifter teammate can be relied on to carry more than His part of the load. "Commit thy way unto the Lord, and He shall bring it to pass" (Psalm 37:5).

I need not pry into His workings, for He is bound by His Word to fulfill desires that have grown out of my delight in my Lord (see Psalm 84:11). I do not have to work things out—just love God, who does the working out. I can sing while He works.

"Abide in me," Jesus said. When you take up residence with Him, everything in His house is yours. "Those who wait on the Lord shall renew their strength" (Isaiah 40:31). If I am weak, I do not need to agonize with Him to make me strong. I need but wait until He starts the pulling from His side of the yoke.

"Be strong in the Lord, and the POWER OF HIS [not your own!] MIGHT" (Ephesians 6:10).

Several years ago I wrote a story about Debbie Barna and her volleyball game. I lost track of her for a while. Then she wrote to tell me that she had moved to North Carolina and asked me to pray that she and Joe would have a baby before her 35th birthday. When her letter arrived, Carl, April and I sat at the lunch table, joined hands and prayed that they would have a child.

Debbie was working as a nurse at a walk-in surgery facility. A woman came in and she and Debbie discovered that they were both Christians. Then the woman apparently felt free to tell Debbie what the Lord was impressing on her, that Isaiah 54 was meant for Debbie personally and that the word of the Lord to her was, "You will have all the children your heart desires."

Despite skepticism about personal messages delivered in this fashion, Debbie did what Mary, the mother of Jesus, did and tucked that secret in her heart. And at the appointed time, Joseph was born healthy and strong. One year later Debbie gave birth to sweet little Maryah. When the doctor found it necessary to tie her tubes, Debbie cried. She wanted more children.

Shortly after that, Joe and Debbie saw a newscast showing three tiny children in Charlotte who had been neglected, then abandoned. They called and asked if they could have them, but were told that the children were being placed in foster care. Filled with love and concern, Debbie and Joe prayed for them.

After a move and in a new church Debbie spotted a woman sitting with a darling little girl. The Lord spoke to Debbie's heart to give her some clothes she had outgrown. The little girl, Debbie learned, was one of three up for adoption. In fact, she was one of the three children publicized on television that Debbie and Joe had so desired and prayed for!

After working with two Social Service departments, battling red tape and waiting nine months, three weeks and one day, a long-overdue arrival of triplets, ages five, four and three, came to live with Debbie and Joe. Now they have five children, ages, five, four, three, two and one!

When this family got bigger, it got better!

When we bought this little house, the interior was decorated in dark avacado and gold. It had a tomb-like atmosphere, dark and depressing. To transform it into a happy house, we opened all the drapes, painted the walls white, laid white Berbour carpet in all four rooms and added splashes of color throughout in yellow, red and royal blue. Then we bought two big, soft, white loveseats to set on either side of the fireplace.

When we purchased them on sale at Sears, the clerk asked, "Are you sure you want *white* couches? We have them in other colors."

"Yes," I assured her.

"Then," she added, "before we deliver them, may I suggest that you have them coated with Scotch Guard, the invisible shield, guaranteed against food stain, perspiration and the prevention of the penetration of dirt and grime."

We bought that package. It sounded like a good idea. I am glad we did. We have put a lot of miles on those white couches and they still look good.

Jean Mosley was cooking with the help of her six-year-old son, Steve. He watched her remove layer after layer of the outer dry skin of a big onion.

"Is that paper, Mom?"

"No," she explained. "It is only a sort of protection for the onion itself. We only use the moist interior. Most everything comes with a peeling, a shell, a hull, a protective covering of some kind."

She started to elaborate, but little Steve, his big blue eyes glowing with knowledge, said, "I know. God's love is our shield."

We learn a lot of Scripture in Sunday school like Psalm 3:3, that carries us through life.

Abram proved that invisible shield in Genesis 15:1. David was grateful for the clear bubble of protection about him: "God is my shield, my refuge; He saves me from violence, keeps me from my enemies" (see 2 Samuel 22:3–4).

Be thankful for the many times you were spared unknowingly from terror or tragedy by that invisible shield; kept from disease during a flu epidemic; from a wreck that could have happened; when there was a robbery nearby. The Lord is *your* shield!

Westminster Chapel in London has one of the most esteemed pulpits in Christendom. It was the platform of G. Campbell Morgan and Martyn Lloyd-Jones and is presided over presently by Dr. R. T. Kendall, one of the most highly regarded theologians in the world today. It is said that the person who speaks there on Sunday morning will be known throughout Britain by Sunday afternoon and throughout the world by Monday.

But when a hobo drops humbly to his knees in a railroad boxcar and speaks one word, "Jesus," he is known throughout the courts of heaven, immediately!

On Ferguson Hill, overlooking the bluffs of West Terre Haute, Indiana, lived the Perkins. The second son, Glenn, had just had a fight with his father.

"There's not room for two men at the head of any household," William declared harshly and sent him away. The 22-year-old kissed his mother goodbye and, looking back, saw her wipe tearful eyes with her cobbler's apron.

Jumping a freight train, the young man rode night and day through Kansas and Oklahoma, hungry and hurt. Weeks later, in the middle of the night, when the haunting *Whoo* of the steam engine indicated they were slowing down, young Glenn dropped to his knees in the railroad boxcar, spoke one word, "Jesus." He jumped from the moving train and hopped the next freight headed in the opposite direction, toward home.

Arriving there several pounds lighter, and a wiser young man apologized to his father and embraced his ecstatic mother. That weekend he met a tiny brunette named Fern. He went off to school then returned to marry her. He became a pastor and they produced five children.

How do I know all this? Glenn Perkins is my father and I was their firstborn. I have heard him tell his prodigal story many times—"Speaking to an Audience of One, Speaking with the Almighty."

Every time a prodigal prays, a recording angel writes his name in the Lamb's Book of Life and the angelic chorus of millions rejoices over the sinner who has just repented.

We thought we had too much insurance. But you cannot be too safe. All our family members travel a lot and we enjoy outdoor sports that can be dangerous. We had what was labeled *Full Coverage* on one health plan, but just to be sure we enrolled and paid two years in advance for a Sun Supplement policy.

When April had her boating accident and we kept getting statements for twenty percent of the bill, we ignored it, knowing we had filed with both companies and were covered. Three months later we got a threatening letter saying we had jeopardized our credit rating and integrity. Then we read the fine print of our policy. It paid eighty percent of all bills. But I called Sun Supplement only to learn they gone under and filed bankruptcy. We were not covered after all.

I rushed the check to cover the discrepancy and right there at the post office, picking up my mail, I found Lowell Lundstrom's new calendar. On the page for that day in bold print, it said that *there are 8,810 promises in the Bible and every one of them is there for us*. We can depend on them, cash in on them. There is no fine print, no overlap and no discrepancy. No bankruptcy with God's funding, either.

"But as it is written, 'Eye has not seen, nor ear heard, nor have entered into the heart of man the things which God has prepared for those who love Him'" (1 Corinthians 2:9).

I loved Uncle Jesse and he loved me. When I was small I said, "I love Uncle Jesse. When I get big, I'm going to marry Uncle Jesse."

He was a living fireball, a one-man entertainment center. He laughed loudly, moved fast and worked hard. When he was a child he picked chickens at a poultry house to make money for his widowed mother. Now he was married to my Aunt Gertrude, worked on the railroad, did carpenter work on the side and ran a body shop for a third income. He never ran low on energy and he sired a son just like him. Uncle Jesse ate on the run so he could get more done, drank six cups of bold coffee each morning to get going and drank six Cokes in hot weather to keep going all day.

Winning may not always mean being first in line. This describes my Uncle Jesse. If you read my first book, *My Glimpse of Eternity*, you know that Uncle Jesse was my hero. He gave me his B-negative blood when I nearly died. Once when I was misunderstood at school, he was there in minutes to defend me. He was a fighter. My dad was not a fighter but a preacher. My dad is still alive in his late eighties. Uncle Jesse died young.

One hot day he was rushed to the hospital, doubled over with uncontrollable stomach pains. The doctor dismissed him with four orders: Slow down and relax, eat slowly, masticate and chew each bite 32 times before swallowing. He could not do it.

There is so much in the Word about savoring life, resting in the Lord and waiting patiently for Him. "In returning and rest you shall be saved; in quietness and confidence shall be your strength" (Isaiah 30:15).

Many times the swift lose the race. But he who endures to the end, not he who raceth to the finish line, shall be saved.

I am somewhat of a free spirit. I do not think one should work at being different, but I do not work at trying to look like a pastor's wife or a writer. Many people wear false faces, costumes and uniforms all their lives, never knowing the joy of relaxing or "freeing up." "Therefore if the Son makes you free, you shall be free indeed" (John 8:36). The best things in life are free, and the people who feel best in life are free.

Walking back from the post office one warm November morning, I thought, . . . *This breath I'm breathing and the sun I'm enjoying are without cost to me—and they are delicious to my well-being!*

I had a heavy parcel in each arm and my hair was hanging in my eyes. I couldn't see out of one eye, so I closed it, but then my hair covered both eyes. What to do? I turned my head slightly and the wind parted my hair free of charge.

Earlier this year while I hiked the same path behind the post office, I stooped and pulled up a clump of fern growing wild in the swamp and transplanted it around the foundation of our garage. That free fern has grown and multiplied though the ones I purchased died.

Last fall I picked some free seedpods from the wild tree of heaven. I now have a little grove growing that gives me privacy and screens the doorway of my writing studio from the view of passersby. No charge whatsoever!

I have joy and a free spirit better than any spirits bottled and for sale at Wilson's cut-rate liquor store. "Freely ye have received, freely give." Lord, help us to daily praise you and not ourselves. Let us set a free example to those who are saying, "Show me what God can do."

Frequently the only way you can reach unbelievers is by your example. Most are not listening to your free advice, but they are watching your free example. Somebody needs *your* example today.

My maternal grandmother, Mom Burns, had a feather bed that she inherited from my great-grandmother Brown. I loved sleeping beside my grandmother, lying on her soft, plump arm on that soft, plump feather mattress. Once you got in, you couldn't fall out!

I was there visiting one early April morning when, with the help of four people, Mom Burns hung that feather mattress on the clothesline to air while the bedroom was being wallpapered. A squirrel chewed a small hole in the ticking and the wind whirled clouds of feathers upward in all directions. It looked like the snow of Christmas!

My brothers and I, along with my Aunt Pearl, worked for hours trying to recover all those tiny goosedown feathers. They were everywhere, stuck to everything. Finally we had done the best we could. Mom Burns mended the mattress ticking and we put it safely back on its springs. But later that fall we found feathers stuck to the green beans and glued to the sides of the cucumbers in the garden patch!

Harsh, hurtful words are like those feathers. Try as you may, you can never bring them back or heal the wounds they cause. Once they are out they cannot be recalled, and they stick into the hearts of the young and injure tender spirits. "A broken spirit dries the bones" (Proverbs 17:22).

I once taught a Sunday school class of little girls. One darling, frail child with big glasses and soft, green eyes seemed withdrawn. Over time I gained her confidence and she told me, "My parents are almost impossible to obey. A year ago I accidentally broke my glasses. They both whipped me for my carelessness. It has been a year, but they haven't let me forget. They keep reminding me. My glasses are fixed, but my heart isn't."

Our prayer should be the old classic *Evening Song*: "If I have wounded any soul today; If I have caused one foot to go astray; If I have walked in my own willful way . . . dear Lord, . . . forgive."

A colorless commodity yet essential to all life—water!

Without it there would be no navigation, no vegetation, no electricity, no steam-powered engines. There would be no pleasurable activities like swimming and boating. There would be no ribeye steaks, because the grass could not grow for the black Angus to graze on. No two grand cups of coffee that wake you up each morning when the sun comes up orangey.

Several years ago I sat in the P & S Clinic in Terre Haute and listened carefully as a cancer specialist instructed my mother, "You must irrigate your system with at least six glasses of water a day. Not coffee, not tea, not Coke, not that good-tasting liquid, but plain, tasteless H_2O. If you will do this religiously, follow a bland diet and consume a half-cup of bran per day, you can keep your ulcer under control, lick this lazy liver, regulate your elimination and flush your colon of irritation and infection."

For a mature woman, I was surprised at her reply: "I hate the sawdust texture and taste of bran, and water is so boring." I have often wondered since then that if she had followed through, she might have prolonged her life.

Jesus is the Living Water. He prolongs life. He *is* life. The Christian walk requires discipline, but "he that comes and drinks of that living water shall never thirst again" (see John 4:14). You need never again experience that inner void. "As the deer pants for the water brooks, so pants my soul for You, O God!" (Psalm 42:1).

Thirst! Drink! Irrigate! Live!

In fall of 1971 when our family moved to Jamestown, North Dakota, I had never seen a snowmobile. They looked like such fun. But after snow remained on the ground for eight months, we realized they were not just fun machines but vehicles to survival. When the highways were closed, you could snowmobile to work or school through the drifts.

When we purchased our first one, the dealer told me two things: "You've got to know how to lean in order not to fall off, and the best way to learn to operate it is to go alone and do it." While my husband was teaching at Trinity College and the children were in school, I decided that, with no audience, I would master the art of snowmobiling.

The machine started for me! I crossed the highway, went down the ditch and into the field west of the little airport. Whee! Such fun! Then I heard a sickening *thud*! In the blowing snow I saw a barbed wire fence. I was stuck. I looked everywhere and couldn't find reverse. We must have bought a faulty snowmobile, a factory reject. It had no reverse.

Wading in drifts taller than myself, I returned home with my insulated boots packed with snow and called the dealer. He informed me, "They don't come with reverse!"

That's not a bad idea. There is no reverse gear in the Christian race. The saddest words of tongue or pen are these: *What might have been*. Stop punishing yourself. Even in a court of law, a man can be punished only once for the same crime, while we keep looking in the rear-view mirror of our lives. If you keep looking back, you will run into something and cause a wreck. Godly sorrow worketh repentance, but only one application is necessary for the cure. Get out of reverse. You are "accepted in the Beloved" (Ephesians 1:6). Paul said, "I press on, that I may lay hold of that for which Christ Jesus has also laid hold of me."

Don't let others remind you of your past, either. Tell them, "I distinctly remember forgetting all that!" And then sing to yourself this song of declaration: I have decided to follow Jesus, *no turning back*!

Our friend Karen Siddle taught pre-school and first-graders for a few months. She told us that she learned more about life and social relations with those little ones than she ever learned in college.

One cool morning on the playground a rumpled little tyke ran up to her and hugged her legs. She stooped down to his level. He touched her face and said, "There you are," then touched his own face and said, "Here I am," then hugged her and said, "Here *we* are!"

That's what I call profound simplicity!

I find this same profound simplicity in the writings of Luella ("Lu") Lee, a professional businesswoman in Olathe, Kansas. I share this from her.

O God, You are and I am. What a beautiful assurance! You love me this moment, because I'm me and You are my Father.

Thank You for letting me know I'm very special to You. It's important to me because, You see, You're very special to me.

I could not live without Your understanding and patience as I grow up. There's something each moment that's different, and I can't always handle it well. Then I see Your smile and, oh, how good it is to know I've made it through.

I'm so glad You have a lap big enough to hold me, as well as the rest of the family, and it's mine to keep. Your shoulders are wide enough to hold each head and soft enough to absorb all tears. Sometimes I feel Yours mingle with mine, and it's like a salve to the spot of pain within.

Your laughter is so loud when I am happy, I can hear and feel it both in and around me. And, yes, I hear the clapping of hands when we've reached a new height together.

Thank You, God, for the sounds of silence that let me know that where my soul drifts, You are with me always.

Be with me as I change from this life to another. Let me know You are, so I am.

We have a birdfeeder we call "the breakfast bar." Each morning we fill it with birdseed and sunflower seeds for the birds and for Clifford, our special squirrel. The first customer at the birdfeeder on the rail of the sundeck is always a young female cardinal. She does not have much color yet and is quite small, but every morning at sunrise I hear her *cheet*.

Recently a large bluejay has arrived about the same time, and it amazes me that he doesn't intrude and take over the feeder. He is a handsome male bird twice her size and much older. When I look closer, though, I see why he does not abuse her: Mother Cardinal is perched in a lower branch, not two feet from the rail.

God is like this. He is not far from any one of us, "for in Him we live and move and have our being." We can rest under His wing.

The *Grit* paper carried the story of a schoolbus wreck. It overturned in the mountains of Oregon. One little fellow fell over the cliff and was hung by his clothing in a scraggly pine. The forest rangers failed in their attempt to reach him. An hour later a helicopter tried and failed. But a crowd watched while a small, frail, middle-aged woman worked her way up the face of the treacherous, rocky slope. This news reporter's bottom line: "She'll get him. She's his mother." And she did.

A construction worker on a highway in New Mexico found it necessary to post a sign, *Closed for two hours*. It was noon and over 100 degrees. He had never heard so much swearing and complaining about the heat and the wait. Suddenly he heard a happy voice: "This would be a perfect time for a picnic." A young mother with three hot, tired tykes spread a blanket under a tree near the dusty road and, brought out a thermos of lemonade and basket of sandwiches. I marvel at a mother's ability to make the best of a bad situation!

Maybe you did not know your mother or had an abusive one. God will never disappoint you. "You prepare a table before me in the presence of my enemies" (Psalm 23:5). And He climbed a mountain, Calvary, *for you*.

Now I know what it means to have your lights put out.

Carol Casey and I enjoy walking a fast three miles from Palm Pavilion to the north point of Clearwater Beach and back. One August day we made it to the end and started back. Water was pouring from our faces and in to our eyes. Even our athletic socks were soaked. We had no idea that at eleven A.M. the temperature was 98 degrees and the humidity almost the same.

Carol was talking to me, but it seemed as if she were a block away. My ears felt stopped up, my hands were numb and I was falling asleep on my feet. Suddenly it felt as though an air pillow had been inserted in the back of my head and neck and the lights went out.

"Get up, Betty!" I heard Carol order. "I can't leave you here alone. There are still no houses yet in sight. You have to keep walking!"

Sometime later Carol hurried back with two paper cups of icy water. God bless her! The milk of human kindness never curdles. I learned later that she had run down the beach to the stretch of land where there were houses, knocked on a door, grabbed the water, asked them to call the paramedics and was pouring the water into my mouth when two men in a four-wheel drive Jeep arrived, slapped an oxygen mask over my nose and said repeatedly, "No blood pressure. . . ." Then, "She's coming around!"

They Jeeped us back to the parking area where an ambulance had been called. I refused it since I felt better and drove us both back home. I have a new appreciation for a cup of water!

Total dehydration occurs when all moisture leaves the brain and paralyzes the body. The paramedics cautioned me to bring along lots of water or Gatorade the next time and not to walk that far in August. A person can survive for some time without food, but not without water.

I used to think that the verse "Give a cup of cold water and you won't lose your reward" was a little extreme. Now I know its full impact! A cup of cold water made the difference between death and life.

Jeremiah and John call Jesus the living water. Drink from His water and never die.

In the mail I received a small box wrapped carefully with foam sheets to avoid breakage. When I got to the center of the packing I found a bottle of clear liquid with a label reading *My Lips Are Sealed*. The idea was for you to apply lipstick, then brush your lips with this clear magic so the color didn't lick off. I laughed out loud. Was this a hint from the friend who sent it that I was a blabbermouth?

I couldn't stop laughing. I would like to buy a dozen bottles and send them for Christmas gifts, and I can name you several I wish I had the nerve to send them to. Don't you have about eighteen on your list right now in whom you would invest if this clear potion guaranteed to cure their gossip?

Proverbs abound: Tell her a secret, and she's sure to chin and bare it. She's always letting the cat out of the bag. She has a tongue that could clip a hedge. Wind him up and he's sure to run someone down. He likes to be first with the worst. He can sling dirt faster than a gravedigger. She burns her scandals at both ends. He has more inside information than a surgeon. Keeping a secret from her is like trying to sneak daybreak past a rooster. She listens in haste and repeats at leisure. Her plastic surgeon was able to do everything with her nose except keep it out of other people's business.

Well, so much for nonsense and idle chatter! Let's turn to Scripture: "A talebearer reveals secrets, but he who is of a faithful spirit conceals a matter" (Proverbs 11:13). "He who goes about as a talebearer reveals secrets; therefore do not associate with one who flatters with his lips" (Proverbs 20:19). "Love will cover a multitude of sins" (1 Peter 4:8). This doesn't mean you lie for someone, but it suggests that if you love someone, cover for him or her.

Mary, the mother of Jesus, set a good example. When the Holy Spirit told her the secret that she was with child, "she kept all these things and pondered them in her heart." She did not publicize. God has great use for people who can keep a secret, who solicit confidence and who pray.

Talk to God about people instead of talking to people about people.

When Fullerton, North Dakota, became a ghost town, the owners of the Ranch Restaurant refused to leave. They felt that if you served *real*, people would drive a distance to taste and enjoy it. The difference between a successful person and another is not a lack of strength, not a lack of knowledge, but rather a lack of will. These owners set their minds, willed to stay and refused to move.

I will never forget the first time we ate there. The president of Trinity College and his wife, Roy and Rosa Mae Wead, took us. When we started driving through the prairies about sundown, Roy pointed out the gorgeous sunset painted across the big sky and reflected on the yellow heads of fields of sunflowers in bloom. We drove farther and farther from civilization. Carl leaned toward me and whispered, "Where are they taking us?"

It was probably thirty miles from the nearest town, and the Ranch Restaurant was the only business that occupied any of the buildings, a row of which was completely deserted. Except for a few farmhouses nearby, I wondered how a business could survive, let alone thrive. The floors, tables and chairs were of hard wood. The menu was hand-printed on brown paper sandwich bags, and their specialty bragged, "Freshest, tastiest northern pike south of the Canadian border!" at prices you could afford.

They were right. We had never tasted northern pike so good. Friends and neighbors fish for it early each morning in the cold streams and prepare it fresh for each evening meal. We didn't mind driving a distance to taste real, and we returned to the Ranch Restaurant with guests again and again.

People will also drive a distance to a church that serves reality. One ole Texas boy put it this way: "Why, some of these old dead funeral parlors they call churches, are false advertising."

Let's work and pray to ensure that people will drive a distance, if they have to, to taste real at your church and mine.

"Behold, I will do a new thing for you."

Sounded like a testimonial at a prophecy conference. The county commissioner was stating his manifesto, hoping to get the citizens of our little Crystal Beach community to vote for him. In exchange for a slight tax increase, they were going to give us our very own fire department! The old folks were ecstatic. No longer would they fear fire, with the nearest firefighters several miles south.

The first night after we got our new fire truck, I sat up straight in bed. Air raid! It sure sounded like one, anyway. What they had failed to tell us was that our once quiet community would now experience "the noisesome pestilence" that stalks at noon . . . and at midnight. I have never heard such a sound—*sqwonk, sqwonk*. The new firemen wanted to make sure we knew they were on the job. They laid on the alert system hard and heavy. Dogs barked, hounds howled.

I'm only 62 and considered very young here, so the old people called me to see what was going on. Were they safe? Was it really a fire nearby?

Scripture assures us that "all things work together for good." In the middle of every difficulty lies opportunity. I seized this change as an opportunity for intercession. Now when I hear the siren, I pray for the firemen's safety; that God will keep them alert; that they can put out the fire quickly; that fear will subside in the occupants; that they will get out safely. Then I roll over and go back to sleep.

Once recent evening the siren went off and I saw smoke just a half-block away. I prayed as I rode my bike to the scene. Two men had bought the vacant lot and were burning off the brush. The wind was wild, the fire out of control and getting too close to the houses. I prayed silently. The wind shifted, then subsided.

Even "the wind obeys Him" when ordinary people pray!

August 25   What Will You *Be Remembered For?*

In the Otter Creek High School yearbook I was remembered for my laugh and my skinny legs. I hope that somewhere between 1947 and 1991 I have made a mark and will be remembered for something more monumental!

I will never forget one of the speakers at a big church meeting last year, Gene Jackson, who said, "Our message used to declare 'What God Has Done for Man,' but it has switched to boasting about 'What Man Is Doing for God.'"

Lord, help us to change that and be remembered for lifting up Jesus. God never called us to build our own little magic kingdom, but His eternal kingdom.

I heard Dr. Robert Ascroft speak many times, but the one sermon I will always remember was, "Jesus did not hobnob with the snobs; He always gravitated toward need. If you don't feel God's presence, it is because you don't have need, or you are among those who have no need, who are rich and increased with goods and have need of nothing."

Vera Bartel was a housemother for freshmen women. They affectionately called her Mom Bartel. In chapel one morning she opened her message with this statement:

It is impossible to look up into the face of God and say, "Impossible." Fay Burks and her husband were in a serious car wreck. She felt the impact three times. She fell out of the seat, her chin split open and her right foot went into the heater fan. She begged them not to amputate her leg. The doctor said, "You've said too many prayers and have too much faith. I'm going to put that leg back on and see you walk." She was in a cast five years, but today she is walking without a cane or crutch. "Nothing is impossible with God" (Luke 1:37). Students, go out and try a little of the impossible today!

At his funeral, the minister said of Hans, "*He had a great God!*"

Will you be remembered in a similar way? Be serious, be truthful, write your goal down in a secret place.

What will *you* be remembered for?

England! I have never been there, yet in our hallway, framed in white wicker, hangs a print of one of those tottery, two-story, bright-red streetcars that still run the streets of "Merry Old." My heart skips a beat when I hear a British accent in a crowd of people or run into a "limey" at the beach, here "on holiday."

Why? Because my roots are there. My maiden name, Perkins, is an old English family. Some of my mother's ancestors came from Ravenscroft, a villa near the saltmines of Middlewich, near Nantwich on the Cheshire border. My first husband's family tree stems from Kent.

Perhaps you have never been to heaven, but if you have trusted in Jesus as your Savior, you're going there. Does your heart skip a beat when you hear someone talk about that place! Walking the road of life, when you hear a voice with a Christian accent, the sound of the blood-washed believer, does it quicken your spirit? When you visualize pictures portrayed by colorful speakers who have glimpsed heaven, or when you read the travel guide, God's Word, does your spirit say "yes" and yearn to go?

It should be so, because your roots are anchored there. God knew you before you were formed in your mother's womb, from the foundation of the world. Jesus loved you and shed his blood to purchase your visa there. "Jesus loved us and washed us from our sins in His own blood" (Revelation 1:5). His blood flows through your veins. You have had a spiritual blood transfusion. Get excited, be homesick for heaven.

You are but a tourist in this land, while your roots are there. Heaven is your native land.

When I was a little girl in first grade, we lived on Lee Avenue in West Terre Haute. It was a little "shotgun" house (called that because it was simply designed, three rooms in a straight line like the barrel of a shotgun). Around the foundation of this humble house was planted lily of the valley. Mother would take my little brother Don and me out to smell them. (If you have never smelled them live, blooming with early dew, you cannot identify with the utter elegance of that delicate fragrance!)

Even if I had been blind, as I walked the four blocks from school, I would have known I was nearing home by that lily of the valley fragrance. No wonder Jesus is called the "Lily of the Valley"! There is none like Him.

For years I tried to find a perfume that could duplicate that smell. They do not grow just anywhere, only in a valley-like atmosphere and climate.

My neighbor on Summerdale Drive, Joyce Yeager, gave me a brochure from a French *parfum* outlet. It boasted that their Lily of the Valley had the genuine fragrance. I sent for it, but it was not even remotely close.

There were times when my first husband died that I would close my eyes in the valley of despair, but the fragrance of Jesus, the Lily of the Valley, was with me. His fragrance filled my room. He said, "I will be with you in trouble."

Just weeks ago with my last daughter away in college, Carl ministering and teaching in Russia, and me facing decisions and crises alone, I closed my eyes. The Lily of the Valley is very present with me.

I have seen the face of a dying woman suddenly express hope, watched her inhale an invisible fragrance, absorbing the Lily of the Valley in the shadow of death.

As we near the time of His coming again to the earth, inhale, expect. I can almost breathe the fragrance. He is the Lily of any Valley. Weeping may endure for the night, but joy cometh in the morning.

Caution: If you are in Tampa today, watch out for that little old lady with the curly perm. I shall never forget the back of her gray head or how she was hunkered down to look between the upper rim of the steering wheel and the windshield. She pulled out of KMart, crossed four lanes of traffic without looking and, drove straight ahead, totally unaware that she had caused a ten-car accident. She left a bottleneck of congested vehicles and shocked drivers.

Our daughter April was home for summer vacation from Wheaton College that June day and was driving me happily to the airport in her very first car. It was a used silver Buick Skyhawk. The title transfer had not even been returned from Tallahassee yet! A seventeen-year-old boy visiting here from New Jersey, who had used his aunt's red Toyota truck without her permission, swerved to miss the old lady, hit the curb right, then bounced left, striking April's fender near the gas tank and destroyed the back end—$2,200 worth.

That boy begged me for a stick of gum to camouflage his breath and promised me the world if I would not press charges. Before the police arrived I did a lot of motherly coaching. You have probably already guessed: I missed my flight out of Tampa.

A nurse driving behind us witnessed the whole scene, yet we ended up paying for April's car (Auntie had the nerve to ask us to pay for her repairs, too!)

That was over five years ago. In the Bible this morning I scanned the verse "Love your enemies" (Matthew 5:44). I prayed, "Lord, wherever that little old lady with the curly perm is, guard her from hurting herself or others. And wherever Rich T. is, arrest his drinking desire. Bring them both to the knowledge of Jesus as Savior and make them aware again this morning of how you protected them in Tampa that day."

Carl spent many years in India. He was amazed that the children who suffered from malnutrition and lacked shelter, sanitation and medication survived, because they were loved. The families of India are close. The babies are carried around all day by older brothers and sisters or on the hip of a mother or grandmother. They are loved.

During the Great Depression our family survived for four days on the broth of one potato and love. My brothers and I were the only born-again believers in our school (with the exception of the Neese children) in an era when we had no Christian television and it was not popular to be Christlike. His love constrains us. We were ridiculed at school and harassed on the schoolbus, but we survived, for we knew that when the bus stopped in front of the house on Stop 18, Mother would always be there. We could depend on her love. My dad's love was evident when he had devotions with us each morning before we left for school. He sent us off with a hearty hug. Because we were loved, we could make it through a day filled with competition, hate and greed.

I wanted that same kind of loving atmosphere for my married family to come home to. My first husband could walk the hard cement of the Sunoco station for fourteen or sixteen hours because he knew that when he returned home, his daughter Brenda would have her little nose pressed against the window, looking for his return. I would run to the door and meet him. There would be a candle on the table, a hot meal and love.

"Greater love has no man than this, than to lay down one's life for his friend" (John 15:13). Jesus loved you enough to die for your sins, to build a bridge from this life to the next. Let His love put wings on your feet.

You can make it! You are beloved of the Father, endorsed by the Almighty!

Before I began writing today, I knew I needed fresh air, exercise and some listening time with God.

As I crossed the Caladesi Causeway onto Honeymoon Island, it was one of those picture-perfect, in-love-with-life and glad-for-God days! Walking fast toward the northern tip of the island, the sun and wind were at my back and the tide was low, leaving the sand packed smooth under my bare feet. Walking in the water burns up twice the calories and is wonderful exercise for the leg muscles, abdomen, lungs and heart. The water temperature was stimulatingly pleasant. I hummed, whistled and sang aloud.

But the one-and-a-half mile return trip was another story. The wind was in my face and had kicked up a bit. It was hard work, leaning forward to keep a good walking pace. I had forgotten my sunglasses and my eyes burned. The front of my legs kept hinting, "Shin splints."

Looking up, I saw a skinny-legged old man perhaps twenty years my senior walking ahead of me, slowly but surely, with the aid of a cane. I caught up with him and started to pass.

"It's farther goin' back," he said.

"My sentiments exactly," I replied. "Let's stop and rest."

He leaned on his cane and talked while I listened.

"Walking out here was like the first half of my life," he said, "a piece of cake. Halfway through I lost my wife, made some bad choices, turned my back on my God. I knew I had to turn around and get back to God, but I found *it's farther goin' back*. I linked up with an unbelieving mate and picked up two bad habits I still haven't been able to kick. But I'm determined to make it to the end."

Thanks, Tom. We all need your warning. "Let the wicked forsake his way, and the unrighteous man his thoughts; let him return to the Lord, and He will have mercy on him; and to our God, for He will abundantly pardon" (Isaiah 55:7).

Helen of Troy sat on her throne in majesty. Then, during a bloody war, she was abducted. Her captors debased her, forced her into prostitution and carried her away as a prisoner to Beirut. She became disoriented and walked the streets deranged.

Years later a loyal subject came upon her in the byways and recognized her. He began whispering in her ear, "You are Helen of Troy. You are royalty, Helen of Troy. You are cherished and revered, Helen of Troy." Love and truth finally penetrated, and it suddenly dawned on her who she was. She eventually went back and did indeed rule again as Helen of Troy.

Satan may be whispering in your left ear, "You are nobody. You have sinned miserably. You are a failure, defiled, washed up, finished." Don't believe him, don't listen to his lies. His vote does not count.

Jesus is whispering in your other ear, the right one, "I have bought you, you are Mine. You are accepted in the Beloved" (see Ephesians 1:6). "If God is on your side, who can be against you (see Romans 8:31)? "The sharing of your faith may become effective by the acknowledgment of every good thing which *is in you* in Christ Jesus." (Philemon 6). Do you know that you and God are a majority?

"You uphold me in my integrity, and set me before Your face forever" (Psalm 41:12). *His vote counts*. He knows who you *really* are.

Rather than asking the pastor on Sunday if a woman is "in tune," ask her on Tuesday after a bad perm or Wednesday when the M.D. informs her she is pregnant for the fifth time. Ask her boss on Monday or her neighbor across the alley on Thursday. Or whisper to her husband Saturday night when she is trying to get the kids into bed, "Is she still calm?"

But if you *really* want to know if a woman has a cool head ask her six-year-old boy on the first day of school when the bacon is burning, the dog is barking, his kindergarten sister is crying, the school bus is honking and Dad is late for work. Here is a poem—author unknown—that says it all.

'Twas the first day of school and all through the house
    The only ones stirring were me and my spouse.
With a little breakfast and lunches to fix,
    I knew in a moment it must be past six.
"Now, Nancy! Now, Susie! Now, Ricky! Now, Paul!
    Get out of those beds—there's no time to stall."
I ran to the kitchen, I had lots to do . . .
    Breakfast to fix and coffee to brew.
As I scrambled the eggs and was turning around,
    Down the stairs they all came with a thunderous sound.
A bundle of words we soon flung at each other,
    Like "Ouch," "Pass the juice" and "Don't hit your brother."
It was hectic and wild, this first day of school,
    And I laughed as I struggled to stay calm and cool.
When the time finally came for them all to depart
    I hugged them and kissed them with all of my heart,
Then . . . laying a finger aside of my nose,
    I slumped in my chair, just starting to doze.
But I heard them exclaim after all of that fuss,
    "Mom, can you drive us? *We just missed the bus*!"

A parent's special: "All things work together for good to them that love their children and God" (Romans 8:28, author's expanded version).

John Poole drives the bus that has taken Lowell Lundstrom and his evangelistic team all over the United States and Canada. John's mother is a nurse in a cancer center. One of her assignments in that medical institution is to inform the patients and family of the patient when they are terminally ill. She tells them, "We are all terminal. Jesus said, 'It is appointed unto man once to die and after that, the judgment.'" She helps build a bridge from this life to the next, removing fear from their hearts when the end comes.

Even if you lose, you win. It is the real country of "no mores"— no more cancer, no more divorce, debt, war, misunderstanding, and no more sin, and no more death. "If in this life only we have hope in Christ, we are of all men most miserable" (1 Corinthians 15:19).

A jolly black minister in the state of Kentucky, Dr. Windsor, told me, "You white people don't know how to die. When the time comes, you kick, you scream, you ignore death, deny it, till the last breath. No wonder you die hard; you don't know how to accept death, don't ask for help to die. We blacks know how to die. When someone nears the end, we gather around him or her and call on the angels to come and give special escort. We sing, 'Swing low, sweet chariot, comin' for to carry me home.' We may hear the flutter of angel wings. Some have even seen them come and take our loved one down the corridor of that grand reception hall for their triumphal entry into that Celestial Homeland!"

He showed me a photo taken at the funeral of a poor woman in their village. You could plainly see angels encircling with wings outstretched behind her coffin. There were no professional singers in that country church, but when the minister finished praying the entire group heard very clearly an angelic choir, singing overhead.

We are all terminal, but how we terminate is determined by whether or not we have our passport in order. Jesus' blood is the way.

September 3   *Snakes, Scorpions and Poison*

I took a serpent by surprise. As I lifted the overhead garage door one Tuesday morning, I went to kick a length of rope aside. But it was not a rope; it was a thirty-inch diamond back rattler. When I kicked, it coiled. I backed away slowly. Snakes are more afraid of you than you are of them. They will escape if you don't surprise, provoke or corner them. I picked up a long-handled, pointed shovel, swung hard, stunned it, then came down behind his head several times before I severed the head from that muscular body. I knicked the cement driveway badly, and was sweating like crazy, but the serpent was dead.

In Mark 16:18, Jesus tells us that we can "take up serpents" and they shall not hurt us. This protection factor applies not when you mess with snakes deliberately, but when by accident you come upon them. This promise was given to people who were working for the Kingdom, ministering to needs of others, and praying for the sick. Another verse tells us, "You shall not tempt the Lord your God" (Luke 4:12). Again in Mark 16:18 "If they drink anything deadly, it will by no means hurt them."

We had a bumper crop of apricots one year. I read that the apricot seed is in the experimental stage as a preventative treatment for cancer. I kept cracking open the apricot seeds and eating them like nuts. When I mentioned this casually to my doctor, he was shocked that I was still alive. He said that just a few can be fatal. The Lord preserved my life because of my ignorance. God will not spare any of His children who try to prove their holiness. If we play dangerous games with God or take foolish chances He's not obligated.

Luke 10:19 says, "I give you the authority to trample on serpents and scorpions, and over all the power of the enemy, and nothing shall by any means hurt you." Resist the devil and he will flee from you. I was walking barefoot in my studio once and I thought I had stepped on a metal staple. I had actually tread on a scorpion. I still have its body taped to a yellow paper to show people and remind me of God's protection.

Have you ever had anyone approach you with, "Can we talk?" (We are talking.) Or "I want to tell you." (Well, just tell me then.) Or "Get serious." (I am serious.) Americans waste words. You would think we are freelance writers who get paid seven cents per word.

Why do politicians, salesmen and people who have the experience of eternal life, beat around the bush so?

Out with it! It's a dead giveaway when they hem and haw, bait and switch. Honesty is the best policy. . . . Get on with it. . . . Grow up. Here is a definition of maturity: "Speaking the truth *in love*" (Ephesians 4:15). Not brutally, don't pry; but try, in love.

This morning I heard the most straightforward approach ever. Donna sat down and told me, "Our fourteen-year-old son, John, Jr., started hanging out at the Jesus Coffee Shop downtown because his dad was too busy with his dental practice and I was too busy staying drunk and smoking three packs of cigarettes every day. One evening Johnnie came through the door for dinner, looked at his dad and then at me and said, 'If I die today, I am going to heaven. If you and Dad die today, you're both going to hell.'"

Donna told me, "I did not even eat any dinner. I went straightaway to that Jesus Coffee Shop to straighten out those strange people. While I was there they straightened me out. I have been straightened out ever since. They told me about the blood of Jesus to cleanse sin, and about heaven's hope eternal. First my heart was cleansed, I was delivered, and the bad habits dropped off."

The lad's straightforwardness was the first bold step of salvation for his entire family, who now work in medical missions in the Philippines.

It doesn't matter if you are a dentist or a drunk, if you will lay aside excuses and be straightforward with God He will deliver the goods. He is not willing that any should perish, but that all should come to repentance (see 2 Peter 3:9).

In 1855 a Sunday school teacher named Kimball stood in front of a Boston shoestore. Should he visit a young member of his class who was working in the store? He hesitated. Finally he decided to do it. Listen to his story:

"I found (him) in the back . . . wrapping up shoes. I put my hand on his shoulder, and simply told him of Christ's love for him and the love Christ wanted in return."

The young man received Christ as his Savior right there in the storeroom. Shortly afterward he moved to Chicago where he organized a Sunday school class for children of the slums. The enrollment grew so tremendously he was called to speak at conventions as an authority on Sunday school work.

That young man, D. L. Moody, later went to London where, through a series of events in which he was directly involved, the life of another great Christian, F. B. Meyer, was changed completely. Meyer said, "I owe everything, everything in my life, I think, to that parlor room where for the first time I found people brokenhearted about sin. I learned the psychology of the soul. I learned how to point men to God."

Meyer, in turn, influenced Robert G. Lee at Furman University, and J. Wilbur Chapman at Northfield, Massachusetts. Chapman's mantle fell on Billy Sunday, and Sunday challenged a group of laymen to witness personally for Christ in Charlotte, North Carolina. Twenty-nine men gathered to pray for revival. As a result, Mordecai Ham began a citywide meeting in Charlotte in 1934. One night a lanky sixteen-year-old boy received Christ. That fellow was Billy Graham.

Seventy-nine years before, a humble Sunday school teacher went into a shoestore to speak to a member of his class about his soul. What if he had not gone?

Someone has said, "You're not a mother until you've borne one and buried one."

On Saturday night, August 25, 1990, a police cruiser pulled into the driveway of a home in Ontario. The officer confirmed the fear in every mother's heart: "Your nineteen-year-old daughter, Marilyn, is dead." Running to Marilyn's room Linda found the Gideon Bible where Marilyn had written of her saving faith in the Son of God. Shortly after, Marilyn's thirteen-year-old brother took his Bible out of a desk drawer and wrote his confession of Jesus as his Savior.

The fatal car crash, the impact of which caused young Marilyn's car to burst into flames, snuffed out the life of a very beautiful young Christian. A fireman on duty said, "This child was in the arms of Jesus in her last moments." Marilyn's mother claimed Isaiah 57:1: "The righteous is taken away from evil." God sees the future and Linda trusted His wisdom.

The following day, this grieving mother met Ian, a weeping, broken, paralyzed young 22-year-old. It was his car that had collided with her daughter's. No one could console him. He was tormented with guilt and grief, refusing to be comforted. Linda's mother heart went out to him. She bent, kissed him and said, "I've come to love you. Now, listen to me, I'm her mother. She pulled out in front of you. Who else do you need to hear this from to believe it?" They talked and he received Jesus. Though his legs had been pinned in the wreckage, he had reached and beaten the window so hard, trying to free Marilyn from the flames of her burning car, that he had broken his hand. His legs were still numb. But thanks to Linda's prayers, feeling was restored the next day. Then Ian's mother talked with Linda and she, too, received Jesus as her Lord.

Four philosophers discussed life's greatest tragedy. One suggested murder and imprisonment. The second considered blindness. The third believed that it was betrayal by a trusted spouse. But the ultimate conclusion: The greatest tragedy in life would be to miss God and not even know it.

Mother Superior, our gorgeous sable collie, was of the bloodline of one the TV Lassies. We had just moved to Sisston, South Dakota, and we wanted to have her wormed and her booster shots updated. We were having her bred for the new litter of spring puppies.

I walked into the only veterinarian's office in town, but walked right out. A dentist living next door had told me what a fine qualified vet he was. I called that dentist and asked, "Did you know Dr. P——was a drunk when you recommended him to me? He was so tipsy he had to lean against the wall and his speech was slurred."

"Oh, I should have told you," he explained. "Doc is in the final stages of multiple sclerosis; he is physically slow, but he's brilliant."

I went back with a different attitude, a different perspective. I pretended I didn't notice when his gentle hands shook during Missy's exam. I got to *know* him, in his skill, in his wit and humor. I got to know him in his suffering, in his love for life in the short span he had left. I got to know him in the strength of his mind and knowledge, his love for the countryside, the traditions of the Dakotans and the prairies.

Carl and I also got to know Doc in his need for God and assurance of life after death. I am so glad I went back to his office. Just a few weeks before he died, Carl and I went to Coteau Hospital and prayed with him and talked about heaven, his eternal home and close destiny.

The reason most people don't love God is that they don't know him. Take time to wait for God . . . *get to know Him*, in His suffering, and His loving mercy.

Pray: "Oh, that I might *know* you." Know Him as Redeemer (Job 19:25). Know Him as the Dayspring (Job 38:12). Know Him as wisdom (Psalm 51:6). Know Him in power (Luke 5:24). Know Him in His holiness (Luke 4:34). Know Him as God, the giver of good gifts (Luke 11:13). *Oh, that I might know Him!*

I had never met Mary, the wife of Doc, our local veterinarian. Several horses died in our county after having been bitten by mosquitos that carried sleeping sickness, or encephalitis. Because of the pond near our barn, we became alarmed and called Doc. When he came to the stable to inoculate our horses, Mary came along.

Just as Doc finished and they were leaving, Carl came into the driveway having just finished his evening walk. He told them he walked for diversion.

Mary spoke up, "That's what I would like to do—walk for diversion."

Immediately I responded, "I've been looking for someone to walk with. It's a date. Tomorrow morning at ten."

The ridge walk overlooking the Red River Valley was heavenly. From that vantage point, we could see 52 miles to Traverse City and almost to Milbank. "What's all the fuss about walking—it's a piece of cake," we joked. Before we knew it, we had walked the eight miles to Clark's Corner.

Coming back was a different story. We had not planned properly. My shoes were the four-dollar variety from KMart, and I wore no socks. Mary's were not much better. The trip back was torture. We literally dragged one foot and then the other every step home. Seven hours, sixteen miles and four bloody shoes later, we could hardly talk. We were hungry and dehydrated and we had to have help up the steps. Before bed, Carl lifted me into the bathtub where I soaked my aching hips in warm water. I suffered serious hip dysplasia for three months.

The lesson? Plan ahead, use proper equipment. "Sit down first and count the cost, whether (you have) enough to finish it" (Luke 14:28).

Whether you're struggling with an assignment, in a marriage, on a job or with an illness like the one that ended a baseball player's pitching career, take a postage stamp attitude. When licked, a stamp "sticks to it" until it reaches its destination. A stamp doesn't come unglued or fall apart. *It keeps on holding on.*

Quoting the old one, "It's not whether you win or lose, but how you play the game," an anemic and shallow approach to a powerful faith report like former San Francisco Giant Dave Dravecky's victory. Cancer claimed his left pitching arm, his dreams, his livelihood and his career. During amputation, Dave's faith in His God and his skilled surgeon came through for him. He declared that the peace of God and his family's love sustained him.

Jesus said, "My grace is sufficient for you" (2 Corinthians 12:9). "Whenever I am afraid, I will trust in You" (Psalm 56:3). It is not what lies ahead of us, or what lies behind us, but our faith in God that lies "within us" that pulls us through.

C. H. Spurgeon once wrote: "We have no more faith at any time than we have in the hour of trial. All that will not bear to be tested is mere carnal confidence. Fair-weather faith is no faith at all."

Family, friends and fans prayed for and pulled for Dave. He thanked them publicly and declared that he drew from their strength. His kids must have inherited some of his faith, too. A St. Petersburg paper quoted one child: "He only has one arm now, but he has a lot of time and it doesn't prevent him from hugs."

There is no substitute for the power generated from the warm, real love of people. As Sam Levenson said, "The tender, loving care of human beings will never become obsolete. People, even more than things, have to be restored, revived, reclaimed and redeemed and redeemed and redeemed. Never throw out anybody."

Lick the postage stamp of faith. Stick to it. Hold on.

I dialed. "Hello, Jim?"

"Oh no, not you again! Don't tell me, let me guess . . . Your M.G.A. has a dead battery."

In less than a year, I had dialed that number three times, paid for three service calls, waited three days to have those two little six-volt batteries behind the driver's seat charged three different times. By now, the Crystal Beach Service Center and I are no longer Mr. & Mrs., but on a first-name basis—Jim to Betty, Betty to Jim.

A couple of hours later he pulled the service truck alongside my old green machine. "These are new batteries, but you don't use them enough to keep them charged." He cleaned the bolts, the cables and the connection clamps. Next, he plugged the charger into the wall socket plug, the source of electricity on my garage wall. He picked up the two clamps, one red and one black, with insulated rubber grips, and clamped them onto the terminal, my negative to the charger's positive and my positive to the charger's negative. The needle indicated that the power was indeed surging through the cord into my dead battery. It worked! My little green machine is alive, humming and purring again.

When Jim picked up his battery charger, he suggested, "If I were you, I would buy my own battery charger. Keep it close at hand." Good advice.

Is your battery weak, dying or already dead in trespasses and sin, or from fatigue in life's battles? He has given his angels *charge* over you, (Psalm 91:11) to re-charge you, to keep you in all of your ways, travels and journeying. You can get a charge out of that statement, but first you have to make the service call. "Call to me, and I will answer you, and show you great and mighty things" (Jeremiah 33:3). Next, you must plug into His current. You are not in *charge* here, you are merely the extension cord. Plug in! Then take hold of the grips and clamp onto the terminal! "Lay hold of eternal life" (1 Timothy 6:12, 19 and Hebrews 6:18). Feel the power surge?

A story is told that while God was creating the world, four angels came by to watch. The first angel watched for a moment and said, "Lord God, You are creating something amazing. Why are you doing this? What is the purpose?" The second angel said, "Lord God, You are creating something out of nothing. How is that possible?" We moderns would say that the first angel had a philosophical mind, and the second one had a scientific one.

The third angel came by and as he watched he said, "Lord God, You are creating something big, wonderful and rich. When you finish it, can I have it?" I have a sneaking suspicion that this angel was a capitalist. The fourth angel watched for a while and then became restless. He said, "Lord God, You are creating something that has not been there before. I don't want to be just a spectator. *May I help you?*"

Susan Moore wrote me from Hagerstown, Indiana: She suffered a nervous breakdown and had nightmares. In them she kept going up a steep, slippery slope, and each time she almost reached the top, a light ahead of her would turn red. In her panic, she cried out to God, "Help! I'm falling apart." Suddenly she became aware of an unseen angel behind her. He put huge hands on her shoulders and *held her together*. Life for her now has become deliciously fun.

One bitterly cold, winter night, a tiny child began choking with croup. Suddenly a bearded man in shirt sleeves appeared at the door and told the baby's father, "This child has an important mission here. Cut out the phlegm." The father had no time even to invite him in from the cold—he vanished from sight, leaving no footprints in the deep snow. The stranger's advice saved the baby's life. That baby grew to be Dr. (Name) Christopher, the greatest herbalist of the century. A stranger saved him. He in turn has saved thousands. Once in a while the earth is blessed with a visit from someone with an angelic rank in direct communication with the divine Source of wisdom and knowledge.

Jesus is calling today, "I am creating a new Kingdom of born-again, blood-bought believers." Make yourself available. Say, "Lord, *I want to help*."

The term *fan* is derived from a word meaning "fanatic," someone who is ridiculously enthusiastic. In England they call them "ranters" because they rant and rave.

When Brenda ran track and April played basketball, I became a fanatic. My kids were out there excelling. I carried an old brass cow bell and rang it when they scored. The loved it when they were in junior high, and even in high school, but when they went to college it was a different story. I used to blackmail them into doing what I wanted by threatening, "I'll bring my cow bell to your next game."

We sat in Denny's one Sunday at noon. It was crowded and noisy. One very obvious fanatic ranted loud and long, making sure everyone noticed that he prayed over the meal before eating.

The other extreme, of course, is being ashamed of being thankful. Even hogs grunt their appreciation. We could easily have Thanksgiving three times a day, 1,095 times a year, instead of the just the last Thursday in November.

It was said of Jesus, "As many as came to Him, He received them." He did not knock on doors and pry into people's privacy, nor did He bang them on the head with a twenty pound reference Bible, but He remained willing to receive those who were ready for the Gospel. I believe we should be available, but not obnoxious. People know if you are sincere.

One man told me, "I was a secret service agent, an undercover man for Jesus for eight years before I even told my wife.

Genuine joy is hard to contain. The Cameron family sings a little song: "The Holy Ghost will set your feet 'a dancing, and set your heart 'a dancing too." Jesus said, "*Let* your light so shine before men" (Matthew 5:16).

And—oh, by the way . . . He made the stars also (Genesis 1:16).

Is this the understatement of the universe! It is written so matter-of-factly, just for the record, *to set the record straight about creation*: And oh, by the way, He made the stars also. No big deal for Him, just routine creation.

Don't put it off, don't delay. Take time tonight to walk away from the city lights, look up and really look at the stars. The first star that God puts out early each evening, the "evening star," is really the trademark of the "Morning Star" Jesus. The angels who saw Him fling it into space heralded His birth.

That same star is the last one that God retracts each morning. That same God walks on the wings of the morning. If you don't or haven't, start loving Him each morning. Job was not healthy, but he was wealthy and wise. He knew God in an intimate kinship. God commands the morning! (see Job 38:12). This is for our generation, too. Start commanding the morning. If you don't, the morning will command you. If you don't seek divine energy at the beginning of the day, and attempt to go through on your own strength, you are likely to stall before sundown. Dominate the morning. Do not let the morning dominate you. Have *your* way with it. Baptize it with prayer, stamp it with gratitude, dedicate it to honest work, unselfish service, quiet courtesy.

Make sure that before you sleep, you have given a hand to someone worse off than you are. Before your day's work begins, draw strength from the Infinite Source, then command the morning, strengthened for your duties, armored against danger and fear. Master the morning.

To be a success in your business, make God your senior partner. Settle the sin and salvation question, make Jesus the Lord of your life, and become partners. Spend time in prayer before you venture, then make God President of your firm, your Business Manager. Let Him make the major decisions and direct the small ones. Give Him ten percent of all your earnings and He will bless your ninety percent. What a great deal!

"Seek ye first the kingdom of God, and all these other things shall be added." Your spiritual integrity must be uppermost and your success second. Those who slide from the faith in their pursuit of wealth eventually find themselves "pierced through with many sorrows." If you search for money, *for money's sake*, beware. It is not a sin to be successful and to have money, but to love it is the root of all evil. To worship it *is* evil.

I knew a man who made a lot of money selling mobile homes, but his integrity was a poor witness. More than one person said of him, "He can sing loud in church, but in business, he is as crooked as a dog's hind leg."

Integrity is your best witness. A shady business never yields a sunny life. One thing that a person can give and yet keep is his word. William Arthur Ward once said, "Earn with integrity and enthusiasm; invest with wisdom and restraint; spend with care and discretion; give with joy and generosity."

Trust God and be content. "Hold steady in prosperity and reverses" (see Philippians 4:11–12). Keep praising Him even when business is slow. He will come through for you because it is His business, too. God directs traffic in front of the business dedicated to serving God and others. "The blessing of the Lord makes one rich, and He adds no sorrow to it" (Proverbs 10:22). "He blesses the habitation of the just" (Proverbs 3:33). "The tent of the upright will flourish" (Proverbs 14:11). "The Lord will command the blessing on you in your storehouses and in all to which you set your hand" (Deuteronomy 28:8).

Word association. The first thing that comes to mind is: "Earn your bread by the sweat of your brow." Jesus talked about free, unearned bread. He was that Living Bread sent down from heaven. His spoken invitation was, *"Come buy bread without cost."*

I believe the manna in the wilderness was a symbol of this free gift of life-giving bread, a free sample, sent down as the forerunner of Jesus. The story is in Exodus 16. I believe we will eat it when we get to heaven. I can imagine that its texture and taste is like angel food cake.

You can actually live on just bread and water. Prisoners do. Jesus said, "I am the bread of life. He who comes to me shall never hunger, and he who believes in Me shall never thirst" (John 6:35). You can carry a sack of bread and starve to death unless you eat it. He said, "I am with you, but *I shall be in you.*" "Unless you eat my flesh and drink my blood, you have no part in me." In order to receive the spiritual nutrients, you must believe that His body was broken for our physical healing, and that His shed blood is able to eradicate all sin. Break His bread, share Him with others.

It is miraculous bread. The boy with two fishes and five loaves offered them and the Living Bread multiplied the natural bread to embarrassing abundance! Talk about leftovers—there were twelve baskets' surplus! That is a great investment, a powerful trade-off. He showed His generosity. He is more than enough—the all-sufficient One.

When you eat bread and drink water at your family meals, remember Him. Whether you have Communion in your home with your immediate family, or look forward to taking Communion bread and wine in public with other believers in God's house, remember Him. We cannot, should not, need not try to live one day without Him, our Living Bread (John 6:35), the fountain of Living Water. "Give us day by day our daily bread" (Luke 11:3). These symbols are meant to remind us that He is coming back.

Have you ever felt like a wiener in a steak house? As out of place as a tuxedo at a swimming pool?

My brothers had an expression, "She's O.K. in her place, but it hasn't been dug yet." They were teasing but the point was valid: Ultimately everything belongs in its place. Gasoline and water are both essential for running any automobile, but each in the right place. Try getting these two liquids confused—put the gasoline in the radiator and the water in the fuel tank—you get nowhere and could even cause an explosion.

And what about gold? Men moved west for it, worked for it, have cheated for it, stolen for it, lied and robbed for it. Yet gold is a transitory thing. Jesus asked, "What shall it profit a man if he gain the whole world, but lose his soul?"

Carl brought me a gift from Russia—a lovely pair of gold loop earrings. He was amazed at the excellent quality, yet he paid so little for them. ("Bought them for peanuts!" he exclaimed.) He returned with a request from our daughter for a gold chain for Christmas. But when he got back he found that there was no more gold available in the stores.

Gold: "It's O.K. in its place . . . heaven. "And the street of that city was pure gold" (Revelation 21:21). At last, gold in its proper place . . . a thing to stand on, walk on and be crowned with. The precious metal gold is paving those streets!

Raising up the hands in praise and petition is nothing new. It was an exercise with benefits that worked for Moses in the Old Testament, and perhaps even commended as a tried-and-true experiment in the New Testament.

During a strategic war, Moses knelt on the mountain overlooking the battlefield. As long as he raised his hands to the God in charge of the battle (the battle is the Lord's; see 1 Samuel 17:47), the children of God won. When he lowered his hands, they retreated. When two officers, Aaron and Hur, realized that Moses was too tired to continue this procedure, they stood on either side and held Moses' hands up for him (Exodus 17:10–12).

The Lord desires that all people everywhere, pray, lifting up their hands, ridding themselves of anger and removing doubt (see 1 Timothy 2:8). Perhaps you have never done this. Try it! Sometime when you are alone at home, either kneel, sit or walk through the house praising and petitioning the Lord with your hands lifted toward heaven.

Have you ever noticed that when a trusting little child wants his father to pick him up, he reaches his hands upward? You'll be pleasantly surprised at the "pick up" you will get from doing the exercise I have just described. Like a TV antenna, you get better reception! The hands lifted upward indicate adoration, a signal of surrender, our empty hands reaching to receive bounty . . . from His *full* and bountiful hands.

Have you noticed that it's easier to get into bed than out of it? You usually fall into bed, but have to be pried or "alarm clocked" out. Birth is easier than death. People laugh at a birth and cry at the death of a loved one.

Have you noticed that sin and temptation are like this? It is easy to get into trouble, but hard to get out. A bumper sticker puts it this way, "Lead me not into temptation, I can find it myself." Another: "I can resist anything but temptation." Satan will help you get into trouble, but he sneers and laughs when you cannot find your way out. He will assist you in your sinning, but leave you stranded when you bottom out.

If you are in a bad situation, bound with sin's chains, pray: "Lord, lead me not into temptation, but deliver me from evil." Set me free from the "arrow that flies by day . . . and the pestilence that walks in darkness, and the destruction that lays waste at noonday" (Psalm 91:5–6). Satan makes his arrows bright, but his wounds are always fateful. Jesus promised that He will be with us in trouble. He will deliver us.

Carl has almost become famous for this line: "Always do what you can't always do." He refuses to get bored, is always looking for a new challenge, yearning for a new mountain to climb, searching for a new path to follow. Musing at the beach early one morning, he told me, "I hate aging. I refuse to get old."

"Don't say that," I told him, "there's only one alternative!"

"I'd rather choose that," was his conclusion. Right now, at the age of 69, he's director of Russian Missions for Zion Bible Institute.

Carl should have been a Marine. The motto of the U.S. Marine Corps is "Semper Fidelis"—always faithful. Jesus said, "Be faithful until death, and I will give you the crown of life" (Revelation 2:10).

On April 21, 1873, Dr. Livingstone wrote the last shaky entry in his journal. The morning of May 4, his servant found him, not in bed, but kneeling at his bedside with his head buried in his hands. In the act of prayer, he traded his tired, worn body for his glorified one, died in the act of prayer, alone in the heart of Africa.

The valley of the shadow of death is very narrow. We pass through it *single file*. No earthly friend can go with us, but if you have Christ as your Savior through life, He will *shepherd* you through the last valley, the valley of death. "I will fear no evil; for You are with me [and] comfort me" (Psalm 23:4). You will pass quickly from death directly into life! (John 5:24).

The late Catherine Marshall shared a concept with me: "The redeeming factor in most conflicts—put a golden zipper on your lipper."

If you cannot improve on silence, don't say anything, keep quiet. Most of us talk too much. Jesus commanded us to let our conversation be that which becomes the godly peacemaker. He said, blessed is the peacemaker, not the pacemaker (see Matthew 5:9). We love to keep things going. If one person will stop talking, there is no quarrel. Usually contentious quarrelers will be embarrassed by the sound of their own voices. An old proverb puts it this way: "When no more fuel is put on the fire, it is quenched, goes out, dies." When Jesus' accusers railed against Him, He opened not His mouth.

A good rule says that when others are talking negatively about a person and you know something bad that you could contribute truthfully, zip your lip instead. Failing to report something negative is not hiding, not lying. Rather, silence is golden.

There is strength in silence. "Even a fool is counted wise when he holds his peace" (Proverbs 17:28). "The Lord is in His holy temple. Let all the earth keep silence before Him" (Habakkuk 2:20). There is even going to be silence in heaven for the space of one hour. Think about it.

Take time at face value. You can force the hands of the clock, but it will never change the time.

God is the timekeeper. There is a time for sowing and for reaping. In between these two is time.

They tell you that there are too many calories in a hot fudge sundae. My friend Laurel refuses to believe this. She went once to Baskin Robbins and ate three in a row, with nuts, whipped cream and a cherry on top. Back home she stepped on the scale and declared, "It's not true. Hot fudge sundaes will not make you fat. I still weigh what I weighed an hour ago." But give it time. If she continues to eat hot fudge sundaes, three in a row, in time she will become obese.

Rick is interested in body-building. The first time he "pumped iron" he still measured the same. If he continues to pump iron, however, he will expand his muscles.

Bruce has a scientific mind. He wants to prove that smoking will not ruin his health, so he smokes a full pack of cigarettes. He then goes by the clinic and orders a lung Xray. The lab report seems to make liars of his parents: His lungs are still clear. But if he continues to smoke heavily, *given time*, he will probably develop lung problems.

"Now is the accepted time" (2 Corinthians 6:2). "Perilous times will come" (2 Timothy 3:1). "My times are in Your hand" (Psalm 31:15). God was before time, and will be after time. He will declare, "Time shall be no more" (see Revelation 10:6).

On the Gulf Coast there is a small island connected by a causeway to Tarpon Springs. Carl says that this little island, Howard Park, looks like an oasis in Egypt. Bedoins and vagabond peddlers yearned for the oasis to seek refreshment and to water their camels. When King David found himself battle-weary, drained and squeezed out by adversity, he cried out, "My soul thirsts for God, for the living God" (Psalm 42:2).

If we also yearn to quench our thirst, we will be satisfied. This drink will eliminate our restlessness, darkness, weakness, sorrow and deadness . . . for he who has God wants nothing. As a young Christian, Sunday morning service seemed to satisfy me. Now that I am mature in Him, in the "big league," the battle of prayer, writing, traveling and speaking for souls, the opposition is getting stronger, and I need the oases of Sunday night and Wednesday night prayer meeting.

Jesus was dying and said, "I thirst." Many times I have squeezed out the last drop of ink in my pen, listened to the needs of others, and prayed until I was hoarse. One Wednesday evening, I dropped into the pew, gasping, "I thirst."

Pastors: Wait on God for those telegrams and prescriptions to deliver mid-week. Put your heart into them, arrange special music, cheer the desperates who come into your service out of the drought of spiritual battle. You are their oasis.

"As the deer pants for the water brooks, so pants my soul for You, O God" (Psalm 42:1).

There are two kinds of people I feel sorry for. I feel sorry for the people who are so super they are not natural (these include the fanatics and religious loonies). Then I feel sorry for people who saunter down the natural path of life, never having tasted the super. I wrote an entire book, *Super Natural Living* on this topic—the good balance between the super and the natural.

A person is like an inflated tire with three compartments: physical, spiritual and intellectual. If a person is deflated in any of the three areas, he is lopsided and everyone in the family, riding along on the road of life with that person, gets a bumpy ride. If a person is overly inflated in any of the three areas, those who ride along on the road of life with that person, get a bumpy ride. If a person is overly inflated in any of the three areas, those who ride along with him are getting a miserable trip, too.

Physical: Interested only in sex, eating, nutrition.

Spiritual: So heavenly minded they are no earthly good.

Intellectual: This person is sometimes "too smart to understand," lacks child-like simplicity to enjoy little things that spice up life. He has no tolerance for less organized people.

If your "tire" is equally inflated in these three areas, you enjoy a smooth ride and others enjoy coming along with you. "Man shall not live by bread alone (the physical), but also by every word that proceeds out of the mouth of God (spiritual completeness). If you have this balance, you will enjoy walking with God, He will give you the ability to get wealth, and he will bring you to a better place of advancement (see Deuteronomy 8:1–18).

Social security to the teenager is going steady in junior high. To the senior "cit," social security is a check he or she depends on to arrive the third day of each month. Our genuine security is the sweet support of God our heavenly Father. "I am poor and needy; yet the Lord thinks upon me" (Psalm 40:17).

We are poor and needy no matter how rich in worldly goods we are. We have every reason to be humble before God. But know this: Before you think of God, He is thinking of you. We have the wealth of His care. How comforting, His abiding thoughtfulness, that all our needs are met in Him. He is our sweet support.

"I have called you by your name; *you are Mine*" (Isaiah 43:1). Remember this Scripture always, it was written for you. Do not limp through life, timid and apologetic. Do not insult your Father by crawling along life's pathway. You were born for a purpose. You belong to the King of kings and Lord of lords.

September 25   Fussy Babies Might Be Smarter

A young mother with a grin on her face handed me this cartoon. It showed a new-born baby talking to his newly found parents. "Have you been sleeping all night, going out after seven P.M., eating in restaurants? Are you used to clean clothes and furniture that looks like new? I'm here to change all that."

If you are reading this and know parents with a fussy baby, share this with them. *The Chicago Tribune* carried an article entitled: "Fussier babies might be smarter." A study reported in the *American Journal of Psychiatry* described how a temperamental baby raised in a middle- or upper-class family would probably have a higher IQ than his less fussy counterpart. A study of 358 children from four months to four years showed that babies who cried and were hard to soothe had higher IQs than babies who didn't fuss much. This seemed related to the fact that in attempting to quiet babies, parents talked to and interacted more with them than did parents of calm ones, who were often left to themselves. The IQ scores of difficult babies who received the extra stimulation reached 134, while the "easy" babies, scores fluctuated between 118 and 120.

I have a writer friend Dawn Wagler who has written, "Is there life after colic?" The conclusion some doctors have come to is that severe cases of colic tended to produce more aggressive personalities. Whether the child learns to be a fighter in life, battling several months of pain, or whether the more aggressive child is the most likely to have colic, we may never know. However, if these children are more equipped to battle the struggles of adult life because of their first few horrendous months, maybe, just maybe, it's worth it. She adds jokingly, "God makes them cute. If they weren't, we'd probably kill them!" If you have a colicky baby, find someone to relieve you for one hour a day, to prevent your emotions from progressing from love and sympathy to frustration, anger, guilt, then hate. Use a hot-water bottle on their stomachs. Trade babysitting hours, hour for hour with another "victim," then pray: "Jesus loves the little children."

The first words out of my mouth each morning are: "Yes, Lord!" This is a positive one word prayer, "yes," that bluffs the devil against any negative suggestions, first hand, right off. Then I pray before getting out of bed, "Thank you, Lord, for a good night's sleep and the light of another new day. This brand new, not-yet-fouled-up day is another chance, another opportunity for another exciting assignment, to be my best for You and for others. Let there be something pleasant in it just for me, too. Help me to complete one work project and to do one thing just for fun today. Keep me busy enough to avoid boredom, yet not so busy that You cannot invade my day with a more rewarding or superior plan. Amen."

Upon arising make a list, numbered from 1 to 10, of the things you feel you must complete before retiring. List the most dreaded or the most important item first and place the less significant items down the line. After the hardest task is completed, the rest will be a lark, a piece of cake, and you will enjoy your day. Putting off the unpleasant or dreaded chore is like carrying a backpack all day: It will dampen your creativity and rob your joy. And if you fail to complete the least important it will be only a small loss or delay.

"To declare Your lovingkindness in the morning, and Your faithfulness every night. . . . For You, Lord, have made me glad through Your work; I will triumph in the works of Your hands" (Psalm 92:2, 4).

She gave what she could . . . the widow offered her mite. She shared what she had . . . the widow who made "pancakes" for Elijah. She sacrificed what she had received . . . the sinner woman with the alabaster box of perfumed ointment. God never expects us to give what we do not have. His requests are never unrealistic expectations . . . pancakes or perfume . . . give what you have.

Susan Bohard in Alaska wrote, "Thanks for your gift (I sent to her what I have . . . books). A family of four moved in with our family of seven. I don't have much, but I am sending you a 'practical box.'" It contained everything practical imaginable: Q-tips, a new red billfold, birthday candles, ribbon, soap, Scotch Tape, balloons. So timely! Some things I had just run out of.

Never underestimate the power of a generous woman. Marianne Crandall in Watertown, New York, gave what she had . . . antiques. She ran an ad, had a sale, paid for my plane ticket, rented the Carriage Inn for a meeting place and invited the public. Twenty-two were saved.

Linda Greenfield in Canada came to my meeting in Niagara Falls. She made and gave away hundreds of tapes of my story. Hundreds have been blessed and no longer fear death. They have responded in a most grateful way. (Although one lady said, "I didn't like the tape. It was too sad.")

The same day a man wrote to thank Linda for his tape: "I got so blessed, bawled so much listening to that tape, I had to pull off the road with my rig."

"For we are fragrance of life unto life of those being saved, and a fragrance of death unto those perishing." And it's the same fragrance.

This year I have already flown 129,082 safe air miles and one scarey mile with a 1,500-foot sudden drop. I do not take God's protection lightly, nor do I take safety for granted. I pray before each takeoff and breathe a silent prayer of thanks giving after each safe landing. Here is my take off prayer:

Dear Father,

I do not take Your loving concern for my safety for granted. This morning I ask You to protect us as we ride to the airport. Bless this driver with peace. I plead your precious blood over me, over the plane while I fly today. Undergird this plane with Your everlasting arms. Keep us under the shadow of *wings*. Keep me in the hollow of Your hand, as the apple of your eye.

I pray that you will assign a crew of guardian angels, dispatch them now to assist, attend and hold the wings of this plane steady for a smooth flight and a safe landing.

Give the pilot and crew steady nerves and clear minds. Invade their day with Your surprise—a new dimension of unexplainable joy.

I won't volunteer, but if it be Your will and You seat someone beside me with a need that You know I can supply, help me to be alert and sensitive, and give me Your comprehension and compassion. I invite the Parakletos, the invisible Coach, the Holy Spirit to come alongside to help.

Upon landing, I bow my head and silently whisper, "Thanks, Lord. I appreciate You. You give Your angels charge to keep us in all our ways, including air ways! Amen."

Nicholas, Czar of Russia, used to dress in ordinary clothes and disguise himself in order to wander through the streets at night to see how things really were in his domain; to see how people were faring under his rule; to investigate what the peasants were saying about him, what they really thought of their emperor.

Late one night he caught a guard sleeping and slipped inside the gate at the army barracks. Beside the guard who had fallen asleep Nicholas found a revolver and some official books. The guard had apparently been taking funds from the treasury. Weighted with guilt, the man had written a suicide note and placed it beneath the loaded revolver:

"To my horror I decline . . . so great a debt. . . .
Who can pay it?"

When he awakened, he lifted the gun and something on his note caught his eye. Beside the question, "Who can pay it?"–was scrawled in official hand: "I Czar Nicholas, have paid it."

You, reader, may be dead in trespasses and sin, but Jesus paid it all: "All to Him I owe. Sin had left a crimson stain, He washed it *white as snow*." He paid a debt He did not owe, I owed a debt I could not pay. And, now I sing a brand new song, *Amazing grace*!

"There's a spot on the elbow of this blouse," I groaned. Mother responded with this old Hoosier colloquialism: "It will never be seen on a galloping horse! If you don't quit going 190 miles and hour you're going to hit something."

There are shakers and there are movers. There are escalators and there are treadmills. You can burn calories on a treadmill, but it will not take you anywhere.

There are even two lanes on the moving walkway at your airport. The right lane is for standers and the left is for passing the standers. Living life in the fast lane . . . the destination makers . . . covering the distance in half the time.

These people are marching double time, to a different beat, to a different drummer. If you ever played an accordion you understand double time. Accordions chord 4/4 time while other instruments are playing 2/4 time . . . 6/8 instead of 3/4 time. Accordionists listen to a different beat. Some hear no beat at all. Many people are standing, spiritually dead. There is none so blind as he who closes his eyes to the truth. None so deaf as he who refuses to hear.

Carl is a minister. He has always said, "You can steer a *moving* ship." Have you ever tried to turn the steering wheel of a parked car? Most people have ideas, but refuse to try them. The prodigal son had a notion to return home to his father, and that is what he did.

There are bathrobes, robes for lounging, priest and choir robes. The prodigal son traded his lounging robe for a robe of prodigal son-ship . . . rulership. Get off the treadmill and onto the escalator.

There are many gates at the airport, but if you care where you are going, not just any gate will do. If you hope to reach your destination, you must exit the *right* one. Dr. Donald Johns, dean at Central Bible College, was famous for his quote to students: "It costs too much to be out of the will of God."

April Stambaugh was driving with excited anticipation toward Talbotton, Georgia, where 39 relatives were gathering to celebrate Thanksgiving. Granddad had given loving instructions for a shortcut from Atlanta, where she attended art school. But April took Exit 11 north instead of south, and ended up in Shawmut, Alabama. The "widest" route had been readily accessible, but if she wanted to reach her destination, Talbotton, she had to take the "narrower" road. A trip that should have taken two hours took five. She got to her destination, all right but very late. Many times the broad road leads to destruction.

Taking time in life to find the right exit is not a waste of time. Many times a shortcut is not a time-saver, and may not be a cut at all. "There is a way that seems right to man, but its end is the way of death" (Proverbs 14:12). Try the spirits. The Holy Spirit is called alongside to help us with life's choices. Let's just be cautious not to confuse the discernment of spirits with the "gift of suspicion."

"Narrow is the gate and difficult is the way . . . and there are few who find it." Have you ever tried to get two pieces of luggage down the aisle on board a small plane? You cannot board with more than two carry-on pieces and they must be trimmed "narrow" to fit the aisle. Trim, get rid of excess baggage.

"Behold, children are a heritage from the Lord" (Psalm 127:3). Offspring may be from the Lord, but they behave many times as though they sprang from the opposite direction!

We joke a lot about children. If you want a few minutes alone and undisturbed, do the dishes. The best way to keep children at home is to make home a pleasant atmosphere . . . and let the air out of the tires! One woman told me, "I put a sign on each of my kid's bedroom door that says, *Your term expires in 18 years.*" One kid wrote, "I know I am responsible for my life and my decisions. I know it is irresponsible to blame others for my problems. I also know that everything wrong in my life is my *parents' fault.*" How about that!

For every mother who would trade her kids sight unseen, there are women who would give up everything they own but their children. I would live in a treehouse and go hungry just to keep the love and respect of mine. We like our children *because*. We love them *although*. They will probably turn out all right, but sometimes it takes strong nerves to watch them.

I heard Andy Rooney remark, "Every kid should have one mother and one father, a few siblings, eat dinner together, and have a room of his own even if it is tiny. A warm bed and blanket to hide under and worry in cozy privacy. . . . Give him enough to eat, enough love and enough discipline. Read aloud to him. Let the child get in bed with you during a thunderstorm. If every kid had these things there would be nothing to worry about the future of the world's adults."

All our kids are not going to the dogs. All are not deceived by the deceitfulness of riches. I watched David Wigginton grow up in the berg of West Terre Haute, Indiana. He is now ready to graduate from Southeastern College in Lakeland, Florida. He made this statement: "You couldn't pay me to be a millionaire." He and many kids, along with their parents, "press toward the goal for the prize of the upward call of God in Christ Jesus" (Philippians 3:14).

Haste makes waste. Marry in haste and repent at leisure. These are old clichés repeated hurriedly, sometimes spoken lightly, that should nevertheless be applied as required social and business principles.

When our youngest daughter went away to college, she deliberately went off-campus to choose a bank so that she would be treated as a client instead of a student. Many times pampered children set up accounts padded by their parents, and banking establishments are aggravated by the doting parents who pick up the slack.

This was a new experience for our daughter, and she needed to find a teller who would be understanding and informative. She asked, "I have eight old checks left from my old account. What shall I do with them? Use them or start using the new ones?"

The sharp nosed, sharp-tongued woman responded quickly with, "That's a personal decision. We don't care *what* you do." But she had already said she didn't care by her attitude.

Avoid abbreviated courtesy. Condensed kindness is no kindness at all. Kindness spoken in shorthand saves time, but not everyone can read or translate shorthand. Don't cut people short. You may feel like cutting them down to size, but they may already have a low opinion of themselves and feel insignificant and shortchanged.

Our little grandson Joshua, hurrying to save time on a school project, slashed his palm. It was no shortcut. Two weeks with almost no use of his hand was valuable time lost. Sharp words can cut, wound and leave emotional scars that heal slowly, too. To virtue, add deliberate kindness.

I was moving down the highway in heavy traffic when I saw a gorgeous, muscular twenty-year-old jogger running alongside the six lanes of traffic. He was bronzed, oiled and coordinated. But if he was interested in his health he should have been jogging in a safer spot, not to mention getting away from inhaling all those carbon monoxide fumes into his lungs.

But out on a country road there would have been no audience to admire his beautiful physique. Television and movies have caused us to be taken up with worshiping our bodies (the creature) instead of the Creator who made us.

In a hiking magazine I read an article entitled, "Run for Your Life! Safety Last." A reporter had photographed the dead body of an enthusiastic athlete who ran religiously for his health. He was struck down by a truck. He was running on a narrow highway in heavy traffic.

He who seeks to save his life can lose it. Be careful where you run in the natural realm and be careful of your motive in the spiritual realm, that you are running in the race for Jesus.

Kevin Shorey, a young evangelist friend of ours from Palm Beach, calls borderline Christians "revolving doors." They want to sound like one, but refuse to look the part. They act the part, yet refuse to confirm it by conforming to the image of Jesus. Admit it—it is just that, "acting a part" apart from God. Kevin is a great communicator and singer. He is impatient with singers who play "bait and switch" with sacred music. It is classified Christian but does not sound like it.

He pulls no punches. Why see how close we can come to darkness? Why go in and out, back and forth, through this revolving door? Why ask, "Can I listen to this kind of music? Can I smoke? Can I drink?" God wants better for us than the sounds of hell, lung cancer and brain damage!

As in a verbal election or parliamentary procedure, sound off. Let your communication be clear. Let your yea be yea, and your nay be nay. This is not the time to compromise. Prayer warriors, guard your heart, from our music to our friends to our every thought. Bring every thought, "into captivity to the obedience of Christ" (2 Corinthians 10:5).

A candle is a pleasant little light. It adds a tender touch of atmosphere for intimate dining. A candle is portable. It can be moved, knocked over or snuffed out. It melts or runs when things get hot.

A lighthouse, by contrast, is a permanent structure built on a rock foundation. It stands the test of time and the storms of life. The lighthouse is a harbor for the needy and seaweary traveler. Because of its high visibility, it becomes an open target for the enemy, a light set on a hill. When the winds of adversity blow, the light still shines. A candle could be puffed out by windy people and boasters, but the solid old lighthouse remains steady through "the blow."

Scripture tells us not to hide our light under a bushel. Hiding a candle under a bushel could be dangerous. But the mighty lighthouse cannot be hid under a bushel. It is constructed to stand the test of time, to weather the storms, to withstand every "wind of doctrine." It is placed in the harbor to warn of danger, to direct us in from the cold, and to serve as a shelter and strong tower where we may run in and hide.

You have known people who try to make their light shine: showing up, showing off, but not shining out. The lighthouse remains firm.

Can you stand this test? It depends on whether you are a flickering candle or a sturdy lighthouse.

My brother Jim operated a small manufacturing firm in Houston. It did well until the oil crisis a few years back when all Texans and the world were affected by it. He also horsed around for a while and eventually got into serious horse breeding—showing, even racing stock. Recently he told me, "I have learned to put something away for a rainy day, to have another income to fall back on, not to bank my future on such investments. When the economy gets tight, people can do without vacations, cars, *and horses*." Jim is a smart man.

"Some trust in chariots [cars], and some in horses [thoroughbreds and quarterhorses]; but we will remember the name of the Lord" (Psalm 20:7).

Dawn Wagler sent me a newspaper story from an Illinois paper, entitled "False Security," recounting that all members of a family perished in a nighttime fire that consumed their home. The father may have locked the doors carefully every night to ensure safety from burglars and made sure every family member was tucked safely into bed that fatal night. Yet they apparently had a false sense of security. Fire inspectors discovered not one but four smoke alarms, installed properly throughout the home—but all four batteries in them were dead.

Many times we place our security in things that are not dependable. Many people committed suicide after the great stock market crash because they had trusted in their financial investments. "Do not lay up for yourselves treasures on earth, where moth and rust destroy . . . but lay up for yourselves treasures in heaven. . . . For where your treasure is, there your heart will be also" (Matthew 6:19–21).

The first thing I do each morning and the last thing I do at night is talk to God. I call the it Oreo cookie concept. Morning and evening prayers are the chocolate wafer on each side, and He fills my day with that sweet cream center, all in between.

The last thing I do after I kiss Carl goodnight is pray silently. This is a wonderful way to fall asleep. I pray, "Lord, I thank You for helping me through this day. I appreciate You especially for helping me with the following difficult assignments [name them]. Erase from my mind anything that will be a 'hangover' in my spirit to weigh me on tomorrow. Remove any unpleasant memories that would prevent me from a good, sound, peaceful night's sleep.

"If I have blundered or been self-centered, forgive me. If I have been wronged, help me to forgive the person [name him or her], and I ask you to eradicate it from my mental computer. I resist any attempt of Satan to disturb my rest. I plead Your blood over my mind and my body, and over my loved ones. I draw an invisible blood line around my home and property.

"I give permission only to You, Lord, to invade my sleep if there is someone I need to pray for. If You have something You wish to whisper to me, or if You know that tomorrow's hectic schedule will be too noisy and I will be too preoccupied to listen, I give You permission to speak to me or reveal to me Your will through my dreaming, if necessary. Goodnight, Amen."

Tip: If you awaken in the night, always pray. If Satan is waking you, he will quit because he does not want you to talk to God. If it is the Lord awakening you, you will know it, for He will answer those prayers.

When my Carl breaks something, he laughs it off and yells, "Piffelberries!" I have never tasted a piffelberry, but it works. Shrug it, shuck it, then forget it. Albert Schweitzer stated one of his many genius philosophies, "Happiness is nothing more than good health and a short memory."

If you spill your coffee, mash your finger, go ahead, scream . . . but with *laughter*. We cannot control such situations, but laughter allows us to control our perception. Worry is like a rocking chair; it gives you something to do but it won't get you anywhere. Scientists have long known that when we are anxious, our bodies release large doses of stress hormones. These are helpful if you are being chased by a wild bull, but for ordinary daily stress these hormones are hazardous to health. So *kwitcherworrien*.

I have a witty, charming young neighbor who lost a breast to cancer. She is still smiling. I asked her how she did it. She said, "No one knows but you and my husband, and he loves me and doesn't care if I have just one breast left. That's why God gave me two, one to spare. I'm just glad both my babies have quit nursing!"

She that loseth wealth, loseth much; she that loseth friends, loseth more; but she that loseth spirit loseth all.

My friend Connie Lundstrom had a mammogram followed by a biopsy that revealed a cancerous breast tumor. "I've never felt so vulnerable and alone in my life," she admitted. I sat in her unseen balcony, cheering her silently, praying for her.

The night before surgery she spent watching the incredible Fourth of July fireworks and read Psalm 94:19: "In the multitude of my anxieties within me, Your comforts delight my soul." Fears rolled back and faith filled her mind. We got a photo of her later wearing a colorful T-shirt—*Repaired in Rochester*, home of the Mayo Clinic. Good for you, Connie!

The best time to examine a piece of real estate is at low tide. Do you want to know what the ocean floor is like "down under" all those gorgeous waves that the surfers worship here on the Gulf Coast? Let's *under*stand it at low tide. You'll find the spiney skeletons of eels, sharks' teeth and rusty cigarette lighters.

Buy a house on a rainy day. You will know if the roof leaks, if the yard stands in water and if the toilet will flush. Do not judge a man's salvation on Sunday morning but when things are stormy. (You don't need an umbrella on a dry day.) Does your religion work? Is your insurance company solvent? Those premiums you pay are not charity; they are your vote that when you need the company, it will come through for you.

Jesus said, "I will be with you in trouble and walk with you through the valley." Jesus said, "If you want to rule with Me, you must know how to suffer with Me." Men want to be a star, pastor a big church, have a big TV ministry, write a magazine, sell a million books. Hidden valleys turn shepherds into kings. Jesus trained thirty years to minister for three. He fasted forty days, suffered harassment from the devil, then emerged from the wilderness and bloomed into a fresh and new ministry of miracles.

The key to prosperity and treasure is to rise to the supreme place where God wants you to be. He will help you soar above your sorrow. There is a stratum in aeronautics called *tropopause*. It is that special place, the calm, quiet place away from pace, above all turbulence, at approximately 35,000 feet above sea level. Sound heavenly?

God formed us, sin deformed us, but Jesus transforms us! "There is a place of quiet rest, near to the heart of God." Lift me up above the shadows where the pure sunshine is found, on the mountaintops of glory! You can walk on the high places, on wings of the morning, "in perfect peace!" (Isaiah 26:3). There *is* such a place.

I hate labels. People judge each other and label according to what sometimes amounts to tunnel vision. There are no classes, no labels in heaven.

We bought a new Anderson window. After it was installed, I worked two days to remove the almost-permanent labels on that glass.

I walked into Kroger grocery store. At the front door was a basket full of cans and a sign: *Missing labels. Take a chance. 10 cents each.* Why not? I picked out three. When I returned home I opened one. It was deviled ham spread. Carl and I spread it on crackers, made two cups of hot cinnamon tea and had a great little treat. Next day while Carl was at work, I opened the tall, thin can. Not a bad deal, probably worth 89 cents—a can of chili con carne. I love chili. I lucked out again.

Later that week Carl ran in the back door unexpectedly for just a few minutes and asked for a quick snack. He decided to open the flat can that looked like another deviled ham spread. After three Wheatsworth crackers piled high with the spread, he slowed down and turned the can upside-down to read . . . *Purina Cat Chow.* You cannot judge a can by its *missing* label, either!

In the beginning the earth was labeled *Without form and void.* Darkness covered the deep, but the Holy Spirit moved, brought order out of chaos, and God created a beautiful earth for us to enjoy. God labeled it *Good* (Genesis 1:31).

Abe Lincoln quit school six times and was labeled gawky, but a concerned, loving teacher went after him, encouraged him, and we later labeled him U.S. President. Close friends labeled Einstein a raving madman. His genius proved that they had mislabeled him. Some labeled Jesus blasphemer, the bastard son of Mary. Easter proved them wrong. God thundered down from heaven and labeled Him, "This is my beloved Son!"

Don't let the turkeys get *you* down. The finest beef at Kroger gets the U.S.D.A. approval stamp. You have God's label of approval, too: "You are a chosen generation, a royal priesthood, a holy nation" (1 Peter 2:9).

He saw people *love* each other. He saw that all love made strenuous demands on the lovers. He saw love require sacrifice and self-denial. He saw love produce arguments and anguish. And he decided that it cost too much. He decided not to diminish his life with love.

He saw people *strive* for distant and hazy goals. He saw men strive for success . . . and women for high ideals. He saw that the striving was frequently mixed with disappointment. And he saw the strong men and women fail. He saw striving force people into pettiness. He saw that those who succeeded were sometimes those who had not earned the success. And he decided that it cost too much. He decided not to mar his life with striving.

He saw people *serve* others. He saw people give money to the poor and helpless. He saw that the more they served, the faster the need grew. He saw ungrateful receivers turn on their serving friends. And he decided that it cost too much. He decided not to soil his life with serving.

When he died, he walked up to God and presented Him with his life, undiminished, unmarred and unsoiled. His life was clean from the filth of the world, and he presented it proudly, saying, "This is my life."

And the great God said, "What life?"

Don't let the cares of life cut into your loving, striving and serving. And do not let discontent rob you of peace. The grass next door may look greener, but it is just as hard to cut. I refuse to allow the things I do not understand to rob me of the things that I do know. We must not lose hope, realizing that there are no perfect people, just perfect intentions. This is an invisible element, an anonymous force . . . the word *hope*. "Every thing that is done in the world," said Martin Luther, "is done by hope."

Jesus' rules for life were basically two: First, love God, then love people. Second: He who loses his life for others shall find it, and he who seeks to save his life [greedily, selfishly] shall lose it." Keep it simple, simply love.

How long has it been since you sang at home alone, no audience—just sang? Stop. Do it right now. Music bypasses the brain, goes straight to the heart, soul, emotions. "Serve the Lord with gladness. Come before His presence with singing" (Psalm 100:2).

How long has it been since you walked in the rain and listened to the patter of raindrops on an umbrella and been thankful for the umbrella? Looked up at the underside of leaves? Tried a new hairstyle? How long since you admitted you were wrong? How long has it been since you listened to your wife until she finished, without once interrupting?

How long since you tucked a real linen hankie into your purse instead of a paper Kleenex? How long since you sang in the choir? Volunteered to take a young mother's baby to the nursery so that she could hear one complete sermon without interruption? Have you sat a child on your lap lately and read a story? How long has it been since you sat on your husband's lap? Do it this evening.

How long has it been since you put a tablecloth on the table for dinner and lit two candles when no one was there but your family? Dress up today for yourself when no one will see you but you. You'll feel better. Draw a homemade birthday card instead of buying one to send. Write a letter longhand, slowly, deliberately, instead of using your typewriter or computer. Send it to someone who never gets mail. Buy a gift for a person who rarely receives one. Get up one hour early this Sunday, fix dinner and invite someone home with you. This used to be the highlight of our week. Fry old-fashioned chicken instead of catering to Colonel Sanders.

How long has it been since you knelt beside your bed just before retiring, as you did when you were a child? You never outgrow your need to empty your mind of the cares of life at each day's end. Kneel tonight. You never get too old to be God's child.

Dr. Paul Goldenfarb informed Grace that she had been attacked with the return of ovarian cancer. The morning before surgery her pastor came and prayed. When he quoted Mark 11:21–24, much of the dread seemed to go: "Jesus cursed the fig tree and it withered."

During surgery it took three doctors to lift the malignant, football-sized tumor from Grace's body. During private prayer the Lord seemed to whisper to her daughter Valerie, *Get Mother on the word; it will heal her.* "He sent His Word and healed them" (Psalm 107:20).

Grace's family bought her many faith-building books, but mostly they read the pure Word of God to her. The Bible and the Holy Spirit ministered to her faith. The reading of the Word, chemo treatments, medications, but always the Word. Sleepless nights: "The Lord is my Shepherd." Three days of hospitalization each month: "He maketh me to lie down in green pastures." Bad day, baldness, bruises, damaged veins: "I shall fear no evil." Lab reports, chemicals flowing into her bloodstream: "Thou anointest my head with oil, my cup runneth over."

After eleven months, reentry and exploratory surgery were necessary. The doctors feared that many cancer cells had invaded her abdomen and that scar tissue had damaged her kidneys and liver. But Grace read aloud, "My words are life to those that find them and health to all their flesh" (Proverbs 4:22). Also, "I shall not die, but live, and declare the works of the Lord!" (Psalm 118:17).

During the surgery, Valerie was reassured by several Scriptures: "Affliction will not rise up a second time" (Nahum 1:9) and "Thou shalt be perfect with the Lord thy God" (Deuteronomy 18:13). Words cannot describe the magnificence of the moment when the report came: "All biopsies negative, no scar tissue. All internal organs and abdominal cavity clean!"

Jesus is the only doctor who cures His patients by absorbing their diseases in His own body. He himself bore our infirmities, and with His stripes we are healed (Isaiah 53:5).

I got so excited a year ago when Sand Key finally opened just south of us. I pulled up to the toll gate and gladly paid my fifty cents, and had a wonderful time. What they failed to tell me was that I had to pay fifty cents to get out, too. I have done TV shows on which I was almost forced to pledge to get off the set, or to be invited back; gone to churches where I almost had to pay to get out the exit door. God help us when we have to buy a ticket to get to hear a man's testimony of what God did for him for free!

If you go to a restaurant and they charge you but do not feed you, you do not return. Many times we get people to come, then place more emphasis on their giving than on their receiving. I believe firmly in tithing, but it seems that sometimes we spend a lot of time taking, raking in, the offering in comparison to the time of prayer and ministry, meeting needs. As many as came to Jesus, He received them and sent them away with their needs met, abundantly, for free and with joy. We must make it worth their trip. There must be something in it for them, some take-home, some carry-out benefits.

"Freely you have received, freely give" (Matthew 10:8).

It is the only way I can get to church. The longest stoplight in the world is at the corner of Pinehurst and Route 580. Some fiendish, sadistic engineer with a sneer on his face said, "Let's make thousands of Floridians and millions of tourists angry this year by designing this "too-long" red light!" Why, you can sit there so long that your cheese molds and a wild palm tree can grow up through the floorboard of your car!

Next time you are stalled at a light, notice what people do. Older men pick their noses. Young women look in the rearview mirror and check their hair and makeup. Young men clean out the ash tray and toss cigarettes onto the pavement while they turn up the music a little louder, a signal to the single girls within earshot. Old women clean out their purses.

One Sunday sitting at that light, I remembered what Dr. Charles Allen from Houston told us he did at stoplights, "redeeming the time, for the days are evil" (Colossians 4:5 and Ephesians 5:16). He sent quick prayers for the people he could see and flashed a fast smile before the light changed at anyone who would glance his way. He felt that two people cannot meet even casually without both parties being changed a little.

I tried it. A couple in the next car were quarreling so loudly I could hear them even with the windows rolled up and the air conditioner on. I prayed for them and whispered, "The peace of God shall keep your hearts." They silenced, looked over at me, smiled and waved as they turned right onto 580 East. I was in the center lane. In the left lane was a mauve-colored Sidekick pulling a boat. Sitting on his mother's lap was a little boy crying, his nose running. His mother was fumbling furiously to open a pack of gum.

On my dash was a single stick of Juicy Fruit, and on the floorboard, a helium-filled birthday balloon my family had given me. I pulled closer to them, rolled down my window and tossed the gum and balloon through their window. The daddy honked, the mother smiled and said, "Thank you much," and the toddler laughed out loud. I pulled through that light feeling good!

This is a feeling book of daily devotionals. One page may make you feel good and the next one bad, but my prayer is that you will have looking eyes, a listening heart and a feeling for folks.

God's ways are not far out, but they are "past finding out." He does not use strange people, but strangers. He picks up an unknown to make known His deeds among the people . . . to declare His glory.

God rarely uses popular people, but simple, trusting ones. Martin Luther married Katie, a runaway, stowaway nun hiding in a herring barrel. Sounds like a fish story, yet it is true. Martin Luther was wrong about a lot of things, yet right about the most important things. After seeing a vision of Jesus, he declared to the Church hierarchy, "The just shall live by faith."

Over 450 years ago he wrote a grand old hymn of the Church:

A mighty fortress is our God,
A bulwark never failing. . . .
The body they may kill:
God's truth abideth still,
His kingdom is forever!

God does not use a popular message but a simple one. The world places Christianity in its lineup of religions, just one of many, while the Scripture says, "There is one God, and one mediator between God and men, the man Christ Jesus." "There is no other name under heaven given among men, whereby we *must* be saved." He was not voted in by popular vote but by God's command—for God has exalted the name of Jesus above every name (see Philippians 2:9).

For the message of the cross is foolishness to those who are perishing, but to us who are being saved it is the power of God. . . . For since, in the wisdom of God, the world through wisdom did not know God, it pleased God through the foolishness of the message preached to save those who believe. (1 Corinthians 1:18, 21)

And Paul adds a postscript in verse 25: "The foolishness of God is wiser than men, the weakness of God is stronger than men."

Have you discovered the magic of the microphone? It has a strange effect on the stagestruck. Once it is in their hands, they come alive and don't know when to quit. All the limelight does to others is show up their ignorance. Phillips Brooks once wrote, "We are haunted by a desire for the ideal life. This is because we have within us the beginnings and the possibility of it."

Jesus said, "Let your light so shine that others may glorify God." It doesn't matter if you are just a flashlight or if you are under the stagelights where the audience is large; let yours shine. Much is said about Jesus as "the Light of the world" and the "Life." John uses the words *light* and *life* interchangeably. Ephesians and 1 John also speak of Jesus as "The Light."

My friend Vicky Hagen gave me a great illustration. She has seven children and several grandchildren and had probably been to one of their school plays recently. "I am glad that in the production of the Stage of Life," she said, "we can never step out of His light."

There is no place so dark that God cannot spot us. You may be ministering in a remote location, unknown to the religious media, but His searchlight is over you—making notes, taking note of eternity. "For the Lord takes pleasure in His people; He will beautify the humble with salvation" (Psalm 149:4).

Pure, undefiled religion, is visiting orphans, widows and ministering to the needy (James 1:27).

Miriam Machovec has a prominent position with Vida and Life Publishers in Miami. I am sure she dresses appropriately on her job here in Florida, yet she has just returned from a humble servanthood ministry to the hungry, needy peoples in Russia, distributing the Book of Life. She talked to us about a practical lesson she learned while there: "how to wear the same white turtleneck for ten days and still look good!" Her message was good too, as she exhorted the teachers there: "Those mighty in Spirit have the heart of a servant! The greatness of man's power is the measure of his surrender to Jesus."

Follow directions. Read the recipe. When it calls for a pinch of salt, do, but don't overdo. Jesus said, "You are the salt of the earth" (Matthew 5:13). We don't salt salt. Salt used in moderation can cure meat, keep it from spoiling and make food tastier. In a recipe for cornbread, if you use too much milk, you end up with mush. If you forget the egg, the ingredients won't stick together. No salt, soda or baking powder and you end up with a flat flapjack. God set the burning bush on fire, but He didn't burn it up. Ever-burning fire!

When you witness to people, feed them salt, make them thirsty, but remember that an overdose of salt produces not just thirst but dehydration. And our motive must be pure. I get nervous when people tell me they love to teach, preach and sing. But when they say, "I love the people I teach, preach for and sing to," we are on the right track.

Jesus also said, "You are the light of the world." The easiest way to overdo the lighting business is to hide your light under a bushel along with a thousand other lights. We cluster with other bright lights in a "holy huddle" while millions are hungry, thirsty and in darkness.

I have a yogurt-maker. I put one tablespoon of culture starter to make a batch of five cups. In the same way, one loving Christian can affect a whole batch of needy people. Don't be pushy, but avoid being stingy with your ideas, your emotion and your affection. Don't withhold from your brother when you see his need. You will win some and lose some. Take the bitter with the sweet, the sunshine with the shadows. There is time for mourning and for dancing. Not everyone will love you as you love them.

No-risk guarantee: You shall do valiantly if you follow the recipe in God's Word. When David reread the recipe, he said he could run through a troop and jump over a wall (not jump over a troop and run through a wall!).

When Jesus was on earth, He healed the sick who came to Him. He did not go door to door offering His miracle services. Sometimes He touched them, put mudpacks on their blind eyes and they saw. Sometimes the sick touched *Him*. The woman with the issue of blood touched His hem and practically healed herself. Even Jesus, who asked, "Who touched Me so that healing virtue went out from Me?" had not specifically directed her cure. Many times He did not make a house call, but "sent His word and healed them" (Psalm 107:20). His methods did not follow medical formulas. But He did not need a formula; He had the Father.

He told *us* to heal the sick, too. He said, "Greater works than these he will do, because I go to My Father" (John 14:12). When He went back, I believe He sent medical concepts that reached farther than He ever could have traveled as one here on the earth. I believe He meant miracles of healing through praying and faith. Pray anonymously for people to receive physical and emotional healing. God will give you many miracles of healing if you do not care who gets credit for it.

Give anonymously and help heal people financially. Loan your spirit; let people borrow your faith when theirs is bankrupt. Specialize in "carryouts." In your gleaning for yourself, leave handfuls on purpose for others. The anonymous healer will be rewarded, his portion "pressed down, shaken together and running over."

I wear a beautiful ivory bracelet, a perfect circle around my wrist carved with tiny elephants. This elegant gift is a constant reminder of God's mercy and redemption.

Years ago following a ruptured appendix, pneumonia, a bowel block, three surgeries and many days in a coma, I had a brush with death, then an unexplainable resurrection. A colostomy was unnecessary, I returned with good health and a love for people I did not have before.

As a result of this experience, missionaries in South Africa, Zimbabwe and Zaire began playing a tape of my story in remote villages and many were saved and healed. Then the Rhema churches in the Johannesburg area, the University of Medicine and the South African Broadcasting Network brought me to South Africa and assigned me a kind and knowledgeable guide, Ruth Nortje.

At the close of a service held in a school auditorium, a beautiful young woman hugged me and sat by me on the front row. "It's not fair," she said. "You are a good woman and you wear cheap plastic bracelets. I am a bad woman, make a lot of money as a prostitute and I wear genuine ivory bracelets."

Then she removed my ten-cent bracelet and put hers on my arm. I never cry, but I cried then.

"I cannot read or write," she told me, "but I'm pretty. I make money by selling my body to goldminers and ivory dealers. I make a handsome living, but am never satisfied."

She and I knelt, arms around each other, weeping together. She asked me to pray. And Jesus gave her real joy in exchange for cheap, commercial lust.

Will you pray for her, too? She wants a new job, a different occupation. She has two children—doesn't know who their father is—and wants a Christian mate.

Rescue the perishing, lift up the fallen. Jesus came to seek and to save the lost.

"When will we learn to take that dumb phone off the hook when we sit down to dinner!" Carl complained. I answered the phone.

"Mrs. Malz, you are one of the first families selected to hear of our special offer for family services. We have just developed a new section of burial plots in the beautiful wooded acres at Peaceful Garden. Select your plot now and save a considerable amount of money and assure your peace of mind for your future resting place." Hustling burial plot bargains!

My hand was still on the phone when it hummed against my palm and rang again. This time it was a sweet-voiced woman wondering if I had considered the alternative to burial. (She really was!) They had a mausoleum shelf, pre-death cremation offer at advance savings.

Carl and I heated the food in the microwave and took the phone off the hook. The rest of the meal we laughed and discussed opportunists. At the scene of a wreck, almost before the impact, two fire trucks, two ambulances, two tow trucks and a helicopter arrive! Well, almost.

Some churches have developed these tactics too, much to our chagrin—opportunists using guilt tactics to get you to pledge, to give an offering. They catch you off-guard in a weak moment. One charity monopolized so much of my time that I asked them to send Carl a brochure for his consideration. Two days later in the mail I received a receipt for a $25 donation, payable within ten days! Wednesday night prayer time can be the opportunist's chance to accuse and gossip under the guise of testimony or prayer request.

We need to be the right kind of opportunists, bold for God to witness and to pray. "Seek the Lord while he may be found." "The Spirit of the Lord is upon me, because He has anointed me to preach the gospel to the poor. He has sent Me to heal the brokenhearted, to preach deliverance to the captives and . . . to set at liberty, those who are bruised" (Luke 4:18). Seize your chance and be an opportunist for Him.

"Poems are made by fools like me, but only God can make a tree."

Let me paraphrase Psalm 1:1–3: If you walk in God's counsel, if you do not scorn but delight in the Lord and think about God in both the daylight and the dark times, you will be like a tree. Not just any tree, but one planted by a river of living water. You will be fruitful. Your leaf will not wither; He will actually reverse the curse. And whatever you invest in will prosper."

That is a tremendous insurance policy!

I have a copy of the children's book *The Giving Tree*. Think about how much trees give to mankind. They release oxygen. They blossom and give off fragrance. They provide themselves for a child's treehouse; they provide lumber to build an adult's house. Trees provide a place to play; yet they have also been used to hang criminals.

We live in Florida where trees give us pineapples, dates, oranges, bananas and tangerines. Trees provide shade from the sun's heat and branches for birds to build their nests. Branches from palms provide fronds for thatched roofing; they break the wind from the force of devastating hurricanes. They bend and take a beating but do not break. The Lord promises that if I proclaim His faithfulness and praise Him, I "shall flourish like a palm tree. . . . [I will] still bear fruit in old age; [I will be] fresh and flourishing" (Psalm 92:12, 14).

Brochures, impressive and expensive, arrive almost daily in the mail: writers' workshops, marriage clinics, charm schools, assertiveness training. Jesus Himself taught two seminars: one on servanthood and one on the ministry of helps (1 Corinthians 12:28). If you are willing to sign up, you will never be without work. God in His overruling, practical providence uses both great and small in the ministries of "door-opening" and "links."

Let me illustrate. Our daughter April was high-point person several times in girls' basketball, Sisseton, South Dakota. At Wheaton College I overheard Coach Brenda Hillman commend April for a great game. When our daughter went to the dressing room I remarked to the coach, "In high school sometimes she scored 21 points. Tonight she only made six points." To which she replied, "This is not high school. This is college-level ball. You should have looked at the stats sheet. Your girl did eight assists that linked the plays together so someone else could score."

Carl's phone call from Rega, Siberia, awakened me from a sound sleep last night at 2:30 A.M. He was "high as a kite" and wanted to share his link story.

On his first trip to Russia a woman had informed him, "There is *one* Aglow group, newly organized, in all of the Soviet Union. We have learned that in the U.S. your wife has spoken to Aglow. Could you, would you, tell her story to us here in Krasnoyarsk?" He did, and the response was overwhelming.

Oh, the power of positive suggestion! Carl mentioned to his listeners that Aglow International would meet later in the year in Orlando, Florida. "Think about it. Link prayer with your daydreaming. Going to Orlando is not a far-out idea. The Lord may want you to go."

The board of five humble, Russian-speaking women dressed in plain cotton dresses did indeed go. And they returned with a spark that has ignited a forest fire in Russia that will never be extinguished!

Try this experiment on yourself and answer two questions: Who are you and what are you?

To the first question you probably responded readily with your name. To the second question, instead of responding that you are a man or woman, you probably thought of what you do: "I'm a writer [a mother, a fireman . . .]."

A schoolteacher friend of ours asked similar questions on the first day of school. She asked her new first-graders, "What does your daddy do?"

One responded quickly, "I don't have one." Ricky raised his hand and reported, "My daddy is a psychiatrist. He helps people think better."

I was talking with a clothing designer who said, in the course of conversation, "At a fashion show I looked around at my buyers. One character stood out like a sore thumb. He looked like a farmer, dressed like a farmer, had a farmer's tan."

I stopped him short. "Don't knock it! Where would we be without farmers?"

I lived in the Dakotas for eleven years with grain farmers. Without them we would starve to death. My grandparents had a farm, milked their own cows and churned their own marvelous butter.

In her book *Cross Creek*, Marjorie Rawlings wrote, "I was part of the earth before I was a part of the womb." Adam was created by God from the earth. When we die we return to the land. "For dust you are, and to dust you shall return" (Genesis 3:19).

Do what you do, whatever you do, as unto the Lord. Do what you do quickly, with sobriety, redeeming the time, for the days are evil. And watch what you do; people are following you!

Procrastination is a thief. While writing this book, if I take time to get a cup of coffee or even "get organized," I lose my zip. I must seize the moment, obey the impulse, strike while the iron is hot!

Every morning when I was in seventh and eighth grade (Mishawaka, Indiana), we had a ten-minute general assembly. We saluted the American flag and the Christian flag. Then our principal, Mr. Moran, prayed a brief prayer and asked us to quote the following: "Initiative is doing the right thing at the right time, without being told."

My father moved us from there in order to pastor a small, red-brick church on North Main Street in Clinton, Indiana. Our family always arrived at church one hour early. Mother checked the music. Dad checked the building, the temperature and double-checked his sermon material, while my little Hungarian friend, Margaret Nagy, and I walked seven blocks to buy an Eskimo Pie. By the time we talked and walked back, the treat was gone and it was time for church to start. Fond memories!

I kept in touch with Marg over the years. She married a minister, Herb Neal, had a daughter and one son who died very young. I put off visiting her, but I did write, especially when she became a widow, since I was widowed myself and lived alone for six years.

Last year, while reading my Bible and praying, I remembered our growing-up times and called her. I learned that she had never been to Florida. So I began saving money to fly her here to spend a week in Florida at the beautiful beaches she had never seen. But Marg had a steady job at the license bureau and drove a decent car. So I put off my impulse. *Oh well, it's the thought that counts, I rationalized. If she wants to come, she can.*

When I learned she was hospitalized, I felt bad. What's worse, she never regained consciousness and was dead in three weeks.

The road to hell is paved with good intentions. "Do not withhold good from those to whom it is due, when it is in the power of your hand to do so" (Proverbs 3:27).

I suffered osteoarthritis in the back of my neck for twelve long years. It was perpetual pain day and night, like a toothache in the top five vertebrae of my neck. Houston Medical Center tried traction, heat packs and medication. No better. They sent me home and advised me, "Learn to live with it."

Three years ago in April, I left the sunshine of the South to speak in a community church in Fryeburg, Maine. They still had snow on the ground. The osteoarthritis kicked up worse than usual. I could not even turn my head. I prayed silently, *Lord, keep my mind on my message and off my neck.*

There were probably sixty people there and only one seat was left in the front row. I took it. Someone whispered, "No, no. Don't sit there. Ruthie is sitting right behind you and Ruthie bothers visitors. Sit on the platform."

"I'll take my chances," I replied. "I'm not a platform person."

Sure enough, Ruthie bothered me. I was trying to concentrate on my notes when I felt a *tap tap* on my left shoulder. I turned to look into the face of a retarded young woman wearing a turquoise sweatsuit. Across her chest were four-inch letters spelling *Ruthie.* She kissed my cheek, drooled on my white blouse and said, "I like you." I hugged her. "I like you, too, Ruthie!" She replied with slurred speech and twisted mouth, "You know my name." She didn't know I could read.

As Pastor Ron Fast introduced me, the Lord whispered to the inner chamber of my heart, *"Lay aside those stale notes. I didn't send you here to impress these people but to love them."*

During my message Ruthie stood and announced, "I like this place!" She could recognize genuine love.

When I finished and sat back down, my neck was killing me. I bowed my head and wished I were home. I breathed, "Jesus," and felt warm fingers trace all five vertebrae. *The pain was gone.* I could turn my neck for the first time in twelve years! The pain is still gone and I can turn my head.

I felt in my heart that there was an undeniable connection between my healing and Ruthie. She was out of tune with reality but in tune with the real Source. She was a most unlikely vehicle for this miracle, but God chooses whom He will. His ways are past finding out.

Reader, you, too, are a likely candidate to be used by God in the miraculous. Not training, not mentality, not religious education qualifies you, but love.

What if the fairy tale *Pinocchio* were true? What if every time *you told* half a lie, your nose grew? You would have to hire a stretch limo to take you to church, and you would have to sit in the back seat to accommodate your long nose!

What if your lips got bigger and bigger when you criticized, talked negatively or gossiped? It would take both your hands to hold up your lips so you could see to tie your shoes . . . and then who would tie them?

What if you looked at a man with lust, imagining just a little? What if while the kids were in school you peeked a wee bit at X-rated video or cable TV, and your eyes grew and grew? When your husband returned home from work he would find this woman with grotesque, oversized eyes. "Explain this!" he would insist.

Men: While you are away on a business trip and are tired of being a good example in your hometown, in front of the wife and kiddos, have you ever wished that God would just turn his head for 24 hours so that you could walk into certain places without being reported? What if, when you did walk in there, your feet grew and grew? What size shoe (size 134?) would you wear? Would they cost $780 per pair?

There are often no immediate consequences to sin. And, thank God, He does not expose and punish us on the spot. "Because the sentence against an evil work is not executed speedily, therefore the heart of the sons of men is fully set in them to do evil" (Ecclesiastes 8:11).

Remember the children's song: "Be careful, little eyes, what you see [little ears, what you hear; little hands, what you do]. There's a Father up above, and He's looking down in love. . . ."

Do not be deceived" (Galatians 6:7). You can be sincerely in error, sincerely wrong, but God never has been, never will be, cannot be, mocked. You can never "pull one over" on God. You are saved by faith, not by works. But "Whatever a man sows [given time], that he will also, reap" (verse 7).

Glorify God with your body.

Both my grandmothers gave me their recipe for homemade angel food cake. They both raised chickens and declared that the success of their cakes lay in this secret: thirteen very fresh egg whites. The yolks were put aside for breading meats, squash, fried green tomatoes and the sort. But for a fluffy, light-textured, high-rise angel food cake, you must separate the whites from the yellows and allow not one string of yolk, or the cake in the baking process will fall flat.

Try as hard as my young, inexperienced, new bride's hands could, I always messed up one of those thirteen eggs and smeared some yolk, ruining the texture of my cake. One day, almost at noon, I heard the familiar honk of Mother's Oldsmobile. When I went to the drive, she flung a small sack out the window and hurried home to get lunch for my brother and dad.

Inside the package I found an Official Egg Separator. The dish-shaped apparatus fit on top of the measuring cup with an indentation that held back one yolk and let the albumen slip through the crack. What a modern wonder, that 29-cent utensil! It save my culinary reputation.

Jesus helped us with our Christian walk when He told us, through the apostle Paul, "Come out from among them and be separate" (2 Corinthians 6:17). You shall be "a chosen generation," wrote Peter, "a peculiar people" (1 Peter 2:9), cherished and rare race being groomed for the Kingdom to come. When Paul used the term *separate* and Peter the term *peculiar*, they did not mean we should be obnoxious and weird, super but not natural. They meant we would be uniquely like Jesus.

Then, when we become separate from the evil of this world, "Neither death nor life, nor angels nor principalities, nor powers, nor things present nor things to come, nor height nor depth, nor any other created thing, shall be able to separate us from the love of God which is in Christ Jesus our Lord" (Romans 8:38–39).

A man can declare himself a police officer and people will believe him; but to function in an official capacity, he is usually required to wear his uniform and show his badge.

You may be a secret follower of Jesus, an admirer of the Lord's concepts, but Jesus Himself commanded, "By this all will know that you are My disciples, if you have love for one another" (John 13:35). He did not say *love one for another*, but made it plain that we deliver that love to others.

I have purchased tickets for my family to see the play *Cats* at Ruth Eckerd Hall in (town?), but if I fail to get those tickets *to* my husband and daughter, they will (sure as you live) miss that performance.

I have just come through a difficult trial. I longed for someone to listen to me, talk with me. Carl was my pastor, but he was on a foreign missions assignment and I needed a shepherd. I am grateful for God's Word that "My grace is sufficient for you" (2 Corinthians 12:9), but it was just barely. A busy pastor nearby showed no concern, did not call to see if I was O.K., did not offer prayer. I translated it as rejection. I learned later that he had been concerned *about* me, but never got that concern *to* me. He had compassion but withheld it, and I never got it.

Express your love *to* people, deliver the *good* goods, show your compassion. Remember, The milk of human kindness never curdles. It is always in style, always essential to someone. Withhold not when it is in the power of your hands to give it to another.

I love the happy, cheerful color orange, I like crisp autumn weather and I love giving treats to the trick-or-treaters in our neighborhood. As a wispy girl growing up, I was always too tall and too skinny. On Halloween I would put on a mask, pad my pencil-thin body with pillows and *pretend fat*. No one would ever guess who I was. Such fun!

Bertha Adams wore a mask, too. It was not Halloween, but March 30, 1975, when a social worker found what he thought was another victim of poverty. It was Bertha's lifeless body in a disheveled apartment. No food and no friends. In her personal possessions he found two keys. They opened two locked boxes in a small bank nearby containing $799,000 in cash!

Bertha wore the mask of poverty. She preferred people to think of her as something she was not. Rather than hiding behind bad choices, though, she could have been, warm, healthy, friendly, even given to those who were poor for real and died with loved ones at her side.

A young husband told my pastor-husband, "Two years into our marriage I discovered who my wife really was. I loved this new person much more than the pretense she thought she had won me with."

Judas wore a mask of charity. He said, "Why wasn't this ointment sold for funds to enable us to give to the poor?" This was a mask; he didn't care about the poor. He was a thief, had the bag that controlled the money and was a traitor at heart.

Get rid of the front. Humility and meekness are of the heart, not the face. A "hang-dog" dejected look is not a holy look. Jesus came so that we might have life more abundantly, that we would prosper and be in health.

Drop your mask. People will like you better, and *you* will like you better. God knows who you really are. In His presence is pleasure and fullness of joy.

He who sows sparingly will also reap sparingly, and he who sows bountifully will also reap also bountifully. . . . God is able to make all grace abound toward you, that you, always having all sufficiency in all things, have an abundance for every good work. . . . "He has dispersed abroad, He has given to the poor; His righteousness remains forever." . . . He who supplies seed to the sower, and bread for food, supply and multiply the seed you have sown and increase the fruits of your righteousness, while you are enriched in everything for all liberality. . . . For the administration of this service not only supplies the needs of the saint, but also is abounding. . . . through the proof of this ministry, they glorify God for the obedience of your confession to the gospel of Christ, and for your liberal sharing with them and all men, and by their prayer for you, who long for you because of the exceeding grace of God in you. (2 Corinthians 9:6, 8–14)

But if you sow to the flesh, you shall of the flesh *reap corruption* (Galations 6:8–9). What is that secret, fleshly thing you are hiding that is displeasing to God? What is that private thing that you are careful about? After you sow and time takes its process, you will reap corruption, corrosion, deterioration. You can sit in a chair alongside the Colorado River and say after one day, "I don't believe in erosion, because it doesn't happen that fast." But erosion by the Colorado River is what caused the Grand Canyon. It did not happen over night. It was a slow process. This is how sowing sin operates in your life.

Maybe you didn't intend that small seed to grow, didn't intend to get so deeply in debt, so deeply involved with an illegitimate relationship. You may think someone wrote me a letter about you and say angrily, "You're exposing me." If you sow the flesh, you will reap temporary pleasure to satisfy your natural appetite, yet you have displeased God.

"And let us not grow weary while doing good, for in due season we shall reap if we do not lose heart" (Galatians 6:9).

A little boy, after looking with fascination at the mean face on a wanted poster in the post office, walked up to the postmaster and asked, "Is that wanted poster a real picture of the criminal?" The postmaster assured him, that yes, it was an actual photo. The little fellow asked, "Then why didn't you keep him when you had him here?"

I stand by watching Jesus knock at the heart's door of my friends and neighbors, and wonder why they do not seize the opportunity, capture the tender moment and want Him, as He wants them. Why don't they open the door, invite him into the throne room of their heart's inner chamber?

"You will find Him if you seek Him with all your heart and with all your soul" (Deuteronomy 4:29). While life is young, early in a situation before it gets out of hand, and early each morning, seek Him, want Him, and He will come to you. Want Him more than food, and He will supply not only your daily bread, but more, much more, exceeding abundance above all that you can ask or think.

The Holy Spirit is a gentleman. He will never be overbearing and push Himself on you. You must want Him, desire Him. The wise men traveled far, searching, desiring, looking for Jesus, journeying perhaps for years. David wanted God—his soul longed for Him, like searching for water in a dry and thirsty land. Job was another wise man who sought for God. "Oh, my desire is the Almighty."

Wise men today still seek Jesus, the Son of God. The Lord is looking for you, wants you. Are you looking for Him? Is He wanted? "Seek the Lord while He may be found" (Isaiah 55:6). Don't wait until it is too late.

Smith Wigglesworth had 20/20 vision.

At the age of eighteen Smith Wigglesworth gathered poor children, spent his wages on their physical needs, and then told them of Jesus. Never a week passed that he did not win at least fifty of them to Jesus.

We have become so preoccupied with selfish blindness and modern-day preoccupation with trivialities that we have lost our vision and become indifferent to soul-winning. Satan has blinded us with the mechanics of the ministry. We train to witness, yet are blind to just doing it.

People with 20/20 spiritual vision sleep better at night. Loving God, then loving others, they can say each night, "My conscience is void of offense before God and man. God is in His heaven, and all is right with my world."

Then, *thy sleep shall be sweet.* "When you lie down, you will not be afraid; yes, you will lie down and your sleep will be sweet" (Proverbs 3:24).

"The Lord is my light and salvation; whom shall I fear . . . of whom shall I be afraid?" (Psalm 27:1).

"In the secret of His tabernacle He shall hide me" (Psalm 27:5).

"Meditate within your heart on your bed, and be still" (Psalm 4:4).

"I will both lie down in peace, and sleep; for You alone, O Lord, make me dwell in safety" (Psalm 4:8).

I love animals and animals love me. There has been a lifelong competition between cats and dogs. Dogs come when they are called, cats take your number and get back to you.

I recently called a friend who is a practical joker. His answering machine said, "This is our cat. I have a message for you. If you are a blood relative or a friendly friend, leave a message. If you are selling something, hang up."

No one pets a porcupine. He has been provided with needle-sharp quills for his protection. He is a prickly ball, like a wrong-side-out pin cushion. His forced hospitality is never challenged. People yield to him in fear, but never love. He always gets his own way. All who have touched him get hurt. He doesn't care what other animals think of him; he is his own man, unpopular and independent.

Many people have porcupine dispositions and wonder why no one loves them. They roll through life in an egotistical ball, wanting their own way, thinking people should jump when they say so. Their attitudes are contrary to Christian love which "does not seek its own" (1 Corinthians 13:5).

Porcupine Christians are rarely bothered. No one comes to them for help or asks their counsel. They do not bear other's burdens, but neither do they share their joys (see Romans 12:15).

Porcupine people pretend to be independent, but really their problem is loneliness. In their jabbing philosophy, prickly attitudes and selfish egotism they have forgotten the truth. "For none of us lives to himself, and no one dies to himself" (Romans 14:7).

A porcupine loses part of himself when his quill pierces another. Likewise, a person injures himself most when his temper or disposition inflicts injury. The bottom line: Be pettable.

We have had the happy pleasure and experienced the hard work of building three new homes. While constructing the foundation of all three, we have taken a Bible, wrapped it in heavy plastic and put it into the eastern corner of the foundation—representing Jesus, the cornerstone of our home.

Upon completion we have had a minister come and dedicate the house as a place of prayer, a temple for God, a place of harbor for our children and a place to serve others in loving hospitality. We have a printed plaque placed near the front entry with the words that are inscribed on the door of St. Stephen's Church in London:

> God, make the door of this house wide enough to receive all
>   who need human love and fellowship,
> Narrow enough to shut out all envy, pride and strife.
> Make its threshold smooth enough to be no stumbling block
>   to children, nor to straying feet
> But rugged and strong enough to turn back the tempter's power.
> God, make the door of this house the gateway to Thine Eternal Kingdom.

We have gotten letters from the people who purchased the homes from us saying, "This is a happy house! This is a peaceful place!"

One of the homes, on Doris Drive north of Terre Haute, Indiana, was hit by a tornado the day after it was finished. It was one of 36 that were flattened to the ground. Brenda and I escaped without one scratch, though only one wall was left standing. The cat was safe under the car, and the dog crawled under Brenda's stomach for safety. Our book *Gone With The Wind* was found two and a half miles away in Rosedale. The *Grit* newspaper took pictures of this quirk. We escaped with nothing but the gowns we wore to a basement nearby. Some people were wringing their hands, some drinking and cursing God, but Brenda and I lay sleeping peacefully on a mattress, waiting for Carl's return home. The insurance company even paid for Brenda's dolls, and built the house back better than new. God was faithful!

"Be sure your sin will find you out," warns Numbers 32:23.

It was November 6, my birthday. Churches in the area of Sauk Center, Minnesota, had sponsored a Saturday night rally and I was to give my testimony. After driving three hours, nonstop, I arrived at the church just ten minutes before time to start. I hurried to the basement and found at the door marked "Women" a line of at least eighteen ladies.

Glancing down the hallway I saw that no one was near the men's room. Who would ever know? I hurried in, locked the door and noticed that the toilet was atop three concrete steps, as if they had built the men's restroom over a stairway. I climbed the steps and bumped my head. Aggravated, I used the white throne, and went to step down. The steps were painted with a gray, porcelain-like finish. I slipped and fell, whacking the back of my head on one of the steps. When I came to , my head ached, my eyes would not focus, my stockings were torn and my belt was broken. I couldn't see my feet. My back and legs were numb and I felt panic, for I could hear singing coming from upstairs.

Rubbing my legs and praying, I realized that I could not find my feet because my high heels had punched through the thin plaster wall. My feet were out in the hallway in a cloud of chalky dust. As I tried to drag my legs back inside I heard two male voices.

"What's this!" exclaimed one.

"Why, I think that's our speaker!" replied the other.

"Not any more," the first one laughed. "She'll never make it. She may be a writer, but she can't *read*." He leaned down and said, "Do you know you are in the men's room?"

"Go away," I begged him.

His next question was the most ridiculous of all. "Are you hurt?"

"No, I'm not hurt! I always exit restrooms this way."

As soon as I could I got up, put my torn stockings and broken belt in my purse, and limped upstairs toward the singing. As I walked in, they broke out with "Happy birthday to you!" I came forward, dragging one leg, and the pastor gave me a dozen red roses. I tried to smile.

Later in the service when I was introduced, I stood on one leg and did the best I could in all that pain. Then I drove home sitting sideways and went straight to the hospital emergency room where I learned that I had broken my tail bone.

Five days later, I got a get well card from the church and the secretary added a little P.S.: "We did not repair the wall in the men's room, but installed a small plaque that says, 'Betty Malz was here!'"

I hope she was teasing.

I walked along the sandy shores at Daytona. The people were bare but the beach was not. Crowded is what it was. There were wall-to-wall bodies who dared to bare (and some dared very much), lying patiently, absorbing the sun to get a great tan. The more exposure they had to the sun, the more they were changed. People knew they had gotten some sun.

I realized suddenly that this principle is also true in the spiritual. The more we dare to bare our heart and soul to the Son, in prayer, Bible reading and fellowship with Him, the more we will radiate with a joyous countenance, and radiate with His light and life. People will know we have been with the *Son*. This change starts from the inside out.

You cannot hope to maintain a rich bronze tan by spending a few minutes in the sun, only twice a year. Neither can you sustain a rich, stimulating relationship with Jesus, the Son of God, by spending a minute or two, here and there with Him, in the sunshine of His presence.

Medical professionals have started cautioning the dangers of overexposure to the sun. But there can never be overexposure to the Son. Retha Gorten once said, "Let Him permeate, then go radiate!"

When I was a small girl, we had a special Sunday school teacher. One morning she brought us a small paper cross with the motto, "Be not afraid." If you left it under a light for fifteen minutes, the cross that had been painted with phosphorus would absorb the light and glow.

Have you lost your glow? How long has it been since you've basked in His Sonshine, absorbed Him, let Him shine on you?

God doesn't require you to give what you do not have, only what you do. Don't sit on your hands . . . do something.

That widow in the Bible couldn't give Donald Trump's millions, but she could give something: her two coins. A Pharisee standing in line probably said, "That's nothing." But I can just hear God exclaim, "Isn't that something!" God doesn't use famous people, just faithful people, and that makes them famous. Think it over. Her story has been told down through the centuries. That's genuine fame!

You will never be called to do what Jesus did . . . but do something!

You may never want to give what martyrs give . . . but give something!

You may not be called to go overseas . . . but go somewhere!

You may not go across the ocean, but you can go across the street!

You may not be qualified to write something like Ephesians . . . but you can write a letter to encourage a friend.

You may not have a platform to preach like Billy Graham . . . but you can invite people to church so the pastor can witness.

You may not sing like Bev Shea or Bev Sills . . . but you can sing something!

One young man has a little investment in a fudge making business. He blesses people with fudge. One couple has a citrus grove. They give away "fruits of their spirit"—love—in the form of citrus fruit and papaya. Give what you are! Give what you have! Give what you can! Do what you can! Don't sit on your hands, do something!

Five-year-old Adam talking of nothing else but being big enough to go to school. The day arrived when his mother walked him the few blocks around the curve to the big brick building. Adam kissed his mother good-bye about a block from the school. He hoped none of his neighborhood playmates saw this. He wanted to be big.

"Son, don't you want me to come for you this afternoon when school is out?"

"Oh no, Mommie, I want to be big. Anyway, at Sunday School yesterday our teacher prayed for our first day at school. She told us that God would go with us and take care of us."

Beth watched the clock. When Adam failed to walk up the driveway after school she went looking for him. She spotted him around the bend, kneeling behind a huge oak tree, his hands clasped in prayer. Slipping quietly behind him she heard, "Please, God, help me. I forgot how to get home."

I know a man named Stanley who wants to be big. For seventeen years he thought it strong to withhold affection from his family. He considered himself too big to show any emotion toward the love of God. He won an argument at home and then walked out. His wife and three children have not heard from him for six years. The two sons are in college and doing well. But Stanley doesn't know this.

His daughter planned to be married at Christmas. She just knew that her dream would come true, that she would find her dad and he would walk beside her, clasping her arm and giving her away. She postponed her marriage until June. She was a lovely bride. But Stanley doesn't know this.

Sometimes winners lose. Wherever you are Stanley, swallow that stubbornness. Like little Adam, humble yourself before the Lord, kneel and pray, "Please God, help me to find my way home."

I pulled into the back parking lot of the Bookstop. I saw a sign I had never noticed before: "Stress and Phobia Center" The Church should be making this service available without cost. Jesus said, "Ho! Everyone who thirsts, come to the waters; and you who have no money, come, buy and eat. Yes, come, buy wine and milk without money and without price" (Isaiah 55:1). Jesus said, "Come unto Me all you who are weary and heavy laden and I will give you rest." The chastisement of our peace was upon Him, and with His stripes *we are healed*. Some churches are merely retail: They do not guarantee; they serve but don't service, are overstaffed, overrated and don't take trade-ins. We should be able to trade in the old garment and put on the garment of praise as new creatures in Christ.

During excavation at Lullingstone, Kent, England, an archaeologist uncovered a chapel of a Roman villa. On the wall was a painting dated 320 A.D. titled "Early Christians at Worship." The people were free spirits, joyously praising God with hands raised. As early as 320 A.D. people were liberated from depression and fear in the House of God. We love to sport labels on our churches like Cathedral. Why not: "Bring us your wounded," "Stress and Phobia Deliverance Center," "This is a hospital" (for the sin-sick soul). Some of our counseling rooms are no more than a place where you play volleyball with your "hang ups" instead of learning how you can get rid of them and have your sins forsaken and then forgiven, once and for all.

But instead we allow heartbroken humanity to come and go. We shake their hands, pat their backs. In short we say, "I've got my nest, now you go get yours." We give them an artificial smile, and send them back home *with their need unresolved*. That is false advertising. We need to start serving what we say we do, or change the menu.

Jesus said, "Peace I leave with you, My peace I give you; not as the world gives do I give to you" (John 14:27).

At the close of a presentation on a campus in Orange County, I prayed, "Father, send the Holy Spirit, that invisible policeman, out there to round up the strays. Place an unseen arm around the offending partner and the runaway child. Let them suddenly feel homesick for God, for their mate and family, and for the Church. Nudge them quickly on their return and help them to turn to the Lord Jesus."

As I was leaving the auditorium, an attractive woman of about 45 was sobbing and reaching out her arms to hug me. She could not seem to find the words to talk, so I took her arm and we went into an adjoining cloak room. She poured out her woe. "You prayed for my husband today. He teaches here in this very college. Over a year ago, he moved out of our home and into an apartment closer to campus. I offered to give up our house and move, too, if he felt the hour's drive was too lengthy. He then told me that he was in love with a twenty-year-old girl who would be living with him. I have kept his secret. I had lost hope until I heard your prayer. The Holy Spirit can arrest him."

Before I left we prayed for "her enemy," the twenty-year-old. Psalm 35:5 instructs us, "Let the angel of the Lord chase them." We prayed, "Bless her Lord, forgive her of this hideous transgression and save her soul."

Two weeks later I received a phone call from a giddy woman. "He's home! The invisible cop found him!"

The same day we had prayed, the college professor had arrived back at the apartment to find his young lover packing. "What are you doing?"

She replied, "I'm leaving. This is wrong. I have prayed with a TV minister. Jesus has forgiven me."

The man called his wife, "This afternoon, coming across the bridge from school, I suddenly became homesick for you. Back at the apartment I found Amber packing to leave. She had gotten religion via television. If I must live with a fanatic, it may as well be my own wife. May I come home?"

My family is convinced that I lead a blessed life.

I jumped into my little 1962 MGA convertible and sped north on Ontario, cut across on Avery, approaching Highway 19A. Before the light could change, I clutched, shifted into low and shot across two lanes of traffic, across the highway, over the hump down into the parking lot, safely . . . almost . . . at the Barnett Bank. I pushed the clutch and tapped the brake. No brakes . . . clear to the floor . . . no brakes! I forced the wheel quickly to the right, rolling faster, then I spotted two parking spaces together. With a quick left turn of the wheel I headed for both of them, jumped the curb and rested only two inches from the glass front of the automatic 24-hour teller.

Our friend Clive Shryer, missionary and mechanic, found the problem. The master cylinder had gone out. We ordered a new one from a British parts house on the Thames River. When it arrives and is installed, I will again be safe. You can get killed without a master.

You may have a good engine (heart), good lights (beautiful eyes), a wonderful chassis (build), good paint job (suntan and make up), even a sturdy seat! But without the Master, you are headed for trouble.

The disciples were out in a boat with Jesus, and a terrible storm raged. They cried out, "Master, we perish!" He spoke to their troubled spirits, and to the wind and waves—and with one phrase, the twelve men were calm and the winds and waves obeyed His voice. He merely had to speak, "*Peace, be still*" (Mark 4:38). He was the Master cylinder of their ship.

In the storms of your life, the Master is all you will ever need. You can trust Him with your safety.

There are two kinds of "hiders" . . . the high hider and the low hider. Both have an ostrich complex, though their heads are not hiding in the sand. On one hand, the high hider may think he is too good to associate with Jesus, the lowly Nazarene. He feels he has already paid his dues to climb that ladder to success. On the other hand, the low hider feels he can never afford eternal life and will never be good enough to qualify.

Jesus always finds your level. He sat on the well curb with a woman of ill repute. He stooped to the ground to touch the eyes of the blind man. He sat down with the children and enabled them to climb into His lap. What a Savior!

Then Jesus became a temporary social climber, looking high and low until he found that miserably rich, criminally greedy tax collector. Zacchaeus went out on a limb for Jesus and, in turn, Jesus jeopardized His reputation to identify with Zacchaeus that miserly man up high in that sycamore tree. Jesus did not wait for an invitation, but volunteered publicly to dine in the home of the high hider Zacchaeus.

What a conversion! Conversion is turning around, about face, and walking in a straight path in the opposite direction. Conversion is going into honest business with the Lord. Mr. Z gave half his goods to the poor, and paid back fourfold to people he had deliberately cheated before he met our Master. Jesus proclaimed Zacchaeus' pedigree. In My book you're a son of Abraham, and today I decree that salvation has come to your house! "The Son of Man has come to seek and to save that which was lost" (Luke 19:10).

Ed Schlossmacher tells an old legend. Each morning at sunrise Zacchaeus rose and went for a walk in the early morning sun. Finally his wife followed to see exactly where he went and why. She found him kneeling, kissing the trunk of that old sycamore tree, the place where he first met the One who lifted him from sin and sadness.

If you have already met Jesus, find a symbol to remind you. If you haven't, look for Him. He is looking high and low for you.

Before Mother died, I sat in her pretty, lavender bedroom in Palm Harbor and helped her read her mail. "Bets, after I'm gone, keep praying for your brother Don. Don't give up on him."

I have four brothers, and Don was the one who seemed to be dragging his spiritual feet. Mother was concerned for his commitment to Jesus. He had experienced health problems while in the military, suffered a financial reversal and was struggling through a domestic disappointment.

During times of crisis, instead of running to God for help, he seemed to run from Him. We were a close family, but at times we wondered if our prayers were getting through.

One morning at 6:50 A.M. my phone rang. It was Don.

"Well, Betty, Mother's prayers have been chasing me and have finally been answered." He explained that he had been laid up with a leg injury, the result of an accident at the tractor company where he is employed. Then, last night, a neighbor carried him and his wife to a revival service.

He explained, "The evangelist opened his Bible but didn't take his text. Instead he walked down the aisle toward me. 'Don,' he said,—how did he know my name?—'before I preach, I am going to pray for your leg—he couldn't have seen my bandages because I wore long pants!—according to James 5:14 and 15.'

"Before I knew it, he anointed me with oil, laid his hands on my head and shoulder, and the pain left my leg. The swelling went down so fast that the bandages fell loose on my shoe! I called to tell you that I got a double dose. Mother's been dead nineteen years, but her prayers are still alive!"

Don is back on the right track.

Ron Billings pastors a church in Sapulpa, Oklahoma, and is a writer. While I visited recently with Ron and his wife, Sherri, we began talking about types of people in the Body of Christ. Ron has concluded that there are basically of two types of people: thinkers and feelers.

A thinker makes an efficient editor, a good C.P.A. or church treasurer. A secretary should be a combination of both, a qualified thinker and a feeler with a sympathetic phone voice. A feeler doesn't make a good C.P.A. Being sensitive to the needs of people won't hack it with the I.R.S.! When I get on that plane to fly in turbulent weather conditions, give me a thinker for a pilot.

Feelers serve well in jobs helping others. A thinker usually will think it through and not get trapped into thankless voluntary service, like tending the church nursery. A feeler will usually come through so that young mothers can enjoy sitting all the way through a church service without disturbance. I think there is a special place in heaven for these volunteers. When I was growing up, if the nursery attendant was late, or didn't show, they always came for me. I was the pastor's daughter and it became my lot. Feelers gravitate toward need, usually make loving parents, and are sensitive to the needs of their children. As a rule, they are good lovers who care about the personal wants and needs of their mates. Thinkers usually make more money.

If both thinkers and feelers stay on the job, do their called duty, what they are best at, there will be no overlapping in the Body of Christ, all jobs will get done, and the Church will run smoothly. One is not better than the other, just better suited for his or her particular task in category.

"There should be no schism (division, separation, disharmony or discord) in the Body (1 Corinthians 12:25). For any body to be completely whole, all organs, large and small, are essential.

Our longtime friend Bruce Schoemann is a crusade director. He called this week for Carl and as always he had a story for me.

Last week he had made several telephone calls to the residence of a noted prayer conference speaker to arrange upcoming meetings. On one occasion the man's seven-year-old son answered the phone. "Hello," the boy said politely. "This is Ronnie speaking."

Bruce decided to have some fun with the proper child. He told the little boy, "This is the office of the President of the United States. I understand there is a very important and influential person residing in your home. Could you ask that person to come to the phone?"

Quickly and loudly the little fellow yelled, "Mom, the President wants to talk to you!"

There are still some moms who are full-time family engineers who have that kind of clout with the kids. "Even a child is known by his deeds" (Proverbs 20:11).

Samuel's mother was that kind of mother, too. Moses' mother was a thoughtful lady who had planned his safety and future explicitly. Aren't you amazed at the diligence, faithfulness and commitment of women who believed that Jesus would rise again and were found at the tomb waiting, expecting?

Jack is a handsome Italian who works at a salon in Clearwater, Florida. He is an excellent hairstylist. He loves his wife and his children, and he is a great armchair philosopher.

About three weeks ago, Jack dreamed that he died. That made him scared so he went in for a complete physical—the first in seven years. The doctor was irate. Jack was overweight; his blood pressure was 169 over 90; his cholesterol was 231; and his triglyceride count was 400. The doctor instructed him to come back in two weeks. In the meantime, the medical office would work out a health program for him. Driving home alone Jack had a talk with himself, *Jack, starting today, you are going to take command of your life.*

Jack had fallen into a pattern—waking up too late, scrambling three eggs in the grease of two sausage patties, gulping a cup of coffee with cream and sugar, propping his eyelids open with toothpicks and squealing around the corner to the parking lot, in the nick o' time for work. Mid-morning hungries set in so he wolfed down two chocolate doughnuts and another cup of coffee. Getting home late, he sat watching television while his wonderful wife, Lorraine, cooked spaghetti. Then off to bed to start the same routine on the morrow.

We can scream, "The devil made me do it" or "Everyone else is doing it this way." But when we get sick we yell, "'Oh God, help!'"

Jack was shaken by the doctor's report and restructured his life. He got up an hour early to exercise, began eating healthy foods and cut out fattening snacks. In two weeks he returned to an amazed doctor: Those high numbers were beginning to go down. Jack has stayed on his new healthy program.

If he can do it, you can do it. I can do it, too. Carl is away for three weeks, and I am determined before he returns to lose those eight pounds I have gained. Thanks, Jack.

The phone rang. It was my friend Joyce who lives in nearby Ozona, Florida. "I feel great," she reported. "I just finished my spring cleaning. I have even cleaned all the grime under my refrigerator." In spite of a heart condition, Joyce could not resist that traditional urge . . . spring cleaning.

I reflected . . . A short time ago I was home alone and I fainted. When I came to, a strange question formed in my mind. *Is there anything in this house that I need to make my family aware of, just in case I should die very suddenly?*

This happened to King Hezekiah. He was sick unto death. God spoke to him and said, "You are going to die. Put your house in order." Hezekiah turned his face to the wall and prayed, and God restored his health and added fifteen years to his life (Isaiah 38:1–5). Hezekiah had a great rule, angels fought for him, he was wealthy and healthy and won wars over mighty nations (2 Chronicles 32:21–30).

God searches the hearts of men. Is your house in order? Think it through. If His divine Xray should suddenly scan your residence, what would He find? What is hidden in the "hidey holes" of your heart? What is tucked away from view in your bureau drawers, under your underwear, 'way back in the corner behind your socks, on the topmost shelf in the closet out of view of little children, under the mattress?

Do you have some good things put away, not being used, that someone could utilize? Do you have money hidden so securely that should you die, it may never be found? Get it out, give it to someone to bring luster to their dull lives!

A minister friend of ours was returning from a revival on a late-night "red-eye" flight to save the small church some travel expense. The airline flight attendant had thoughtfully given each passenger a blanket and pillow, and had all the flyers "bedded down" for sleep.

Long after the lights were turned out, a small girl seated with her father toward the front of the cabin continued to whine, fret and cry out loud. Person after person made remarks, "Can't her daddy get her quiet? What is wrong with that fretful child?"

Our minister friend was suffering compassion fatigue from preaching, praying, listening to needs of others following a five-night revival, and he was mentally wrung out. Hoping to get some sleep, he rang his call button and asked the stewardess, "Can't you do something to help quiet that child?"

The flight attendant leaned near him and replied in whispered tones, "The little girl's mother is in a coffin with the cargo in the belly of the plane. She is crying because she wants to go down there with her mommy."

We should be hesitant to question and judge a person or situation until we learn what kind of cargo they are forced to carry. Jesus said we should be kind, tenderhearted—forebearing one another *in love*.

"Why was I ever born?" "Is there any reason for me to go on living?" Most of us have heard people ask one of these questions.

Perhaps we should ask of them a question: Why has God made such a wondrous universe? The splendor is too awesome for the human brain to try to take it all in—golden daybreaks, stunning orange sunsets, the sun, the moon, the Milky Way, a tiny lavender crocus bursting through the chill of snow to bloom in earliest spring.

God brought down from heaven's paradise a sample of glory for us to see and created the Garden of Eden. Then He created man. Why? To worship Him. This is the reason we were born, it is our reason for living, and we are happiest when we are doing what we were created to do, worship Jesus, the Son of the living God.

In Luke 19:28–40, we read that people lined the streets worshiping and praising Jesus, so hilariously happy, casting their garments before Him as He rode a colt down from the Mount of Olives. They praised Him with loud voices for all the mighty words He had done for them.

Among the crowd were those who were jealous of the applause, or perhaps blind to the fact that He truly was the Son of God. They told Jesus to silence the people, but He replied: "I tell you that if these should keep silent, the stones would immediately cry out."

Soon after, the people did hold their peace. Many changed their minds about who He was and they crucified Him—and the rocks cried out: "And behold, the veil of the temple was torn in two from top to bottom; and the earth quaked, and the rocks were split. . . . (Matthew 27:51).

*I am grateful to Paul Hamelink for the content of this message.

It was the third and final session of a prayer clinic in a church in Oklahoma. Up to this point things had gone smoothly. The audience was warm, friendly and unusually responsive . . . laughing, crying, learning.

I was introduced, but my opening remarks would not come. It was either the piece of peppermint caught in the left side of my throat, a dry cough or a neck spasm. My eyes watered, my nose ran, I cleared, I hacked, I coughed, but I couldn't speak.

The look on the people's faces was kindly sympathetic, but what I needed at this point was not sympathy but a glass of ice water. All I could think was, *Somebody do something.* The session was being video-taped, and I had certainly gotten off to a bad start, making a pitiful impression.

One young man named Bob sprinted from the sound booth, left the audio controls on remote and returned with the marvelous "cup of cold water in His name." It was what the doctor ordered. It worked!

Now, Bob is youth pastor of the church and really "overqualified" for this humble task of working in the sound booth. I am sure it is not part of his job description. He is a reverend by profession, but a servant/shepherd by possession. I immediately thought of Jesus. He was overqualified to be a carpenter, too.

"Master, where shall I work today?" And my love flowed warm and free. He pointed out a tiny plot and said, "Tend that for Me." But I answered quickly, "Oh, no! Not there, not anyone could see, no matter how well my task was done. Not that that little place for me!" His voice when He spoke was not stern but kind, and He answered me tenderly, "Friend, search that heart of thine. Are you working for you, for them or for Me?" Nazareth was just a little place, and so was Calvary!" . . .

Anonymous

November 23   What They Don't *Tell You*

When you buy a box of powdered milk, you see that the pouring spout is indicated by a dotted line. What they don't tell you is that the spout is not necessarily aligned with that dotted line.

Advertisers brag, "Child proof bottle." My three-year-old grandson brought me an open bottle of pills from his parent's medicine cabinet, announcing, "Mamaw, this is a child-proof bottle." It was supposed to be. And those that are, *really* are. How on earth do they expect an older person, feeble or arthritic, ever to get that bottle open to get relief?

Have you gone to a wholesale outlet at the last minute on Christmas Eve and bought a present for your child? What they don't tell you is that it's knocked down. What a line of propaganda printed on that box: "Some assembly required!" That is the understatement of the year! You stay up all night putting it together before your tykes awaken on Christmas morning.

My latest gripe is with the litter you supposedly just scoop out. You never have to change your cat's litter box again, the ad says brightly, just lift out the waste matter. What they fail to tell you is that those magic granules are actually dried-out glue balls. If you spill a few and your husband accidentally sprays a few drops of water over the shower curtain, you can never get that litter pan off the floor again. That thing is cemented there permanently.

Satan makes his arrows bright, even misquoting the Scripture, telling you to "enjoy the passing pleasures of sin" (Hebrews 11:25). But what the devil does not tell you is, "The wages of sin is death" (Romans 6:23).

Satan won't tell you that the soul that sins shall surely die. He also fails to tell you about John 3:16: "Whosoever believes on Him, Jesus, shall have eternal life at its fullest here on earth, then heaven forever after" (paraphrase). And Satan surely won't tell you the last half of the story . . . the Good News that Jesus is coming back to the earth again and that "the gift of God is eternal life in Christ Jesus our Lord" (Romans 6:23).

Every furrow in the book of Psalms is sown with seeds of Thanksgiving! James Whitcomb Riley wrote: "Oh it sets my heart a-clickin' like the tickin' of a clock, when the frost is on the punkin and the fodder's in the shock."

At age nineteen I had a wonderful wedding on Thanksgiving. One of my daughters was born on Thanksgiving . . . floods of memories. Our family members, 31 all told, always gathered together at my grandparent's house for the occasion, all born-again, Bible-believing Christians.

C. H. Spurgeon said, "When we bless God for mercies we prolong them, and when we bless Him for miseries we usually end them. Praise is the honey of life, which a devout heart sucks from every bloom of providence and grace. As well be dead, as to be without praise; it is the crown of life."

There must be sprinkled a few disappointments here and there to make us thankful for the blessings.

It was Wednesday P.M., closing time before Thanksgiving. I was working at Edward's Jewelry in New Castle, Indiana. A wealthy owner of a men's clothing chain was buying an expensive new watch.

"Bought your turkey yet?" he asked me.

"No," I admitted. "I can't afford one, so we're eating with my parents." Then I laughed and added, "If I had your money and you had a feather, we'd both be tickled!"

I was surprised when tears came to his cool green eyes and he said, "I'll trade you places. I have liquidation assets of four million dollars, but I can't eat. I'm terminal with stomach cancer."

Since that day I have never forgotten to be thankful for the ability to eat and digest, every day, not just Thanksgiving Day.

If we can't be thankful for what we receive, we should be thankful for what we escape. I'm not sure any of us gets what we deserve. Be thankful for your car. Be thankful for food. Before their first harvest, the Pilgrims survived for many days on rations of just five grains of corn per person.

Thanksgiving. It contains twelve letters—six for thanks plus six for giving. Give thanks!

It would be a long drive to Tallahassee, so I grabbed a tape and shoved it firmly into the tape deck of my car, not even looking at the label.

Out came the booming voice of Big John Hall singing: "In everything give Him thanks." As I played the tape over and over again, the Holy Spirit brought two different stories to my mind that happened years ago.

The day after Thanksgiving 1950, a hospital chaplain in Houston, Texas, visited a young woman, an airplane accident victim. The pilot of the small plane had died from the impact. She had regained consciousness, realized she was alone and panicked from fear and pain. Five hours later she was found.

She was alive, although she was frightened and in pain. Her reaction was to complain to the chaplain about how cruel fate had been to her. The hospital staff said she complained constantly the two months she was their patient. She was discharged and walked out a normal woman, but still complaining.

By contrast, the following February the chaplain ministered to a young woman named Linda at the scene of a hideous wreck. A truck had thrown her car against a telephone pole. When he arrived, her body lay crushed inside. One of her legs was completely severed. Somehow, numb to the fierce pain, she remained calm, which prevented additional strain on her heart.

The chaplain climbed into the car and rested his hand on the side of Linda's face as a rescue crew tried to work her body free from the wreckage.

The chaplain said her first remark was, "Am I glad you're here!"

"Linda, we're going to sing," he told her. He began to hum softly, "What a Friend We Have in Jesus." Over and over for more than an hour they sang together, "What a Friend we have in Jesus, all our sins and griefs to bear." She never lost consciousness during the entire ordeal. The physicians said they had never seen anyone with such severe injuries stay so kind and patient during the many operations that followed and the long weeks of convalescence.

The pastor said her attitude during the whole experience was absolutely positive. She praised God constantly, and remained cheerful. At first the physicians thought she was denying her true condition. But they came to realize that Linda's attitude resulted from her genuine belief that something good could come from any situation, no matter how bad, if she praised God. Linda knew the magnitude of her loss, but was thankful to God for what she had left.

In everything give thanks (Ephesians 5:20 and 1 Thessalonians 5:18).

"Drink water from your own cistern, and running water from your own well" (Proverbs 5:15). Strange Scripture? Many times the citizens and city dwellers would pollute the cisterns and wells at the city limits, to kill strangers and intruders. Only the city dwellers knew this, so they only drank from their own cisterns and wells.

The writer of this proverb used this illustration to warn young men about prostitutes. "The lips of an immoral woman drip honey . . . but in the end she is bitter as wormwood, sharp as a two edged sword. Her feet go down to death, and her steps take hold on hell. . . . And do not go near the door of her house, lest you give your [vigor] to others" (Proverbs 5:3–5, 8–9).

I grew up in Terre Haute, Indiana, near the Indiana State Normal College, now called Indiana State Teacher's College. They were more normal back then, I guess! Students at the State Normal College were warned, "Never go window-shopping in the red-light district." Any student found even near the streets of 2nd and Cherry was automatically dismissed from school.

We received the newsletter today, "Sounds of New Life Ministry," from Tim and Cheryl Youngblood in Loveland, Colorado. They have been traveling extensively in foreign missions. Cheryl became suddenly and inexplicably ill. For two months she suffered. They prayed, believed, visited several doctors and she underwent numerous tests. At long last a specialist discovered that Giardia parasites had gotten into her system from drinking the water.

Linda is receiving treatment and recovering. This illustration serves as a warning to missionaries and folks on the home front: Don't drink from strange wells.

As a pastor's wife, I always try to sit with the "newcomers" at choir practice. One young woman joined choir and had faithfully attended for three weeks. She had a sweet, resigned nature and wounded-dove eyes. She dressed poorly, seemed to feel poorly and was about thirty pounds overweight. I learned that she had three small children, and her good-looking husband was abusive, and an alcoholic. She worked long hours at a local nursing home.

This particular Thursday night practice I wore a bold blouse printed with leopards and zebras. She whispered behind the song book, "I love your blouse. I would give anything to have one like that."

At the close of practice, in the choir room, I removed my blouse, gave it to her and wore a choir robe home.

Only days later I was speaking at a women's convention in Sacramento, California. Following the singing the person in charge of the meeting said, "Move around and shake hands with someone you don't know." I confess, I hate these "howdy doody" times. I would rather shake hands on an impulse, because I want to, and don't get much out of people shaking hands with me upon command.

I decided to walk all the way back and shake hands with a woman my height on the farthest pew. I told her laughingly, "I love shaking hands with a person tall enough that her nose doesn't strike me at my belly button!" She introduced herself and said, "It's turned cold and you don't have a coat with you."

Next session she showed up with a gorgeous, full-length, soft, black leather coat and handed me a wild, black and white striped bag. Back at my room, I found in the bag two beautiful jump suits (tall size).

I use that wild bag for a purse, and travel to cool climates in the jump suits and that pretty coat. Not bad . . . one equals four. I gave away one blouse for four garments.

Jesus said, "Give, and it shall be given unto you" (Luke 6:38, KJV).

"The liberal soul shall be made fat." Do you want a fat soul? I believe that God rewards the motive of the giver many times even when the recipient is totally unappreciative.

The small church Dad pioneered could not support him, so he planted and harvested two acres of crops to feed his family. As we drove by a poor, run-down farmhouse on the way home from church one Sunday, Dad remarked to Mother, "Look at those skinny pigs. There's not enough on those hogs to be worth butchering." He slammed on the brakes of our old Hudson car, and pulled into the drive.

He told the farmer, "I have lots of corn—in fact, more than we can use. If you will come by, I'll give two bushels to help fatten your pork."

The man's reply was not, "Oh, thank you," but a question: "Is it shelled?"

I shared this with Carl and he told me of a similar experience, a Thanksgiving story.

It was during hard times, and Carl was living in a small Ohio suburb with his wife, Wanda, and their three small children. Even though they did not have a lot, they were thankful for what they did have and looked for someone less fortunate to invite over for Thanksgiving dinner.

They invited as their guest a widow living alone in poverty. Wanda prepared turkey, mashed potatoes with gravy, candied sweet potatoes, vegetables, two pies—banana cream and the traditional pumpkin—iced tea, hot tea, egg nog and coffee.

They lit a couple of candles and, being seated, looked at the woman, expecting, perhaps, that her eyes would be wide with wonder at the magnificent meal she would soon enjoy. Instead, she tightened her lips and inquired, "Where be the cranberries?"

God rewards the benevolent—"in spite of." Consider the Scriptures: "There is one who withholds . . . but it leads to poverty. The generous soul will be made rich" (Proverbs 11:24–25).

My neighbor and I were digging in the sand at Clearwater Beach with her little three-year-old. Just inches from our eyes, a pair of young women were strolling along. One girl had a strawberry tattooed on her left hip and the other sported a butterfly, positioned at the same spot. Later, walking toward the refreshment stand to get a lemonade for the child, we saw another "bathing beauty," asleep, lying in a yellow lounge chair. Near her heart, over her left breast was printed, "Phil." My neighbor almost lost it, laughing, making jokes later, "What if she changes her mind?"

In a restaurant, a character in line had tattooed proudly on his left arm, "Gert." What if it's his wife's name and he remarries? Wouldn't Lillie be intimidated to sleep on the arm bearing another's name?

Ancient mariners bore tattoos. Men in military did the same—a love link to mother, sweetheart or country, the good old U.S.A., complete with eagle and American flag.

Tattoos are nothing new. God bears a tattoo, too. He said "I have inscribed you on the palms of My hands" (Isaiah 49:16). Times are tough; life is hard. But God is aware of your need. He has *your name* in the palm of His bountiful, miracle-working, loving, giving hand.

The world's largest nation with immense natural resources, looked for oil and gold, denounced the Bible, refused to see Jesus. The U.S.S.R. is now bankrupt spiritually, economically and politically. Pray for America, that she will continue to *see* Jesus. Churchill once said, "You can expect America to do what's right after she has tried everything else." "Righteousness exalteth a nation. Sin is a reproach to any people" (Psalm 34:14, KJV). "We wish to see Jesus!" (John 12:21).

St. Augustine "saw" Christ and walked out of his life of shame.

St. Francis of Assisi "saw" Christ among the poor and heard Him in the songs of birds.

Lady Huntingdon "saw" Christ, refused royal attire, ceremony and nobility, and instead gave all her money and energy to advance His noble causes.

John Huss "saw" Christ, was so enamored of His reality that his praises could not be muted, and were heard above the crackling of the flames when he was burned at the stake.

John Wesley "saw" Christ and his heart was strangely warmed; the world became his parish, and he set a flame in the hearts of millions.

Catherine Booth "saw" Christ, chose to live in poverty so she could touch society's rejects. More people filed by her coffin to honor her in death than those who shortly afterward gazed on the bier of Queen Victoria.

Corrie ten Boom "saw" Jesus and declared around the world: "Look around and be distressed; look within and be depressed; look at Jesus and be blessed!"

Spurgeon, Moody, Bunyan, Whitefield, Calvin, these and more "saw" Christ and affirmed with the disciple Thomas, "My Lord and my God!" (John 20:28). Reader, pray as Mary Relfe did: "My Lord and my God, place me in touch with my spiritual moorings. Enable me to see Jesus."

"Let us lay aside every weight, and the sin which doth so easily beset us, and let us run with patience" (Hebrews 12:1). I have already guessed that my "besetting" or "ensnaring" sin is impatience.

Gritting my teeth, wrists rigid, I jerked open the plastic enclosure that housed one hundred Christmas napkins. When the seam finally gave way to my pressure, and shuffled napkins all across the six-foot breakfast bar, I realized that they had been contained in a Zip-Lock bag. I had forced open the bottom. With one look, one motion, I could have separated the bag, and both the contents and container would have remained intact.

But I rationalized that I was trying to hurry and get this one little job done, so I could relax and enjoy the "season to be jolly." We can always explain, rationalize our sin (weakness). I learned this tactic of rationalizing from Carl and the kids, so it's really not my sin. Right? Wrong!

When will I learn? Looking at the clock, I quickly slid the mixing bowl onto the same counter, tossed in an angel food cake mix, added 1 1/3 cups of water, snatched up the portable mixer, plugged it into the wall socket and hurriedly pressed the "on" switch, and *sssssllllhiiipppp zzzzzzoooooom*, the bowl whirled like a tornado onto the floor, flinging that sticky stuff all over the wall, the refrigerator door, the louvers on the laundry room door, and left a glob under the overturned mixing bowl on my newly installed, black-and-white-checked kitchen tile.

I surprised myself when, without saying any bad words, I quoted Scripture: "In your patience, possess ye your soul." Good job, Mrs. Malz! But then I looked around to see whom I could blame. No one. I had to rationalize. I am not a kid and I cannot blame it on immaturity or inexperience. I'm not quite old enough to plead senility. Now, I was here alone, just me and my conscience with my Lord.

Oh, good. I knew I could find the culprit. A tiny tangerine seed had caused the slide. A small thing but, nonetheless, big enough to blame. Still, a tiny drop of patience would have saved me a lot of trouble.

During the holidays a box arrived containing the strangest presents for Carl and me.

"She's lost her marbles!" we laughed.

Carl and I each received a hand-painted rock from a friend in Florida. On the front of the flat, smooth stone there was painted a little fleecy cloud and a sun in the sky. Below in the meadow was a little white lamb.

Looking closer Carl burst out, "The woman is a genius!" Turning the rock over he found written in small white letters, "St. John 8:7." Looking quickly in the Bible I read, "He who is without sin among you, let him throw a stone at her." On the front of my rock she had printed, "Betty's First Stone," and on Carl's rock, "Carl's First Stone." We both have them on our desks to remind us to think before we judge others.

Reading on in chapter 8, where Jesus forgave the woman who had been judged, Jesus commented, "I judge no one. And yet if I do judge, My judgment is true; for I am not alone, but I am with the Father Who sent Me" (verses 15–16). The Pharisees wanted to debate this. They digressed from an interview to an interrogation and put Jesus, not the woman, on trial.

I have had several of these rocks made since to pass on to people who have a tendency to criticize others. Why do we feel we must comment on people and subjects that we know almost nothing about?

In the small town where I grew up, there was a self-righteous family of four sisters who met every Tuesday morning to shop, then have lunch together. When seated to dine, they donned their judges' robes and for the next two hours felt it necessary to solve the world's problems, talk about church business and the affairs of relatives and neighbors. People joked about the need to avoid their close scrutiny. "Judge not, and you shall not be judged" (Luke 6:37).

Fists are for fighting, for holding, grasping, and for keeping. When I was little, Mother would call from the kitchen, "Bets, come here quickly. I need you." Fists were small and I could reach down into a jar and wash the inside for her.

Make a fist, make a statement. Lie down on your back, in a relaxed position, hands limp at your side, and try to scream, yell and be angry. Usually when anger sets in, you rise to the occasion, on your feet, raise your voice, raise your hand into a fist to show you mean business. It is a stubborn gesture.

You can catch monkeys this way. When the zoo keepers go to the tropics to replenish their monkey cages, they attach jars to a perch. Inside they place peanuts or a banana. A monkey will run his little hand in that jar, grasp his catch stubbornly, and let himself be captured before he will release his grip on what he wants.

At the Exodus, the children of Israel clutched onto some personal possessions. Their jewelry formed the golden calf and Moses beat it up, poured it in water and they drank it.

We can be spoiled by one miracle that demands another, until we worship or become addicted to miracles, always wanting more miracles. Let us rather "hold fast the confession of our hope without wavering" (Hebrews 10:23). Make a fist, hold on. "Ask in faith, with no doubting, and you shall receive" (James 1:6). Make a fist and refuse to let go.

When Mother wants to go to bed, she straightens up the house,
sets the breakfast dishes out, airs the cat, mends a trouser seam,
checks the doors and thermostat, soothes the baby's troubled dream,
rinses nylons, sets her hair, and plans tomorrow's clothes.

When Father wants to go to bed . . . He goes.

As a mother, O Lord help me to be,
  A lighthouse beside life's troubled sea.
When storm clouds sweep my family's skies,
  Let me light hope in my husband's eyes.
Help me be kind during the tedious hours,
  That my offspring may blossom like buds into flowers;
Then, when stars darken and wild winds blow,
  Help me show my children which way to go.
When a crisis comes to our home and hope seems lost.
  Give me the strength, dear Lord, to guide the tempest-tossed.
Please God, help me to live so close to Thee,
  That a lighthouse each day to my family I'll be.

                                        Author Unknown

I have heard that the man who invented the guillotine was beheaded, died under the knife of his own invention.

This is a kind of boomerang effect that happened in reverse in the case of three Hebrew lads.

In the book of Daniel, chapter three, we find that Shadrach, Meshach and Abednego refused to worship any but the true and living God and would not bow down before the gold image that King Nebuchadnezzar had set up. The king, full of fury, commanded, not the privates, not the corporals, but the mightiest men of his army to bind the three Hebrews and cast them into the burning, fiery furnace. It had been heated seven times hotter than it had ever been heated before.

These boys had on their garments, but their clothing was not scorched, nor was a hair on their heads singed. The Son of God came down and walked with them in the fire. But the men who threw them into the fire were consumed by the flames that would not hurt God's children. The fire they kindled for another killed them.

As if that was not enough of a backfire, the king declared that anyone who caused the Hebrew children further trouble and refused to worship the true God would be cut up into small pieces and their houses made into ash heaps.

The evil queen Jezebel, wife of the wicked King Ahab, had massacred many of the Lord's prophets and sent a message to the prophet Elijah that she was going to take his life as well. Now Elijah had done great wonders in the name of God during her husband's reign, but he had also overseen the deaths of the prophets of Baal, whom Jezebel served. She hated him still and wished him dead. It boomeranged on her. Elijah was taken up to heaven in a whirlwind. Jezebel was thrown down from the upper palace window. By the time the guards got to her, all that was left for burial was her skull, her feet and the palms of her hands. The dogs ate her flesh. (See 2 Kings:32–36.)

The Lord is our defense!

The Door to Discipleship Is Now Open

I attended a very lively black church. The choir swayed joyously while they sang, imploring Jesus to use them in His service.

When the pastor stood and declared, "The door to discipleship is now open," and the audience echoed loudly, "Make it plain! Make it plain!" I knew I was in for a treat and started taking notes, hard and fast.

Pastor: "We are pardoned from sin, but we are not excused from service. Christianity . . . stow it in your heart, know it in your head and show it in your life." The audience echoed: "Make it plain! Make it plain!"

Pastor: "If Christ is *truly* Lord, this prayer can be uttered: 'Lord, I'm a broom. Take me and sweep the world for Your causes; Lord, I'm a rag. Wad me up and use me to clean all the grime off this earth.'" The audience echoed, "Make it plain! Make it plain!"

Pastor: "Lord, I'm a car, drive me whenever and wherever you desire. A bandage, apply me to the wounds of hurting people. A handkerchief, use me to dry a tear from my sister's eye. An umbrella, open me up to keep the cold, drenching rain off my brother." The audience echoed, "Make it plain! Make it plain!"

Pastor: "Lord, I'm your piano. Play Your tune on my keys. My money is Yours, Lord, Spend me for anything you desire. I'm a brush, Lord. Paint with me . . . You choose the color and the object. Your cargo and take me anywhere in this world. I'm a sacrifice . . . lay me on any altar, dead or alive, now or later, for suffering or both, use me Lord. I relinquish all right of ownership to my life. Please never give me back to me again. Consume me with your will. 'Do not be afraid, for God is with you wherever you go.'" (Joshua 1:9).

And the lovely voices echoed: "Yes! . . . Make it plain!"

If you have ever been "ticked off," or "tocked out," you will like Gloria Lundstrom's message:

Did you hear about the clock that had a nervous breakdown? One day it began thinking how often it must tick in the coming year. Figuring two ticks a second, 120 per minute, 7,200 each hour, 171,800 a day, and 1,290,600 ticks every week. The clock nearly fainted when it figured it must of necessity tick 63 million times the next 12 months. The poor clock became so anxious and distraught, it suffered a nervous collapse.

Confiding in a psychiatrist, the clock complained that it didn't have the strength to tick that much, that long. Doc asked, "How many ticks are you required to tick at a time?"

"Only one," the clock replied.

"Well, the solution is simple. Simply tick one tick at a time and don't worry about the next one," advised the doctor. "You'll get along fine." That's exactly what the clock did. As all good stories end, it ticked happily ever after.

Gloria, along with her evangelist husband, Larry, and their family have "lived" in a bus, traveling for 25 years. She is wife, mother, speaker, school teacher, counselor, secretary, writer . . . it takes all the "ticks" out of me just thinking about it. They are in a new city daily, new church, new audience, new challenge. At midnight when they finally return to the bus or a room, she falls into bed feeling like that clock—not . . . one . . . "tick" . . . left.

You can identify. Your life is too hectic, but you cannot run away from it all. That's too easy, sounds too good. Reevaluate your priorities, make new resolutions, come to understand that you cannot do everything. Give up the least important to save your sanity. If necessary, juggle your jobs to find quiet time with God. "Be still, and know that I am God" (Psalm 46:10). Let Him soothe your anxieties. Wait long enough to receive His "peace, be still," rest in his presence, His Word, and pray. He will strengthen you to forge ahead again. Take this advice and He will add many "ticks" to your life.

Don't worry about tomorrow, just take "one tick at a time."

The state of Missouri is the "show me" state. Indiana Hoosiers; Kentucky Hillbillies; Ohio Buckeyes; Oklahoma Sooners; Georgia Peaches; Florida Crackers; Arkansas Razorbacks. You either accept the state you are in or move to another state.

The word *state* has many meanings. We talk about the state of confusion, the state of depression, state of the art, state your preference, state your case, make a statement. Actions speak louder than words. By saying nothing you make a statement. If you can't be smart, you can be quiet.

I met a couple of "Brits" at the beach this summer. They asked me, "What is the proper time here?" They refused to change their watches from London time. That's loyalty.

Paul said in Philippians 4:11, "I have learned in whatever state I am, to be content." That's *royalty*. He had practiced and arrived at a good attitude about his whereabouts and called it the "state of contentment."

State of mind determines the difference between failure and success. When we call on God we can reach our goal, rise above handicap, above average and above mediocrity. We become more honorable.

Joshua and Caleb had the right attitude. Others complained about the giants—sour grapes. Josh and Caleb saw and got the big grapes. Quality is never an accident; it is always the result of sincere effort, intelligent direction and skillful execution, it represents the wise choice of many alternatives. Excellence can be attained if you care more than others think is wise, risk more than others think is safe, dream more than others think is practical, expect more than others think is possible. "I can do all things through Christ" (Philippians 4:13).

Harold was the first boy who bought me a box of candy. He was the first boy who made me feel grown up, taking me to church in his car. I was thirteen. Years later, he married a girl prettier than me, one of my best friends. He was helping his son start his car alongside the highway one day when a careless driver sideswiped him and left him paralyzed. I have asked Harold to tell us how he has become *happy*. Here are the top six.

1. Have a personal relationship with God. Become happy with Christ. If you are not and do not know how, call a minister or Harold (812–533–1263).

2. Learn to be an optimist. Develop a positive attitude. It is a proven fact that this enables the brain to secrete endorphins. These are pain blockers that actually help a person with chronic pain.

3. Don't bemoan the fact that your are physically down. Hard places are a part of life. There is no life without a set of troubles.

4. Do not blame God for your misfortune. Job was righteous and lost everything. But because of Job's attitude, God multiplied him. He had twice as much as ever before. Don't waste your time trying to affix blame on anyone if you are victim of yourself. If you smoke for years, for instance, and come down with lung cancer, don't blame God. Harold explained: "My second cousin was dying of lung cancer in an Indianapolis hospital. There was a hole in his throat for him to breathe through. I visited him, and there he sat, propped up in bed, with cigarette protruding from the hole in his throat, puffing away."

5. Take care of yourself. Look your best all the time. If you look in the mirror and see a sick person, unshaven with messed-up hair and wrinkled clothes, then you will automatically feel worse. If you are well groomed, pleasant-faced, you'll say, "Not bad, for an old geezer." Looking your best helps build a positive attitude.

6. Think of the welfare and happiness of others.

My Christmas shopping was done; the gifts were all wrapped prettily, the out-of-town packages mailed in plenty of time; the tree was up and decorated; the Christmas cards were all signed, addressed and mailed—all but eighteen of them. I had scraped the bottom of my budget and there was no money left to buy stamps to mail them.

I told my daughter April, "This is 1990. I can't remember having to pray for postage stamps since the Great Depression!"

Later that day I inserted the key into our family's brass post office box. I hit the jackpot—sixteen Christmas cards! One was from Dawn Wagler, my walking, talking, coffee-drinking, writing friend from the Dakota days, now living in Illinois.

It was a pretty Christmas card. Just above the signature was a brief note, "Enclosed is a very dumb present!" It was a tiny package, about the size of a stick of chewing gum, wrapped in green paper with a thin red ribbon. Opening the miniature gift I realized it was no dumb gift at all, but a very smart present. It was twenty postage stamps! I sent away my eighteen cards, which would now arrive in time, and had two stamps left over.

You cannot judge a package by its wrapping. One of our relatives gives gifts wrapped so fancily that the packaging must surely cost more than the content. And a person wrapped up in him- or herself makes a very poor gift indeed.

Carl's grandfather gave Grandma Strait a strangely wrapped gift as they sat by the fireplace early one Christmas Morn. She unwrapped a large box, then layer after layer of brown grocery bag wrapping paper, then a smaller box and more layers. Finally when she saw another box inside she thought it was just an empty joke, and tossed the last remains in the fireplace. Grandpa grabbed the poker and quickly beat out the fire to show her that inside was a $100 bill.

Jesus came wrapped in swaddling clothes, common packaging, and we did not esteem Him (see Isaiah 53:1–3). But what a Christmas present He was!

When television was first introduced to America, one of the first and most interesting programs was hosted by Art Linkletter, with this well-known statement: "Kids say the darndest things."

On one broadcast little Joey told Art, "My daddy is gone away to the Army." Art comforted him with the fact that his father would return for a furlough or discharge soon, and asked, "Do you get to sleep with Mommie while Daddy is away?" Shaking his small head he reported, "No, Uncle Billy is sleeping with Mommie right now." Art tried to cover for the brutal truth, and the cameramen had a heyday. They focused the camera on "Mommie" who had turned ashen white. I hope her husband wasn't watching Channel 13!

Kids rarely tell a lie. They tell it like it is, and are brutally frank. As children grow they learn to be merciful in their truthfulness.

Ferne shared with me that when she was eight, and old enough to know better, she did something bad. Then she climbed up on her father's lap while he read the paper one evening. "Dad," she confessed, "I did a terrible thing today. You must punish me."

She told me, "I really understood the love, mercy and forgiveness of the heavenly Father by my earthy dad's response. He held me close for a long time while he searched for words. Then he spoke, 'You don't have to explain. I'm your father. You are my daughter. I understand you and I love you. Therefore, I can easily forgive you.'"

"Let not mercy and truth forsake you; bind them around your neck" (Proverbs 3:3).

The children's Christmas play at church . . . sometimes people who work hard to put it together wonder, "Who needs it?" Perhaps grandparents enjoy it most, seeing their young offspring, one generation removed, singing little songs offkey, too softly to be heard anyway. The audience hears only the teacher. Some moms and dads are disappointed that their kids were not chosen to take leading parts.

I have heard children's church directors say, "We would love to celebrate Christmas without rehearsals, without the hassle of hustling little bodies across stage over and over again, only to have them forget their parts at the performance. Wouldn't it be grand to stay home in front of a nativity scene of tranquil pleasure?"

Carl was pastoring a church in Ohio. Christmas Eve fell on Sunday, and the kiddos were ready. The sanctuary was packed, the organ played first "Jesus Loves the Little Children," then faded softly into "Away in a Manger." Five little tykes from the nursery were to begin the celebration. Each had a bigger-than-life cardboard letter, which, when aligned in proper order (which they had practiced eleventy-five times perfectly), would spell to the congregation: H—E—L—L—O.

Following this, the junior choir was to march down the center aisle carrying real lighted candles, trying not to set on fire the kids' robes in front of them.

The organist played the prelude, not once, but three times all the way through, and still no opening "HELLO." Junior candles burned lower than low!

Behind the scenes, four-year-old Bradley, carrying the last letter, "O," had wet his pants and refused to go on. What to do? Finally their distraught teacher just gave them a shove and said, "Go!"

Little Brad, crying out loud, rushed in first followed by his wee friends clumped together and they greeted the churchgoers with this sentiment: OHELL!

It's true, we can do without it. But the warm smiles on the softly lit faces watching the reenactment of Christ's birth every year make it all worthwhile.

When someone asks, "What is he like?," we most likely identify that person by his attitude about himself, others, about life.

Charles Swindoll says, "The longer I live, the more I realize the impact of attitude on life. . . . It is more important than the past, than education, than money, than circumstance, than failures, than successes, than what other people think of us, what they say or do. It is more important than appearance, giftedness or skill."

Attitude will make or break a company . . . a church . . . a home. the remarkable thing is that we have a choice every day. We cannot change our past; we cannot change the inevitable. The only thing we can control is our attitude. I have heard it said that life is 10 percent what happens to me and 90 percent how I react to it. And so it is with you. We are in charge of our attitudes.

The quality of a person's life is in direct proportion to his commitment to excellence, regardless of his chosen field of endeavor. The difference between a successful person and others is not a lack of strength, not a lack of knowledge, but rather a lack of proper attitude.

Don't confuse humility with fear; contentment with laziness; faith with passiveness; small thinking with spirituality; smugness with meekness. Don't worry about what you do not have. Use what you do. God has all you will ever need. If He doesn't have it in His storehouse, He can create it.

"Anything is possible to Him who believes" (Matthew 19:29). Grow in faith. You can enlarge His power in your life by prayer. When you pray, "Keep me from evil," He places a hand on you. When you have the right attitude about prayer and God's source, you can never "out-ask" God; you can never "out-imagine" God; and you can never "out-dream" the God of creation.

Lean on Him . . . adjust your attitude toward others . . . and let your faith soar.

This story was mailed to me by a man from Shoals, California.

A New York businessman who was also a Sunday school superintendent was invited to speak at a convention for Sunday school teachers on the West Coast.

He told the audience a story of how, one Sunday morning years ago, he was walking through the slums of New York City to round up recruits for his Sunday school class. At one corner he met a barefoot boy with uncombed fiery red hair and invited him to go.

"The lad asked why he should go and I told him that we taught boys to be good," explained the man to the audience. "And he said, 'I don't feel good because I'm hungry.'

"It was nine o'clock and the boy had not yet eaten. I had gingerbread and crackers and set them before him. He ate in a way that showed me how keenly hungry he really was. When he stopped eating I asked, 'Will you go with me now to Sunday school?' He said that he would go.

"He had never been to Sunday school. He thought it was a place where you went to get your hands slapped with a ruler. When he found himself in the hands of a pleasant young lady who treated him with love and didn't notice his shabby clothes, he was greatly surprised. He became a regular attender. He told all his friends and persuaded most of them to come along with him.

"Two years after that he and some other boys were adopted by farmers on the West Coast. I have never heard from him since, but I have no doubt that he is doing good wherever he is," the speaker concluded.

Suddenly a man stood up in the audience and said, "I can control myself no longer. I have tried to find this man for years to thank him! I am that red-haired boy who ate this man's gingerbread. I am here for this convention because I am now a Sunday school superintendent. I owe all I am and have in this world, and all that I hope for in the next, to the man in that New York City Sunday school who taught me about Jesus."

"Those who turn many to righteousness [shall shine] like the stars forever and ever" (Daniel 12:3).

I was speeding to get to the Smokey Mountains before dark. Carl was sleeping soundly, curled up in the back seat of our car, his head resting peacefully on a fluffy blue pillow. The sound of the siren accompanied by the flashing red and blue rotating lights atop the highway patrolman's official vehicle awakened Carl and he sat up to hear the policeman say, "Mrs. Malz follow me to the county jail."

"Jail," I wailed, "what kind of justice is that? Can't I pay my fine, or just mail it in?"

He firmly assured me, "You have your way of doing things in North Dakota. This is how we do it here in Tennessee. You state your case before the sheriff, and he judges it and decides your fine."

By now baby April was awake in her little car seat and was crying, "Please, Mister Pleesmum, don't take my mommie away!"

I tried to be brave, but as the three of us walked up the stony steps jailward, my legs trembled. I had sung and played my accordion at jail services, but I had never been a prisoner.

Standing, waiting forever, Carl spotted a sign and jabbed me with his elbow, while he shook with inward laughter. The sign stated, "Relatives may bring prisoners candy and cigarettes."

The judge showed mercy. I paid my fine and we were on our way. Carl stuck out his hand to the arresting officer and said, "Well, if she had to get arrested, it couldn't have been by a nicer guy."

In the car I gritted my teeth at Carl. "Thank him for arresting your wife? What kind of sadist are you? Why didn't you just leave him a tip?"

Carl replied, smiling his stiff, German grin, "Would you rather have justice or get mercy? You should be grateful right now for the many times you should have been stopped and weren't."

"He has made you alive together with Him, having forgiven you all trespasses, having wiped out the handwriting of requirements that was against us. . . . And He has taken it out of the way, having nailed it to the cross" (Colossians 2:13–14). Jesus didn't give us what we deserved either.

That one liner started wheels turning in my mind. "You don't waste cannon balls on a snow bird" any more than you would think you can use a toy water pistol as a fire extinguisher to put out fire and brimstone from the bottomless pit. You are no match for Satan. He is acquainted with those consuming flames, he walks through them, but someday he will be cast into the lake of fire to burn forever.

We walk in the natural, take steps in the flesh, but we do not war in the natural or dare fight in the flesh. We are ordinary, weak, human beings, but we do not fight our spiritual battles with ordinary weapons. Our weapons are not carnal, but *mighty through God*.

"I can do all things through Christ who strengthens me" (Philippians 4:13).

Some have tried to war in their own strength without adequate spiritual weapons. But "the evil spirit . . . leaped on them, overpowered them . . . so that they fled out of that house naked and wounded" (Acts 19:16).

But if you are genuinely fortified, "no weapon formed against you shall prosper" (Isaiah 54:17).

The devil, your invisible enemy is second in patience to God. He will wait ten years if necessary until the evil he plants in you grows and weakens you, then he will attack when you're down and destroy you. But take heart, there is no place so remote, no corner so dark that Satan can hide from God.

Don't stretch yourself beyond your measure, rely on Him and God will approve you, and come to your assistance.

We have an anchor that keeps the soul,
Steadfast and sure while the billows roll,
Anchored to the Rock that cannot move,
Anchored sure and safe, In the Savior's Love.

Paul found himself on board a ship containing 276 passengers, sailing toward Italy. A horrid storm broke upon and beat them for fourteen days. This was in a day when there were no shortwave radios and no Coast Guard. Paul used the only available radar: prayer. In response to his S.O.S., an angel appeared and told him, "Be of good cheer, not one life will be lost" (see Acts 27:22–24).

"They dropped four anchors and prayed for day to come" (verse 29). They also thanked God in advance (verse 35). "Faith without works is dead." They ate, they celebrated, they cheered (Acts 27:34–36). By faith, Paul promised them, "Not one hair shall fall from off your head" (verse 34). Those four anchors worked. "They all escaped safely to land" (verse 44).

I believe that for survival in modern times, we need a cause that is grand, something that to survive must be anchored to Jesus. In the storms of life we also need four anchors. I believe they are:

Pray: Talk to God daily, every day, all day.

Listen: Let God talk to you, instruct you, give you direction and guidance.

Read the Log Book: Devour and digest the Word. In it are the issues of life.

Have fellowship: There are no "lone rangers." We need the love of other believers.

I have discovered that if I don't write things down, I am sure to forget them. Spoken words, no matter how eloquent, are soon forgotten. I write everything down.

An elderly man living nearby in a mobile home park asked me a question. I said, "Let me jog your memory," to which he replied, "Honey, my memory ain't joggin'; it ain't even draggin'!"

I dropped my grocery list in Ulmer's Jack and Jill grocery in Ellendale, North Dakota. An elderly lady passing by saw me with my head down, looking at the floor. She asked, "What's wrong?"

I told her, "I've just lost my mind." She ran from me. I caught up with her, running down the aisle to tell her, "I was kidding. I write everything down. I wrote down my grocery list and lost it, so I had lost my mind."

Writing stamps indelibly on the mind things you need to recall later. All through the Old Testament we read the words "It is *written*!" Writing can be a form of prayer. Written prayers are the best kind. If you're in public and don't want to be overheard praying aloud, or if you're being distracted by a lot of noise around you, write your prayer out. God sees it.

Another advantage to writing your prayers is this: When the answer comes, you'll remember: *Yes, I asked for that. I had forgotten that I asked for that.*

Keep a record also of your answered prayers. It will blow your mind at God's faithfulness. It will eliminate your doubting and restore your faith in the power of prayer. Communicate with God, the Source of supply of *all*.

Two of my brothers kept this joking game going for years until they finally outgrew their prankish boyhoods. We would be driving through town on the way to church, with the windows down in our old Hudson. Don would yell loudly, "What's your dad do for a living?" Jim would yell back, "Nothin', he's a preacher!"

Their second favorite was to catch a rather shy person and ask, "Does your face hurt you?" When he would rub his cheeks and slowly answer, "No," they would retort, "Well, it sure is killing me!"

Carl said he went through this stage. At about the age fifteen several of his "hot dog" buddies thought they were men about town. Near their house was a rather pious church, know for its lack of joy and enthusiasm. If it were the 1990s, they would say it had no charisma. One long-faced old gent always stood on the street outside the church and invited people to come inside. Carl said that at one invitation he answered the man, "No, thank you. I have troubles of my own."

That "hang dog" look was not a good witness.

A plastic surgeon can give you a face lift, but only God can give you a "faith" lift. "The spirit of a man, is the candle of the Lord" (Proverbs 20:27). "Thou, O Lord, wilt light my candle" (Psalm 18:28, KJV). Everyone is an ordinary candle, complete with tallow and wick. Wait in His presence until He lights that wick with the fire of the Holy Spirit—then your spirit will glow and burn, warming you and making light the hearts around you.

Pray aloud the following prayer if you have a sad countenance and need a faith/face lift: "Why art thou cast down O my soul? and why art thou disquieted in me? hope thou in God: for I shall yet praise Him for He is the help of my countenance. . . . Why art thou cast down, O my soul? and why art thou disquieted within me? hope thou in God for I shall yet praise him, who is the health of my countenance . . . and my God" (Psalm 42:5, 11).

My father received an emergency call. The coal mine north of Clinton, Indiana, had collapsed and trapped several men inside. There was little oxygen left. As a minister, my dad prayed and drove (faith with works).

At the site one man ran to the trunk of his car, pulled out a drill with a diamond bit and drilled a hole through a steel plate that covered the shaft. The men put their noses to the small hole until heavy equipment came and lifted the steel housing.

There is praying, then there is praying through, drilling into the opposition. "From the days of John the Baptist until now, the Kingdom of heaven suffers violence, and the violent take it by force" (Matthew 11:12). This is not dabbling in praying, this is war. Let us earnestly contend for the faith that was once delivered unto the saints—that old-fashioned kind that Daniel had. Accept no substitute. Don't be satisfied with anything less than the authentic. "You shall receive power after the Holy Ghost has come upon you." We can pray in the Spirit, war in the Spirit, tearing down strongholds for our family and friends, for our nation. Intercessory prayer is praying for the needs of others, as though they were our very own. Are you a mixer or propeller? Circling the throne room, or praying through? Like a hot poker that melts the wax of opposition, you can be endued (that's *your* endowment) with power *from on high.*

"The effectual, fervent (feverish, red hot) prayer of a righteous man avails much." Be sure you are righteous. It was said of Hudson Taylor, "God has had His way so long with him, that now Hudson Taylor gets his way with almighty God." You obey Him, and He will respond to your praying. He promised that if we abide in Him (take up residence with) and His Word abides in us, we can ask what we will and it *shall* be granted."

He will scatter our enemies (Psalm 68:1). The enemy comes against us one way, but when God arises to confront him, he flees before us seven ways (Deuteronomy 28:7).

To little Evan, heaven is a place where he wants to see angels again. A drunk driver plowed into the back of the two-door car, in which he was riding in the back seat. His mother and two sisters escaped as the car exploded into flames. They were horrified for Evan ... but looking up, they saw him standing safely in the middle of the road. "Don't worry, Mommie," he called, running to them. "A big angel picked me up out of the car and set me on the road!"

Linda Greenfield, whose teenage daughter, Marilyn, died in a fiery wreck, wrote, "I am not troubled by a comparison of these two stories. The angels came to my daughter Marilyn and escorted her home before she knew pain. I can just hear her, when they arrived, say 'Cool!'

"I gave Marilyn's clothes to some of her friends. Their mothers and I discussed heaven. We are planning a Mother-Daughter Banquet up there, perhaps even a picnic for mothers and daughters along the bank of the River of Life."

Heaven ... a place of no sorrow or pain. A place where, as the song says, "we shall see Him face to face."

I have a kid brother who is five-and-a-half weeks younger than my daughter Brenda. They were very close. When you bought a gift for one, you had to purchase one for the other, and if one of them got a spanking, the other came to the rescue and you almost had to spank the second party. When they were probably three, Gary fell in love with a coon-skin cap like the one worn by Daniel Boone. He played with it on all day, and slept in it at night. Brenda found it hard to respect him properly and never did call him Uncle Gary, but affectionately named him "Boonie."

When they were probably fifteen, a friend came over with his guitar. Three teenagers with three guitars thumped, chorded and hummed till Mother called, "Lunch is ready." They ignored her. They were neither hungry nor thirsty. Finally at the table Gary lamented, "Iced tea. Is that all you have to drink? Bring out the good stuff. Mother, where are you hiding the Coca Cola or the home-made lemonade?"

I proceeded to preach at them, telling stories from the Depression era: "When we four older kids were your age, we had two choices, water (if we wanted to go out to the well curb, prime the pump and pump for it) or buttermilk, served at room temperature. If you wanted it 'on the rocks' you could get an ice pick and chip away at a fifty pound block of ice in the ice box—no refrigerator." They hooted when I told them that we didn't have a television either, and they began accusing us of living in the Stone Age and shaving with a sharp stone bound to a stick.

When their friend left, Brenda helped with the dishes and Gary mowed the grass in the July heat. "Job well done, son!" my dad complimented him, as Gary came through the kitchen door, and sighed happily, "Iced tea? Yes!" The July heat had intensified his thirst and appreciation.

Looking back, I'm glad for what we have now. But we sometimes need to remember the past to see how far we have come.

Standing on my front porch were an attractive young couple and their three tiny daughters. It was almost Christmas. He asked, "In Christ's name, help us." My mental computer raced, jealousy gripped my grieving heart. What could I do for them? They were a complete family unit. My 37-year-old husband had recently died after open-heart surgery. I had just paid off an $8,000 debt of hospital, surgical, medical and funeral bills. Shock and disappointment still lingered like a morning mist. I had a lovely home on two acres, but the two girls and I were a fragmented little family.

They pointed to their old-model car in my driveway and explained that it contained their only possessions. "My construction job ended and I tried for weeks but couldn't find another. This morning our mobile home was repossessed, and we were left standing on a bare rented lot, with our clothing, a few Christmas gifts, and one section of carpet that we don't need now."

Their children and mine ran and played happily together, unaffected by material loss. He asked to stay in my guest cottage rent-free until he could find employment and another place to live. I had mixed emotions of sympathy and caution. In the past years vacationers had taken advantage of me, yet I heard my voice say, yes.

They hummed and whistled Christmas tunes as they carried in and arranged their personal belongings. They were so appreciative to have a "place," and be together. And would you believe it? That remnant rug, the piece of carpet they brought, fit that one-room cottage to the inch!

The following morning, my yard had been raked. At noon he announced, "I found a job!" Five months later when they moved into a lovely home, I could not take the rent money they handed me. They had given me more than I had given them. They sang duets at church, our children played, she cooked and served us on the picnic table under the palms. Their example taught me to laugh and love in spite of conditions. Their genuine possessions were greater than mine.

What is truth? I know some people who are so brutally frank that they offend and hurt and drive away. There is a legend told of two seers named Ernest and Frank who sat down together to philosophize. One said to the other, "You be Earnest and I'll be Frank."

Much is said about truth in the Bible. God never intended us to be Pharisees, nor for truth to be judgmental, so He instructed us thus: "Speaking the truth . . . in love." Love shelters, shields, protects, even covers. It does not cover up, however.

The letter kills but the spirit gives life. We search the Scriptures, not because they are life, but because they bear witness of Him who is life and truth, Jesus (see John 5:39). We must worship God, not the facts about Him. It is not just knowing the Book of the Lord that should be our goal, but knowing the Lord of the Book.

Truth is not given to us so that we can know and judge, but so that we can become. When the fresh truths cease to change us, we have departed from the way. As Rick Joyner said, "If we do not know Jesus as our Life, we do not really know the Way or the Truth either."

Inflexibility destroys the ability to receive truth. The ability to receive correction is essential to walking in truth. "Reproofs for correction are the path of life" (Proverbs 6:23). He who heeds instruction is in the way of life, but he who refuses correction goes astray" (Proverbs 10:17).

He who seeks truth must seek Jesus. Do not seek new things, but the old truths, ever new. He is Truth.

One legend of the Christmas tree is told by the Germans.

Martin Luther, the sixteenth-century Protestant reformer, was walking through the woods on a winter's night when he came upon a little fir tree. He brought it home, decorated it with candles and explained to his children, "As we look upon this evergreen tree with its lights, it will ever remind us that Jesus was, and still is, 'the Light of the world.'"

Many German communities stage plays about Adam and Eve on December 24. An evergreen tree is decorated and hung with bright red, polished and shining apples, to represent the Tree of Life. Many people copied the custom and started setting up decorated trees in their homes.

Peter Marshall gave suggestions about the approach to the holiday of holidays: "Let's not 'spend' Christmas nor 'observe' Christmas, but let's *keep* Christmas, keep it as it is . . . and all the loveliness of its ancient traditions. May we keep it in our hearts, that we may be kept in its hope."

We spend a lot of time looking for that perfect gift. This a good attitude, since it is probably, with the exception of Easter, the finest hour of celebration for the Christian. "Every good gift and every perfect gift is from above" (James 1:17).

You will undoubtedly share many gifts today. Be sure to remember the greatest Gift of all, and share His peace from your heart.

Merry Christmas!

When the ham is cold, many bulbs burned out, and the candles have melted, keep the warmth and love of Christmas . . . let it linger in your heart, and let it radiate after the letdown of the "high" of the season to others around you.

God has given Jesus the name above every name. Let us continue to honor Him every day of the holidays and beyond. Continue to show good will, to love the unlovely and to heal the sick. "Paul went down and put his arms around him" (Acts 20:10).

Harv Springer tells the story of a friend who came down with infectious hepatitis. He was isolated in quarantine, and his optic nerves had deteriorated. Doctors pronounced him legally blind. In spite of the sad report, a few friends gathered around an old-fashioned altar following the Wednesday night prayer meeting at church. They prayed that Jesus would send His word and heal Bob's blind eyes.

The following morning the nurse came in to administer Bob's medication. When she turned on the light he said, "What is that?" She dropped the medicine and ran down the hall calling for the doctor.

When the doctors were convinced that his sight had been healed, he was released. They teased him, "Remember, you're blind."

No way! Bob works as a guard, but his real vocation is strengthening people whose faith is weak.

Up with Christmas! Christmas continues . . . after the tree comes down.

December 27   Holiness—The Invincible Virtue

Manoah and his wife could not have children. They prayed to the living God, and the angel of the Lord came and told his wife that she would bear a son. She was instructed to practice holiness, and to teach her son, Samson, in the same manner, in holiness. The power of the miraculous is no accident, it is the byproduct of holiness. Samson was the strongest man who ever lived. Holiness is essential to God's energy, an invisible virtue that brings visible results. (see Judges 13).

Pastor Don Lunsford puts it this way, "We can't just preach the gospel of holiness, but we must live this same gospel. The drifters' votes don't count. They try to push the remote control, changing churches as they change channels. By their behavior they say, 'Please me or lose me' and many pastors are more concerned about ratings than righteousness. But people are searching for absolutes. Our message should be clear, speaking the truth in love. We must show and live the Gospel. Holiness is expensive, but worth it."

We must avoid cut-rate religion. Jesus was straightforward when He said, "Without holiness no man shall see the Lord" (see Hebrews 12:14). He Himself was put to His own test. In Matthew 4:5 and Luke 4:9, we read that Satan came to Jesus and said, "Kneel down to me and I will give you the kingdoms of this world." Most half-hearted, cut-rate Christians would have gotten down on one knee.

Can you pass the test? Will you go all the way, pay the full price of holiness so that you may see the power of God here on earth, and see Him face to face?

Windows and doors. Both are openings, but don't be confused—there is a difference. You look through a window and walk through a door. Windows are for looking, viewing. Drive-in windows and teller windows are for getting and receiving. But you don't dare jump through a window. Look before you leap.

"The Lord made windows in heaven" (2 Kings 7:2). Wait for Him—He will open the windows of heaven and pour out such a blessing there will not be room enough to receive it (Malachi 3:10). God may call you through your heart's window, or the window of your eyes, as you read His Word. You may receive a call to minister to foreign nations. Wouldn't it be wonderful to take Jesus everywhere that Coca-Cola is? "Go ye into all the world."

Wait and be sure before you walk through the door of opportunity. What a waste to be good at something that doesn't have eternal value! He speaks in whispers to the heart, but we must wait for Him. An apple picked too early is bitter to the taste. That same apple, given proper timing, is sweet satisfaction.

Doors are for entering, going, doing. You go through by invitation, a key or someone inside opening it. There are doors of opportunity. Before you walk through them, you have seen through vision's window. "Make the best of opportunity, redeem the time, the days are evil" (Ephesians 5:18). But don't get "trigger happy," you could kill your future. We destroy God's best, by "jumping the gun" with our impatience. The Holy Spirit's power is to that marginal. If it's God, nothing can stop Him.

Automatic doors are no modern invention: "I will open a door that no man can shut, and I will close a door that no man can open" (Revelation 3:8).

What happened to "In honor preferring one another"? It's written twice for emphasis—Romans 12:10 and again in 1 Timothy 5:21. In Sunday School, they taught me that real JOY was *J*esus, *O*thers, *Y*ou and in that order!

Now don't misunderstand, I am not a prude. I am somewhat of a non-conformist myself. My front door welcome mat reads "Go Away!" and the back-door mat reads, "I Gave at the Office."

In a little book nook at a strip mall, I picked up an interesting book written by an interesting little lady titled *I Gotta Be Me*. It made me wonder, where did the old songs go? "To be like Jesus, all through life's journey from earth to Glory, all I ask is to be like Him!" And "Oh, to be like Thee, Blessed Redeemer, pure as Thou art. Come in Thy meekness, come in Thy fulness. Stamp Thine own image, deep on my heart!"

Jesus said, "Deny yourself and follow Me." We must guard against magnifying ourselves and . . . deny. He will help us, walking alongside. But oh! Where he is leading! I have had a 28-minute glimpse of eternity's heaven. Whatever it costs you to buy the ticket, *go there* by all means. It will be worth denying here to get *there*.

Jesus said, "He that seeks his life shall lose it, but he that loses it for My sake, shall find it." I was extremely concerned about preserving my own life yesterday. In heavy traffic I realized I hadn't fastened my seatbelt. I reached for it and while wrestling with that dumb, wonderful life-saving device, I swerved into the left lane then to the right, just missing the ditch.

I gained control of the car and learned a valuable lesson. I gotta be me, but first I gotta be His. Wherever obedience and good sense are called for, it is my duty to employ them.

Carl used to read a popular author until he found out that the man likes cats. B.C. Before cats, we used to have more birds, more squirrels. B.C. Before cats, I didn't have hair on all my sweaters and claw marks on both my hands from playing with the little scratchers.

When Carl and I first met he was a city boy from Cleveland. I'm a country girl from Indiana. On his first visit he looked around at all the animals and said, "What a zoo!" After we were married he told me, "I don't like cats."

"Carl," I informed him, "you cannot hate any of God's critters and be a Christian. He created all the animals. Anyone who is cruel to cats is not a good witness. Verbal and mental cruelty to animals is sin."

Early one morning at four A.M. I slipped downstairs to see why the kitchen light was left on. I heard Carl's resonant voice whisper, "What's the matter, Disco? OK, so I will warm your milk. You don't like it cold." Her name was "Disco" because she danced a lot. He learned to really like her.

Now we have Sinner Man and the only reason Carl lets me keep him is because he is male. All of our other pets have been female.

B.C. Before cats, I didn't know that they lie in the sun just to absorb the rays of solar energy for vitamins, health and energy. A doctor told me you rarely see a cat with arthritis. They spread out their hair follicles and take in much-needed nutrients from the sun, a valuable lesson people can learn.

A leading psychiatrist prescribes a special therapy to cure depression. He recommends you imitate the cat and sit relaxed for twenty minutes each day in the sunshine. If it is cold outside, sit near a window where the sun comes filtering through. Sit with your eyes closed and your hands outstretched, yet relaxed. The solar energy and warmth of the sunshine on the thin layer of skin on your eyelids and on the backs of your hands are readily absorbed and will help cure depression.

Thanks, Kitty, for your silent example. I vow to start doing this daily, taking time to relax in the Sonshine of God's presence and absorb from him the strength to face the tasks ahead.

I guess we will keep our "Sinner Man" since he taught me this object lesson. Who knows, I may change his name from Sinner Man to B.C.—Beautiful Cat.

Harold Bowden has contributed this message. It is a good note to end the year on.

Years ago in days of childhood,
I used to play till evening shadows would come,
Winding down an old familiar pathway,
I heard Mother call at set of sun.
"Come home, come home, it's supper time.
The shadows lengthen fast.
Come home, come home, it's suppertime."
We're going home at last.

Recently I heard this old song again. I grew up on a wedge-shaped farm, the Bank Place. It was owned and leased by the West Terre Haute Bank, located on a plateau that dropped off to the river bottom. In Indiana, we ate breakfast, dinner and supper. So if you invite me to dinner, I will arrive at high noon.

After my old pocket watch got tired and died and went to wherever old watches go, I would stick my hoe handle into the muddy, heavy soil of the Wabash River bottomland, and if there was no shadow, I knew it was noon and time for dinner.

Supper was at sundown when Dad arrived home from the coal mine. When the evening shadows came, we looked for a white cloth hung by Mama on the barnyard gate. From the plateau it could be seen for four miles. My brother John, and the Cox boys (hired hands), and I would come in famished and staggering from cleaning out Johnson grass, cocklebur, Lamb's quarter, horse weeds, and wild sweet potato vines from the forty acres of corn. Mama had the table heavy laden with bounty from our land—vegetables, fried chicken, pork chops, spare ribs, country ham, souse meat or plump sausages. There would be a large pitcher of milk and sweet potato pie. None of us was fat, we didn't go to the health club, we just worked and then worked.

That was fifty years ago. We are growing older, some of the "hoeing gang" has died. Father time has taken its toll. Mama is in heaven now. I catch myself looking up for her white flag. God's banquet is nearly ready and I can almost hear Him say, "Come home, it's supper time!"